ANNE
O'NEILL-BARNA

*

HIMSELF
AND I

HEINEMANN

LONDON MELBOURNE TORONTO

William Heinemann Ltd

LONDON MELBOURNE TORONTO

CAPE TOWN AUCKLAND

THE HAGUE

*

First published 1958
© by Anne O'Neill-Barna 1958

Printed in Great Britain
at The Windmill Press
Kingswood, Surrey

CONTENTS

For E. Savell Hicks

*

I MARRIED AN IRISHMAN

IT WAS APRIL, 1951. We had disembarked at Cobh and continued by train to Dublin—Jimmy aged three, Bridget, two, Dorothy eight months, and I. What a train trip! Next door was a high-spirited rugby team with an illusion that compartment walls gave privacy. "Let's have no funny business in here," announced one of them cheerfully, and a few minutes later he called out, to the laughter of his companions, "Take your hand off me. Take your hand off me! I give you ten seconds. I give you ten minutes. I give you ten hours."

In the dining car, the man at our table asked, "What would you do if you won the Sweeps? Never mind, I'll tell you what I'd do. I'd buy a harem."

His wife nudged me with her elbow. "Listen to him," she snorted, "me ould Ali Baba!"

And there was a great commotion as a bagpipe band came down to one of the provincial stations to meet, I supposed, a returning war hero. We all put our heads out of the windows to watch, and saw a prize-winning greyhound emerge from a first-class carriage and walk delicately down a gangplank, while the band played 'O'Donnell Abu'.

This was quite an introduction to Ireland. As a matter of fact, none of these incidents made any lasting impression because we wound up in the midst of the Irish countryside, surrounded by propriety and the past, and far far away from bright young men, would-be harem owners and winning greyhounds.

Bill, my husband, The O'Neill-Barna, had gone to Ireland a few months before, to open up the family place for us, near Glennasmol in County Wicklow. Instead, he decided it would not do, and we eventually bought a 'modern' house, a hundred years old, forty miles from Dublin. The modern house had no electricity, no heating, no water and, as it turned out, no well, so I don't see how we could have been worse off in Kilbarna House, but perhaps we could. Anyhow, for three months we had waited in New York, getting glowing letters about this place and that, photographs and long descriptions, and when finally a cable arrived saying "Come on over," we received it with pure joy and got on the next ship. *Then* we learned that no home had been bought after all—we were to live in an hotel and I was to join the search. At any rate, here we were. But to go back to the beginning and explain why is almost like being psychoanalysed. It all hinges on the fact that I married an Irishman, which had seemed a very American thing to do at the time, but as you see, led me far afield.

The Irish are odd, and what's more, they are contagious. There we were, snug in New York, having children with alarming rapidity but otherwise quite sensible, and then came this infiltrating notion to go to Ireland to live. Bill, who has absolutely no 'mass' on money, as the Irish say, was feeling uneasy about making all those dollars—green, queasy-looking old things. Not that there were so many of them as all that, but to use his favourite word it was bourgeois, pronounced 'boorgose'. It was unfit for The O'Neill of Clan Barna to be bothering his head about money, when all we had to do was go to Ireland and live on his income there, which was in sterling of course. Nice, clean, devalued, unconvertible sterling.

2

Bill often says that being Irish is a state of mind, and that's what I mean by contagious. In a very short time I was as keen as he on going 'over'. It would be like re-entering the past, the unspoiled, undeveloped nineteenth century. I thought tenderly of old-fashioned virtues implicit in home-made bread and grandma's apple pie, barefoot boys and one-room schoolhouses. Bill never suspected these wayward thoughts which—it goes without saying—were completely inappropriate. He gathered, though, that I didn't grasp the real situation. I remember his looking at me askance a couple of times and asking if I was *sure* I wanted to go.

Was I sure? By this time he had resigned from his position with one of the big steel companies, and we had given away most of our possessions. I thought he was touched.

"Go? Why, it's all settled."

"We don't have to go, even at this point. Remember, the climate is damp, the rooms are cold. I think you're seeing it all with a romantic eye, and you'll be disappointed."

"Who, me? Nonsense."

"You won't get crime waves or atom bombs or TV commercials, but neither will you have Fifth Avenue or the library."

I brushed all that aside. "Think how good it will be for the children—space to grow in, and a sense of the past to grow with, folk tradition and all that."

"Ha!" he said.

"Well, it's there, isn't it?"

After all, had we, or had we not, cemented our friendship under the benison of Irish folk-lore? And had we, or had we not, lived at least in part off the profits of radio scripts on traditional music, etc.?

"Perhaps. But remember too, you will find a country two hundred years behind the times, a country in which, in terms of education, there simply ain't none, as Canon Sheehan said.

3

And as for folk-lore, even the scholars there realise that it is no more. To the generation today, it's as foreign as feathers to a frog. So, lassie, don't be starry-eyed about Ireland."

"Fine time," I muttered, "to tell me."

"Well, never say I didn't warn you." Then he was off on one of the bits of song he likes to break into——

"I kissed her everywhere between
The weeping willow and the village green."

He certainly seemed nonchalant. Naturally, I felt we were irrevocably committed to that steady income in sterling, and so I said, "We'll go."

Thus—so casually—the die was cast.

Of course I had been romantic about Ireland long before meeting Bill. In the first place, something about Brooklyn, where I was born and bred, inclines one to world brotherhood. Old-stock city folk, who were never west of the Hudson or east of Jones Beach, can get quite maudlin about the banks of the Wabash and the isle of Capr*ee*. In my childhood we wouldn't have known a plough if it bit us, and yet we sighed heavily for the good old days down on the farm. And probably because a sprinkling of us were Irish-American and rather dedicated about being Irish, the rest fell into line and whooped it up for the Ould Sod.

That is, all but me. I was a literal-minded type who couldn't reply to a simple "How do you do?" without introspection, and while others marched in St. Patrick's Day parades and identified themselves with the masses, I stayed at home with my nose in a book. That sort of thing led naturally to solitude and good marks, and the next thing you knew I was at Vassar, majoring in Greek.

The reason for Greek was that all the reading brought on a

4

curiosity about mythology. At one time, I can safely say, I knew more about myths than anyone this side of Apollodorus, a feat which was of great help to my father with his crossword puzzles. But the classical gods and heroes, it presently appeared, had connections with later folk-lore, so that became my special province. A fellowship in Rome was centred on Italian fairy tales, and then, back in the States, I took an M.A. in English and Comparative Literature. Mind you, Greek, Latin, Italian, English, Folk-lore and Comp. Lit.—and what was the result? A thesis on "The Irish Influence on the Bowre of Blis Episodes in Spenser's *Faerie Queene*." (I only spent five years writing it, and now I *think* that was the title—which shows what four children can do to you.)

Later on I held a Guggenheim Fellowship on New York City folk-lore and song, but the common denominator in everything I studied was the fact that Irish origin kept bobbing up. Greek and Roman myths had Celtic parallels; King Arthur and his knights seemed a development of the Red Branch cycle; American tall tales smacked of Finn MacCool; and, above all, American folk music sounded preponderantly Irish—certainly inherited from Irish singers. I remember how irritated I would become over references to our Anglo-Saxon culture. Indeed! U.S.A. tradition seemed far more Gaelic than anyone had ever indicated. Talk about St. Patrick's Day parades, I was now wearing the green with a vengeance.

My father used to tease me with remarks like "The radio? Great Irish invention," and "Washington and Lincoln—oh pardon me, they were Irish too, weren't they?" But I was very lofty about it all. I collected enough 3-by-5-inch slips on Irish ballads to fill two filing cabinets and six shoe-boxes. In university circles it became known that Ireland was my particular pasture and I read more and more about it; no allusion was too remote, no fetch too far. Irish influence was mine, all mine! Academically speaking, Ireland was practically virgin territory, and I guarded it jealously. To me, it was the country of the ancient chivalry, where a chieftain would bankrupt himself out of hospitality, where a man's honour was worth more than herds of white cattle, and a noble act was framed for ever in song and story.

Into this heroic setting stepped Bill.

A classmate named Gloria and I were in the Columbia University library one evening, shivering gently in our adjoining cubicles because the climate in the stacks is fine for books but not for humans. A figure strolled down the aisle and settled itself in another cubicle. Gloria, who had a better view than I, pulled on my sleeve and said "Psst! Do you know him?"

"Who?" I asked, blinking.

"The one who came just in—the man with the face."

Considering most people are similarly equipped, it seemed an odd way to describe him, but one look and I saw what she meant. The true Gael has modelled lips, a strong but chiselled nose—distinctive features which identify him all the way from the Hebrides and Arran to Australia and the Argentine. This was a Gael of the Gaels. Cuchulain reincarnated. A profile from an old coin. Pibroch of Donal Dhu and all that! Oh dear, you couldn't call it love at *first* sight, because I'd been seeing that face in every legend I read. After all those books, what could you expect? On the other hand, is there any love that doesn't come at a glance?

The man turned on his desk light and the stack light and moved in our direction. He searched the shelves right behind my cubicle. Then, to my utter confusion, I realised he was talking to me.

"—most extraordinary. I've read in libraries in several countries and never, but never, until now, have I found the

6

books I was looking for being used by someone else. This is a most happy occasion."

"Oh," I stammered hurriedly. "Here, you take them." Most scholars glared, or waited drumming their fingers, if you had the only copy of a title they wanted.

"After you. I'm very pleased." And he was.

One thing led to another and presently we were out having tea. Then he joined the one of the two Irish clubs at Columbia that the rest of our group belonged to, and we all saw a great deal of him, especially me. I heard references to his being a member of the I.R.A. and hadn't the remotest notion what it meant—I mean folk-tales never went into *that*. Needless to say, I learned. He had fought all during the Trouble and afterward and had some very moving and some uproariously funny stories to tell about it, and apart from that his hobby is Irish history, of which, one gathers, little that is true is known. The English view? Written by the conquerors. The Irish view? Written to incite emotion. The facts are still to be dug out of libraries and archives, and that is his delight.

The campus had two Irish societies at that time and a complicated feud between them, which included the other one's stealing our book of guests and copying the addresses, picketing our meetings, etc., etc. I hadn't been at the university when it all started, and neither of course, had Bill, but we kept hearing about it.

"Do you know what They've done now," word would go around. "They've started a hurling team and they're going to practise outside our hall."

"Do you know what They've done now!" Gloria would announce excitedly. "They've taken to wearing saffron-coloured kilts and they're recruiting undergraduates like mad!"

"Do you know what They've done now," the president

said in great worry just before our annual dinner at the Men's Faculty Club. "They've threatened to keep our guest of honour from speaking!"

"He's here already, isn't he?" we asked.

"Oh, yes."

"Then I wonder what they have in mind . . . Hmm . . . Now just leave it to me," said Bill omnisciently, and everyone was most grateful.

What he did was quietly rearrange the tables and the seating at the very last minute, taking the place originally intended for the guest of honour himself. Halfway through the main course there was an explosive noise and bong! a chandelier fell on—guess who? Me. Bill had misplaced the siege perilous by one.

Incidentally, he and all the other native Irish in the room disappeared under the tables at the first noise, while we Americans sat there stupefied. The Trouble, you know.

Well, no one was hurt—they tell me that I calmly picked chicken and green peas out of the broken glass and continued to eat—but as you can see, this was rather an earnest feud. Every club member was expected to help in the strategy to which the officers felt committed; every move had to be carefully weighed, because the other society was ready to pounce; alliances had to be studied and built up or spurned, as the case might be, and all in all an exciting time was had.

Part of the strategy involved our attending the affairs of non-university Irish groups, and that, let me tell you, is a world to itself. There are hundreds of Irish organisations in New York, and though we were restricted to those which had Gaelic language programmes or some other cultural aspect, we could have been at an honorary dinner or social meeting every night of the week. We met new people, devoted young Gaelic students, who called themselves by Irish names and eventually married each other and had babies named Colm, Deirdre, Brid, Donal, Maeve, Diurmuid, etc.

And they might have been a little shaky in speaking Gaelic, but they could dance it fine. Every dinner, class and meeting ended with Irish dancing, which is about as gay as a drumhead court-martial. I shouldn't criticise since I can hardly waltz without fearful concentration and counting *one*-two-three under my breath, but I've since found that it's the same here in Ireland, and even the newspapers comment on the gloom. That rather bacchante phrase, "On with the dance, let joy be unconfined," with its suggestion of nymphs whirling with mad abandon while Nero fiddles and Nebuchadnezzar gets drunk, was the caption under a photograph of stern-faced little girls rigidly dancing at a country fair. And it's true—step-dancing and joy in Ireland have hardly a bowing acquaintance. The participants can't talk or smile, can't even move from the knees up. but do the exacting steps dead-pan and stifle their gasps for breath. Attention is riveted to the feet, and any expression or grace above the ankles is against the rules.

While this sort of thing was going on at the New York Irish societies, the rest of us—the frivolous ones—would find a restaurant and discuss philosophy and relativity instead. We soon discovered that Bill, besides having the rare quality of complete, international understanding, had the more common but ever wonderful Irish wit. I remember one evening when we were all sitting around a table. "Tell me," said Bill to the waitress, "do you love me as much as ever?"

"Arrah, go on with you," she said, blushing, and handed us all double portions.

Someone in the circle laughingly commented, "Leave it to The O'Neill! When I die, I wish you'd have the key of heaven, Bill."

"Why?"

"Because you'd let me in."

"It would be better for you," Bill retorted, "if I had the key to the other place, because then I'd let you out."

He would, too. His irreverence is most reassuring. In fact, come to think of it, I'd say the Devil is one of his favourite people. He likes to repeat traditional sayings like, "Bid the Devil good morrow when you meet him," and the old

> When the Devil is sick, the Devil a saint would be.
> When the Devil is well, the Devil a saint is he.

Despite this, he is an incorrigible idealist. He goes around trying to improve people—like the girl on the crowded subway who accepted his seat without thanking him. Stations later, he said pleasantly, "Excuse me, I think I must have left my handkerchief. Is it behind you?" and when she got up, he slid quickly down again. "There," he said, wagging his finger in her astonished face, "let that be a lesson to you."

But his typical slant on humanity crops out most often in a remark which I think he has occasion to quote every day of his life: "Get thee behind me, Satan—and push!"

Part of what attracted us to each other was, I suppose, the fact that we are so different. Bill is as Irish as one can possibly be, that is, Gael, with a mixture of Norwegian, Norman and English, while I am American without any Irish ancestry. That's rather rare, even in America, while to be an American without any Irish ancestry and to be living in Ireland is, I think, unique. Every "Yank" I meet in Ireland is a returned Irishman, only here they are called "returned Yanks" with a fine air of disdain. (Bill calls them "returned empties".)

One of my grandfathers won the silver skates for being the best ice-skater in Harlem, and had stories of *his* great-grandmother from Holland, who put sand on her floor in Manhattan and spoke only Dutch. She communicated with her small great-grandson by means of special cookies, which we still make. The other grandfather fought the Indians in the west, taking part in the campaign against the Sioux in the 1870s. The heritage from him is cowboy stories salted (for children's benefit) with memorable phrases like "I ups to him and he ups to me", "Curses, Jack Dalton!" and "Bang, bang! And forty Indians bit the dust." He was stationed in Bozeman, Montana, and from what he said, we have Indian relatives there today. But Grandpa's western adventures are our family's only connection with wide open spaces. Otherwise we are strictly urban, every last leaf of us on the spreading family tree. That is, everyone but me, since entering rural life in Ireland.

Bill's family, unless you happen to know Ireland, is hard to explain. They are very peculiar by normal standards. I mean they sit around and discuss other families and grieve that the such-and-such's have come down in the world and have to work for their living. In Bill's direct line, the chief of the clan does not work. It is up to the peasants and tenants to work, because presumably they like to work, but The O'Neill does not. Bill's father didn't, his grandfather didn't, and so on back, and Bill doesn't. The interlude in New York before we came to Ireland was his one lapse, and I notice that he keeps it dark.

I hasten to explain that the family is not one of the fabulously rich Anglo-Irish gentry, but strictly 'native', old, old Irish, and the fact that the chief has never worked is due, not to canny investments in 1850 or so, but to ancient loyalties within the tenant families, who in spite of confiscations kept up a community co-operation. In return the O'Neills supplied leadership, advice and, when they had it, capital. The system is quite dead now, it might be added; we have seen only a final gasp or two, and Jimmy, the only male in the next generation, will have to supply leadership and advice elsewhere, or run his own tractor. Thank goodness.

The women who married the O'Neills of recent times, anyhow, have not thought too much of the traditional arrangement. Bill's father led his mother a merry dance, giving away the family bank account to various needy followers, so that she imbued all her children but one with a hearty respect for security.

Bill's younger brother is a professor. He specialises in certain insects which are found only in inland streams—very obliging of them, as his hobby is fishing. None of the family sees him any more, though we heard from him once when Bill sent him waders from New York.

There's an older sister, but she lives in London. All I know about her is that she could have married a rajah but married an Englishman instead. And there's a far-out cousin-in-law in California, widow of someone. Bill met her once, at her wedding, and I never; but every Christmas she sends us a card and writes all over the remaining space, "Dear Bill, You will be glad to hear that my blood pressure is 280 and my basal metabolism is plus 60. My sister has shingles and gall bladder trouble. I'm sure my gall bladder isn't quite right either and I'm going to see Dr. Seawash, he's much better than Dr. Erntmint, the one I had last month. The sinus trouble I wrote you about last year is better since the operation, so I would be in pretty fair shape if it weren't for my heart attacks and strokes. Happy New Year, Sophie."

The most notable member of his family, after him of course, is Bill's sister, Enid. In one respect she is quite like him. She not only grieves over people who work for their living, she even feels sorry for those whose ancestors did, and who consequently have a lot of money. To her and her husband, there's something plebeian about being wealthy, something not quite acceptable, not top-drawer. The only correct, morally sanctified, in fact the only *possible* way of life is to manage gracefully on your income.

Enid can do this, too. If she absolutely has to have 'help', she has them, and if she doesn't she copes beautifully with a charwoman. She and Noel go away on holidays—though always in Ireland—and buy things at fine art auctions and eat enviably, and all in the most matter of fact way, without any symptom of tight halo. Enid couldn't understand why Bill and I didn't do the same, and she was delighted that, after our regrettable life overseas, we had finally come to our senses and were about to take up our proper post.

I was somewhat overawed on meeting her for the first time. This was in her perfectly appointed house in Dublin, before we had even seen the hotel where we were to stay. I am always frightened of efficient, intelligent people. I am sure they detect the real me in a glance and tabulate mentally with little clicks: "Not logical, muddles at house-keeping, doesn't dress for dinner, cheque-book in bad order, children noisy, reads when she should be making beds, doesn't like brisk walks."

Enid is slim and dark and handsome. She has worked out her own salvation so successfully that she feels she is in a position to advise others how to work out theirs. For years, according to Bill, ever since an aunt who filled the same rôle, died, everyone has gone to Enid when in difficulty, and Enid has figured a way out.

Our conversation beside the drawing-room fire was not a marked success. I had expected a cosy *tête-à-tête* and the usual feminine topics—the mere male and his ideas, *la vie chère*, household hints, servants, etc. But Enid refused any common ground. She has blue eyes and black lashes and she gazes.

"It's a pity about Kilbarna," she said. "We were all so happy there as children. Of course without the furniture it would be quite a job to fill it again, but still it would have been big enough for all of you." She has no children herself and she always speaks as if our offspring were innumerable— vaguely, as though the total were something only advanced physics could accurately express.

"He says it's too big."

"He hasn't the heart to put the steward's family out, you may be sure of that. He let them in once when he was on one of his visits back from America, and for all I know he's made out the deeds to them this time. There was nothing I could do about it."

This was news to me, as Bill's larger-scaled benevolences always are, but I said nothing. She handed me a cup of tea and went on with what seemed to be a survey of the situation. "I've gone about with him daily, for months, looking at houses. The stairs I've climbed, the dry rot I've viewed, the damp I've endured! It hasn't been easy."

"We're *so* grateful," I exclaimed. "You've been an angel——"

She cut me off. "The trouble is Billy. I needn't tell you, you must have him taped by now. Every ruin in Ireland is for sale, and Billy would have bought them all. I barely persuaded him to wait till you got here."

"Er—thank you, but . . . I mean, do you think I'll be any use?"

"You? Of course not. One couldn't let him out alone, or both of you out alone, I'm sure. We'll all three have to continue the hunt, now that you're here. What a bore! We've been shown so many abandoned rectories, for example, that I began to call Billy 'Reverend'. Abandoned guest-houses. Abandoned semi-detached surburbia. Abandoned towers. But we have at least eliminated most of the field."

"You've been wonderful——"

"Perhaps you'll be able to keep him in line," she said with

a heavy sigh. "We'll begin again next week. Now the first thing *you* must do," she continued kindly, "is to forget that you are American."

"Well, gee, I don't know about that," I said uneasily.

"*I* do. Of course it's your home and a country of a sort, I suppose, though nothing like being Irish so far as national character goes, but you mustn't live like that here."

"Like what?"

"Extravagance. Throwing money around. Disgusting."

I brightened up. If that was all, it was going to be easy to make her happy. "Oh you're quite right, Enid! But really, I spend very little, only what I absolutely have to. As a matter of fact, Bill——"

"Yes. I know. You don't have to tell me. Billy's the spendthrift. He's notorious for it."

"Oh dear!"

"When he was thirteen years old, he was discovered late one night, in the back room of a pub, betting £1,000 on the turn of a card."

"Where did he get it?"

"On a horse."

"You mean—he sold one?"

Enid looked at me like a Catholic who has just discovered that there are Protestants in heaven (incredulity, horror and an immediate lowering of standards). "Surely," she said, slowly and painstakingly as though she were sounding out syllables to a child, "surely, e-ven in A-mer-i-ca, there are horse rac-es and hun-dred to one shots?"

"Oh yes, how stupid of me!" I exclaimed, mortified. "What happened?"

"What happened?"

"Yes, when he bet the money?"

"Lost it, of course."

"But what happened to him?"

"Spanked and put to bed. Then, a year or two later, he was in the midst of the Trouble—which of course he took part in without any of us knowing. He was still in short trousers actually. We only found out about it when they put up notices for him: 'Wanted, notorious irregular. Dead or alive, £5,000 reward. Drinks champagne and brandy and frequents only the best hotels'. Our Billy! And while he was on the run, he organised a scheme of poaching for the relief of the poor families whose men were off fighting, and do you know, he made ten pounds a day, for weeks and weeks. But what he didn't give to the poor he spent on ammunition.

"Really it was Daddy's fault, I suppose. He was delighted with him and encouraged him. He even lent him a motor-car, a Rolls-Royce, which in one of those recurrent alarums Billy buried in a field. He was afraid the enemy would get it and intended to dig it up again, but someone went and built a house on top of it.

"Previous to this, when we couldn't find him, we looked up in the air. He was off with Lord Coolavin in Coolavin's aeroplane, little more than a motorised box-kite, as I recall. But now the Trouble took precedence over everything—a horrid time."

"Bill never speaks of it as 'the Trouble'."

"No, he wouldn't, because to him it was one great game. But to the rest of us at home it was anything but a game. I remember one night, about 2 a.m. actually, he had just come in from some ambush, and information must have been given about him, because within minutes the British had surrounded the house. Doors were being smashed in, front, side and back, rifle butts cracking on the panels—a terrifying sound. We were all frozen with fear, knowing that from the record he had already established he would receive short shrift. Billy was covered with mud from the waist down, sure evidence that he'd been out. Daddy said, "I'll open the door before these fellows wreck the house. Billy, you sit at that table and don't get up, no matter what.'

"Then he went to the door and the officer in charge barked out his questions. 'Yes', Daddy said, 'I am O'Neill, and my son is inside, but I'm afraid you have the wrong house. Anyhow, come in, man, and have a drink.'

"The next thing we knew, Daddy was calling the cook to get up and make tea for the poor soldiers. We were still petrified. Annie reported to us afterward that she found Billy in the dining-room with some officers—bottles and glasses on the table—and Daddy and himself chatting away with them like old friends. Lamp-light, you see, and all that. They never looked under the table to see his muddy boots."

"I'd chalk that one up to your father's credit."

"Credit! Billy is much like Daddy, and it's all right to talk about it now, but my skin creeps when I think of what Mama must have gone through. We didn't usually have such direct knowledge of Billy's activities, but even to this day I hear stories of him. And the worst of it is, they're all true. Like the time he was captured in Ballyshanmore and they held him for three weeks and then released him, convinced that he was the village idiot. It was bad enough his taking on the British, but apparently they weren't enough for him—he also had to take on the Church. And when the bishop excommunicated him and the rest of them, he wasn't in the least put out, even though he never knew the moment he might be killed. But he was worried that his men might take the decree to heart, and so he decided to punish the bishop."

"You mean the time he led the parade the bishop had forbidden?"

"Oh no—that was nothing. A new hall had been built and the bishop was coming to dedicate it. The ceremony was to take place at three in the afternoon and Billy heard about it. What do you think he did? Tunnelled under the hall and set land mines to blow up the platform on which the bishop was to stand. Unfortunately, as he would say, he had forgotten all about Summer Time, Greenwich Time and such, with the result that his mine went off an hour too early. I think to this day his one regret in life is that he didn't blow up the bishop. That's how he got his big excommunication, bell, book and candle."

"I should think one would be enough."

"In normal times, for a normal man, it is. But everything about Billy is bravura. Finally the Trouble came to an end, and Billy was a brigadier and the rest of us were grey. Then the Civil War—he was on the losing side, of course—and he was forever raising money for his men or their widows. He was always able to make it, but he always gave it away. Eventually Daddy tied up the estate, what a mercy, so that Billy could only have the income, and Billy went off to America. Goodness knows what his transatlantic extravagances have been. Would you like some more tea?"

I felt like saying, "In the absence of adrenalin, yes," but thought better of it.

"Don't tell me you didn't know all this," she murmured innocently, cocking an eye at me over her cup. "He has other faults, too—far worse."

Upset as I was, this seemed to be a final thrust. A lurid montage ran through my mind. Full-of-the-moon murder? Dope? Drink? Rape? Jekyll and Hyde?

"Wh-what?" I quavered.

"Well," she said, speaking loudly, clearly and slowly, "he's *most* famous, with the family, for liking Low Company."

When I repeated all this to Bill he shared none of my indignation. "Good old Enid," he said fondly. "Our family ties are all family knots, you know." Then, impatiently, "Never mind what *she* told *you*. What did *you* tell *her*?"

"Nothing."

"That's all right so. Don't worry, tell her anything you like. The only thing you could tell her that would shake her is that I was working in New York."

Boorgose, you know.

*

CHAPTER 2

THE HOUSE-HUNT BEGINS

GLENNASMOL, where we went to stay, was on the coast some twenty miles from Dublin, yet it was so wild and isolated that a feeling of timelessness possessed me after only a few hours. Because of the sea, it was a summer resort and all the emptier out of season. Enid settled us into one of the little hotels, manœuvred a freckled, fair girl who lived nearby and who 'helped', into the rôle of Nanny, and gave us a week-end of rest. It was there that Bill was sea-changed into Himself, for like the Grand Dukes at Estoril, an O'Neill in the glen has his title. This was ancestral territory: almost within the memory of the oldest inhabitants the men of the clan had defended it against the English.

It was long, narrow and curved like a sickle, touching the beach at one end, yet hidden between snow-covered mountains. Until a year before, it could be reached only by the military road, but now a new highway connected it with Dublin. A foaming river ran the length of it, crossable by fords; waterfalls tumbled down the steep sides to join the stream and its rushing sounds. One could see how this hard, secret place had been kept intact. The far end slipped softly between the mountains with a promise of fairyland a step away—actually, it led to stormswept heaths and forlorn ravines, and ultimately to the Pale, from which raiding O'Neills had extracted 'black rent' for centuries.

But today only a dozen families were living in the glen, in stone houses not visible from the one road, and of these less than half bore names associated with the clan. How odd that our improbable offspring, Jimmy, Bridget and Dorothy, were the last in circulation of the real thing.

They loved the glen immediately. Jimmy was an active little boy, thin and dark. "You could blow him off your hand" was the glen comment on him. Bridget has blue eyes and black lashes and is, by courtesy, blonde. "Good morning, film star," was the standard greeting to her.

Jimmy was a child of many questions; he inquired and investigated all day. Bridget on the other hand was a child of one question, "And me?" based on fear that Jimmy would be taken somewhere and she would be left behind. The two little figures, one dark and chattering, the other fair and anxious, made a striking contrast as they played near the hotel, while Dorothy, always laughing and impish, was 'aired' in the arms of Lilly, the local girl, who, thus encumbered, also chaperoned the other two up hill and down dale.

Their favourite destination was the big rock near the river which 'belonged' to their own great-great-great-, etc., grandfather. According to legend, the huge boulder had been a sling-shot for Fergus Mac Hugh O'Neill, who had hurled it at Elizabeth's invading forces and dispersed them. Lord Grey had been in command then; he was, I think, the Lord Deputy of Ireland and, in the surprisingly cosmopolitan way of the Irish chiefs of that day, Fergus married one of the Greys. The poet Spenser, my old preoccupation, was Grey's secretary. A small world! Spenser wrote home disparaging remarks about the Irish (and advocated a scorched-earth policy which starved out thousands of them), but he didn't do what family tradition says Fergus' wife eventually did— betray him and five of their sons to the English. Was she a

Lorna among Doones, or a Doone among Lornas? Was this deliberate or inadvertent, domestic or national, highest tragedy or lowest politics—who knows?

Whichever way it was, Fergus was captured. Some time before, he had had his men bury the family treasure in the glen. "There were potatoes on the fire, and he sent the men out with the treasure, and they were back and it hidden before the potatoes were boiled."

"Has it ever been found, Daddy?"

"Never. Shall we have a look?"

"Oh yes! Come!"

"And me?"

Meanwhile we explored in a leisurely way—Fergus' ruined castle, the old mines, the ancient fords, the paths up to dizzying heights. It rained fine misty rain most of the time, and the children and I froze under layers of woollens. No one else did; cold, I gathered, is not felt in Ireland.

The hotel, run on proper, sparse lines, lit diminutive fires only at night, though we were charged extra for these at bonfire rates. The meals, likewise, were picnic on the board and banquet on the bill. The proprietress and Lilly ate at the same time we did, and I could not help noting that the proprietress had an egg for tea while Lilly did not.

"Oh, that's the usual thing," Himself said when I commented.

"What if Lilly were to ask for an egg?"

"She'd be reminded that she had one two weeks ago Sunday."

Still, the hotel was pleasant enough. The children played in the garden with the guinea fowl and peacock. An English girl climber came and went. An old man arrived for the week-end—he had been a guest there, on and off, for at least forty years. His hands shook and he spilled his soup.

"Ah, he's a respectable old soul," said the waitress to us.

"We give him a wee table to himself." She added, as though to fill in the sketch, "We do find him in the dining-room at half seven, waiting for his breakfast."

Another 'feature' of the place was a handsome young man named Tom Malone. His people had some land near the hotels, and Tom used to till the fields, guiding and speaking softly to his horses, while all the lady visitors watched him and sighed, "Isn't he graceful! Isn't he lovely!" in the same tone of voice they used for exclaiming over the mountains and waterfalls. Tom's family had been associated of old with the O'Neills, and before we left the glen Himself engaged him to come to work for us. Tom was tanned and tall and extremely well-proportioned, almost a giant of a man: an all-round farmer, dependable and capable, and an expert hunter and poacher. A man's man, and yet a man of the ladies—and he knew it. There must have been a great falling-off in patronage at the resort when word got around that he was leaving.

Himself picked up a lot of old threads as the men of the glen came at night, in ones and twos, to reminisce with him. But the children and I went to bed early, needing the rest after our long trip, and the quiet, remote days were welcome. It was a diversion for us when tinkers camped by the river in bright red caravans, loosing their calico horses and spancelled goats on the sparse roadside grass. We watched them with interest. Two tinkers, a red-haired man with broken teeth and a red-haired woman wearing a blanket shawl, tried to buy cigarettes in the hotel, but the proprietress refused to let them in. Bill stopped them as they walked away, their weather-beaten faces expressionless, and gave them a pack.

"Thank you, sir." Then a glance of recognition and the faces lit up. "Ah, it's Himself! God bless you! Sure, we heard you were back! The Brians were askin' for you. The

Sheridans are off the road, they're tryin' the houses. Welcome home. Bless you, God bless you. We pray for you all the time."

"Oh dear, I'm disappointed," I said when they left, having expected—what? Phrases new-minted as the dawn? Similes drawn from Nature and the Tarot pack? "Are they always so pious?"

"They're playing it safe. It isn't what tinkers say that's interesting, it's what they do."

"You do like them, don't you?"

"Why wouldn't I? Wasn't I in their keeping when I was wounded and on the run? No house would have been safe, but the British didn't think of raiding a caravan. The Brians and the Driscolls passed me from tribe to tribe, and I was accepted as one of themselves."

"Did you learn any of their customs?"

"I certainly did. How to grow hair on a bald head, how to make an old horse act young, and how to talk to an animal."

"Bow wow?"

"Don't laugh, I do know."

"Tell me, then."

"I can't, it's a tinker secret."

Time was flying. That night the tinkers departed, and in the morning it was found that the hotel's guinea hens had vanished. There was a great commotion, sending for the guards, tears of vexation from the proprietress, imprecations, to no avail. No one seemed to know which way the tinkers had gone except Himself, who murmured to me, rather wistfully, I thought, "if we had time now to go for a bit of a drive, we'd have a *good* dinner for a change."

But we were just as well out of it, because Enid arrived with a folio of house listings. She and Himself sat down over them and winnowed away like old hands. I was supposed to join in but couldn't come to grips with it. Everything was either 'a charming detached non-basement unique bijou semi-single-storey villa-type bungalow with verandah' or 'a magnificent gentlemen's residence, choicely situate on 500 acres of prime fattening land; electricity, plumbing and drainage expected shortly'. However, they seemed to be getting somewhere after hours of slogging through the heady mists of words.

"Ha! Check that one."

"No, not this."

"Vicarage?"

"No good, it will only have four bedrooms, the clerical limit, you know."

"Rectory?"

"In view of the size of your family, Reverend, I'm afraid Protestant church property is out."

He shuffled a fat pad of papers. "Well, we've six places to see in the midlands without these, and about six others. Should we quit?"

"We've more than enough, the pick of the lot. This is the best selection we've had yet. I'll be down in the morning and we'll start right out."

The glen was full of melancholy stone ruins, and indeed so is all Ireland. The next day when we began our trip, this was the first impression that struck me. Even in Dublin I had spotted rows of boarded-up houses, and in the countryside there seem to be more deserted than lived-in buildings, not all of them ancient by any means. This one might be a barracks set on fire during the Trouble; that one a BIG HOUSE with trees growing through the roof and ivy holding the walls together. Tiny labourers' cottages with one or two walls left, the room divisions still visible in different colours of paint. Historic ruins, old castles and monasteries listed in the guide-books, the castles usually reduced to a square tower and a rubble of stones and grass on which cows would be grazing. There's an incongruity in driving through Ireland, modern car, modern speed, with this great, sad countryside silently around one, speaking volumes about people past and gone—gone through emigration or eviction or war or famine or just, in the case of castles and BIG HOUSES, the will of God.

Most of the country is beautifully varied, a continual surprise to the traveller; changes can sometimes be measured by the yard—hill, valley, stream, field, dell, woodland, ruined abbey, avenue to an estate, group of country council houses, pasture, pond, fields, church, new concrete-block shops, hill and glen again. Almost all new building is in concrete-block, usually very ugly and in bad contrast to the older more rambling cottages. The houses of the gentry, even if falling apart, are still very lovely, being set carefully in place with a regard for the countryside as a whole.

The one thing acutely missing is—trees. A 'woods' might be any straggle of bushes. But, apart from these and lines of stately, shady trees marking nineteenth-century driveways, most of Ireland is treeless. The scenery is in miniature, exquisite immediately in the foreground, disappointing in the distance. Wild flowers, vivid in colour and larger than ours, make every roadside a picture; but lift your eyes beyond and the most you can hope to see is a field, a bare rocky hillside and a cloud-filled sky.

The Irish, however, get great value out of these rocks and clouds: poets go on about them, painters paint them and see in them infinite colours. A proper tree-filled landscape might ruin the national arts. Yet in pre-English days Ireland was a land of forests. They were cut down during the conquest to facilitate the capture of rebel natives. Before, according to an old saying, a squirrel could travel the length and breadth of the country without ever setting his feet on the ground. But of course the national arts were different then, consisting as they did of illuminated manuscripts, the richest folk-tales of the western world, and some fancy spear-work in the shade.

We drove west along the military road through which the glen had finally been invaded. Desolate, it laboured its way over the mountains. Startled sheep leaped away from the car. Once we passed a Nordic-looking hiker headed for the youth hostel which had been Parnell's shooting-box. Otherwise, not a soul. The road was precarious at best, and at times it simply went out to lunch. A rough sign would announce 'Closed to Traffic' at eroding canyons grossly misnamed 'the Sally Gap' and 'the Wicklow Gap'. Himself took this as a challenge, of course. He just set the car at the precipices and, mind over matter, somehow we got through.

"Whew!"

"What were you saying?" he asked.

"Oh nothing. Just Donner Pass, Death Valley, Thermopylae and other things that came to mind."

"You can relax now. The mountains are behind us and we've nothing but level road. See?" His idea obviously was that the faster he went, the leveller the road was proved to be.

Himself had been no slouch at driving in America, but I was unprepared for the exuberance which he threw into getting from here to there in Ireland. This was terrible. In America I had kept him in check because it was after all my car; but here, what could I do, because it was after all his? My customary cries of "Sssss!" "Look out!" "Watch!" were now answered with a snarl; even when I went to the trouble of putting things politely, like, "One doesn't drive as fast now as usual, does one, because the brakes are not holding," or, "The road is a bit slippery here, don't you think?" all I got was a nasty look for my pains.

Fortunately we saw few cars, because to see them was to pass them; but we did lunge through teams of horses, herds of bullocks, flocks of sheep, tribes of donkeys, and solitary addle-pated hens, who lay down and gave up the ghost when they saw us coming. The narrow curves, the speed, the animal world—all reduced me to a state of paralysis. Fat lot of Ireland I was going to see! I was done up in curls from my toes to my eyelids.

"Heavens," said Enid, "I thought all Americans were mad for speed."

"N-n-not th-this o-one."

"Remember when you used to race with the maharajah, Billy," she asked brightly.

"I do, I do," he chortled, surging up to eighty with the nostalgia of it all.

"We used to hide behind trees. You both had *such* an exciting way of skidding into the bystanders when you went around bends. Like this one."

ScreeEEECH went the tyres.

"Oh dear," said Enid sadly, as we remained on the road, "I see you haven't your old form back yet."

"Heh heh," I laughed feebly, meanwhile wondering what was wrong with me anyhow. Why should remaining alive be to me of such absorbing importance, when obviously, in this car at least, the majority voted otherwise?

"Whatever happened to the maharajah?" Himself asked.

"Did you not hear? He was assassinated."

"No! Where?"

"Back in India."

"By whom? When?"

"By outraged passengers," she said sweetly, "when he was skidding around a bend."

"Oh."

After that, however, he did slow down. By the time I had recovered my composure sufficiently to give my kind attention to the scenery, we had reached fairly flat country. On either side of the road were smallholdings with whitewashed farm cottages, some thatched, more of them roofed with 'galvanised', a corrugated tin. There were occasional low hills and Himself pointed out green mounds called raths, which are carefully left untilled as the people believe they are fairy forts. Mostly the view was flat and monotonous compared with the glen, but change was provided by the weather—in two hours we had had sun, rain, fog, sun, drizzle, snow, hail, wind, sun and finally a misty continual rain.

"Don't think this is going to be pleasant," remarked Enid morosely as we flew past a town. "Once one is out of Dublin, it's very difficult to find a bit of comfort. However, we shall see. Pity we're going through Naas now when it's too early to eat. There's an excellent hotel there."

"What does it matter," I said cheerfully. "We'll find another."

"Is she weak-minded?"

"My dear girl," said Himself, "this is Ireland. Outside of Dublin and Cork there are possibly two places fit to eat in."

"One, I should say," said Enid thoughtfully. "This."

"If we strike a bad restaurant, can't we just order sandwiches and have a big dinner later?"

"My God!" said Enid.

"Look, there are no restaurants, and there are no sandwiches. You go into a hotel and you get what they have that day and that's all about it."

A magnificent detached non-basement residence was our first call. This turned out to be a red-brick Victorian affair miles from nowhere, which looked as if it had strayed out of a city. It could have been in Flatbush or London. Not my taste, but with Enid I tagged along after Himself, who tramped through it from attic to non-basement and was stopped only by the outgoings.

29

Outgoings are the sum-total of payments due annually on a house, quite apart from mortgage and running expenses. For instance, there is ground rent—literally, rent to be paid to a landlord for the ground on which the house is located. Some places are free of such rent and consequently called freehold, but most property is not. On farm land, instead of paying ground rent, an equivalent sum is handed over to the Land Commission. Then there are rates, one for the dwelling and any out-buildings, and another for the land, and these are based on valuations made long ago and not related to actual value. There's an electricity rate. Sometimes there's a water rate.

Many houses appear to be bargains, and are—except for the fact that their rates are so exorbitant no one will buy them. For some reason, the misplaced town house was in this class. Himself calculated the outgoings for us in the car and reluctantly decided to give it up. This startled me.

"How could you possibly consider it? It's so ugly and inconvenient. Did you like it, Enid?"

"Compared with some he's been ready to buy, this was a *chef d'œuvre.*"

I began to feel misgivings.

"See here," said Himself in a tone of strained patience, "we've been looking for a house for three months. It's time we bought one."

"Well," said Enid, "let's have lunch first anyhow."

The nearest town had an hotel, and she decided it might as well be here. A dingy, dim hall, filled with large black Victorian furniture, vases full of artificial roses, a grandfather clock ticking loudly, dusty torn draperies at windows and doors, no one in sight. Farther on there was a dark corridor and, to the side of this, a dining-room where two 'travellers' were eating in silence. We sat at the only other table, which was set, dustily. The cloth was not spotless.

Enid started tapping her foot. A thin, worried-looking girl hurried in—the waitress.

"Tell me, lassie," said Himself, "do you love me as much as ever?"

"Arrah, get along with you, sir," she replied, blushing.

"Well then, will you join us in a glass of sherry?"

"No sherry," she said smiling. "No licence, sir."

Enid looked her over coldly (torn apron, dirty uniform). The smiled faded away. "Bring us luncheon, please," said Enid rapidly, "as we're in a hurry." Freezing look at Himself. "A mercy there's no bar. You'd have her chucking us under the chin and singing Moore's melodies, doubtless. Same old Billy, I'm afraid. Do have sense."

"Ah, who has sense around here anyhow?" he said cheerfully.

"You have, if you choose. You could sell it. Tell me, Anne," (turning to me), "is it true that in America you have lemon pies with no nourishment in them at all?"

Talking about low-calorie foods when one is ravenous does not enhance them, but I was interrupted by the soup course, which we all greedily attacked. I gave up after two spoonfuls, Enid after three, but Himself emptied his plate.

"Ah well, he has no taste," said Enid. "Hunger strike, you know, and all that. Never the same since."

With lowered eyes, the little waitress removed the soup and served us each a plate on which was a thin slice of grey meat in white gravy, a boiled potato, a browned potato, some violently green, canned peas. "No butter?" I asked.

The waitress looked puzzled.

"We don't eat bread and butter with our meat," Enid explained.

"I mean, for the potatoes?"

"One has it at home of course, but since the war it isn't customary in restaurants."

31

"Oh. And what about napkins?"

"Napkins?"

"Serviettes?" asked the waitress.

"*Table*-napkins," said Enid firmly.

The girl retreated.

"They've been cut out since the war too."

"Well," said Himself, "whatever that soup was, the meat is the same."

"Mutton or beef?" said Enid, tasting. "Hmmm, I'd say beef."

"Is it boiled or roasted," I wondered.

"Both, of course. Boiled for the soup, then roasted for the dinner."

"Do they always serve two different kinds of potatoes?"

"Heavens no, one. It's always boiled potatoes, you know, titivated up a bit."

"Really? I have a booklet called 'Twenty-seven Ways to Cook Potatoes'."

"Well, don't show it in Ireland," said Himself, "or they'll cook all twenty-seven kinds at once."

Dessert was jelly (Jello) and custard made from custard powder. Coffee came last, a mixture of hot milk and chicory served demi-tasse. The bill came to two pounds. Enid was livid. "My household would eat, and eat well, for three days on two pounds. Two pounds is a week's wage for my cook. At the worst, one pound should have been the limit. Some hotel-keepers have shopkeepers' mentalities—charge the traffic as much as it will bear, and that's why" (in a loud voice), "no one ever comes a second time."

Himself overtipped the waitress as Enid stalked out.

We saw a house right on a river, but it was in the shadow of a derelict granary, six storeys high, that loomed like a city tenement over it. A fascinating weigh-bridge went with it, but Himself passed it up. We saw a house originally built by an English land-agent—the windows were little more than slits in the walls and the doors so narrow that only one person could squeeze through at a time. Himself got talking with the owner and embarked on a lecture on absentee landlords, rack-rent and so forth, which Enid cut short by wanting to know how one was expected to move furniture. So he passed that up too. He also passed up a two-storey bungalow surrounded by an acre of greenhouse.

We had tea at five in a drapery shop with a back-room restaurant (you never know where the kettle may be boiling); no complaints, as tea is tea and excellent anywhere in Ireland, but now we wanted dinner. Heading north-west, Himself whizzed through mile after mile of bog road, unadorned by houses, much less inns. Eventually we found a hotel in a town, checked in for the night (vast lumpy brass beds in dusty unaired bedrooms) and went down for dinner. The décor was as before.

Soup came. We all tasted in silence. Meat course came. Grey slice in white gravy, violently green cabbage cooked to a mush, boiled potato and roast potato. Dessert was jelly with custard sauce. This time we had tea instead of coffee, and Himself asked the waitress if she loved him as much as ever at dessert, instead of first off, and then retreated into the bar.

Enid dismissed it all with a long indrawn breath. We had the empty lounge to ourselves, and a good warm fire.

"Tell me, Anne, what do the Americans think of the Irish? No, I'll tell you—they think we're gallivanting around with shawls and bare feet."

"Oh no."

"While really the young women here are all trying to dress like film stars."

"Oh dear," I said apologetically, "the movies. In America we have so many other distractions we don't pay so much attention to them."

33

"Don't belittle them, they've been a boon to our people. They were the first to show another way of life, the first to make women here rebel, if only a little. We're a far way behind other countries, you know. I think Ireland was the only place in the world where the suffragette movement was laughed at *by the women*. We were encouraged to laugh at it, of course, told our place was one of virtue and sacrifice."

"But women took a great part in the activities of the Celtic revival, back in the early 1900s."

"Oh that. No one bothers about those days except Americans."

"What do you mean?"

"My dear, the dollar scholars, we call them, here to pick up Ph.Ds. One sees them in Dublin, notebooks in hand, asking how to get to Joyce's Martello Tower, or Yeats' lake isle, or Gogarty's house on Ely Place. Then they go home and write books about brawling, poetic, witty Ireland, and the likes of you is influenced to come here."

"*Touché*," I said, blushing.

"Whereas we natives know it's all a lot of As I Roved Out. That's the secret of the Irish, in case you ever want to know."

"But you do want visitors, you must admit. You have, not one, but three tourist agencies urging travellers to come to Ireland."

"Tourists? Gawking loud creatures. The government wants their money, but the rest of us would prefer their absence. That is, the English ones anyhow," she added more kindly. "Haven't you noticed?"

"I can't tell anyone apart. How do you know which are English?"

"They're the ones who eat ice cream on their steaks."

Himself came in, sank into a chair and arranged his feet cosily on the fender. "We were talking about American films," said Enid, edging toward the fender herself.

"Ah yes, the super-spectacles they make over here. With knights jousting o'er the lea."

"Those too. We don't like them either, do we? Littering up the place. We go about picking up limbs on pointed sticks."

"Well, at least it's an industry that employs the Irish, and as such has government blessing."

"Government!" said Enid.

"Do I detect, dear sister, a note of cynicism?"

"I'm a government man myself," said a voice from a chair in the corner.

"Come and join us," invited Himself. "We need an opposition."

They talked and talked, solely, exclusively and at length on the Irishman's favourite topic—Ireland. The Irishman's only topic, you might say. No one in the country wants to hear about anything else. That's why questions beginning, "Tell me about America," really mean, "Tell me, what does America think of Ireland?" That's why the national papers contain no news. (Once Himself and some friends were talking about this deplorable condition and suggested starting a new, internationally-focused Irish journal. Their idea of cosmopolitan interest was to have articles on "The Irishman in Australia", "The Irish in Canada", "India and Ireland".) This night it was all new to me and hazy. Once I roused to ask, "Do you have women in politics in Ireland?"

"Oh no, not women," exclaimed Himself, shocked at the idea. "Only widows!"

*

CHAPTER 3

THE HOUSE-HUNT ENDS

THE NEXT MORNING we set off again. We were now well into what is called the Midlands, the flat central part of Ireland which contains the huge bog of Allen. Up, up climbed the speedometer, as Himself sideswiped a dozen panic-stricken cows and passed an ancient car and almost turned us over in the ditch. The hunt for the next house on the list slowed him down presently, so I was able to open my eyes and observe the country.

A seldom-used waterway called the Grand Canal and a quiet river crossed each other and our road from time to time. Occasionally a barge chugged into view on the canal, or a fisherman leaned over a bridge; swans and water-hens paddled serenely by. Thatched cottages and whitewashed little villages made calendar art for us; everything seemed very permanent and peaceful.

We were headed for a 'charming gentleman's residence', which by now I realised clearly might mean anything, the words in which houses are advertised being a sort of literary convention which has reached a high form in Ireland. Only by seeing each of them could one determine if it were ready for *House Beautiful* or demolition.

But this one, Beaumont House, was ideal. We entered a circular hall, in which an assortment of riding crops and shooting sticks were still hanging. The family had already departed, but a left-over elderly parlourmaid showed us around. A door led to a sunny drawing-room which was lined with books, leather-bound, old and fascinating, and the doors in it were masked with false books and shelves. Adjoining this was a study. Off the round hall in the other direction were a long panelled dining-room, a morning-room and an old-fashioned kitchen with larder, scullery and storage rooms. Underneath was the cellar, a labyrinth of small stone chambers, with a laundry set up in one of them. A stairway, curved like a shell, led from the main floor to the bedrooms—five of them, a huge bath too. The bedrooms were airy, sun-lit and spacious—the kind of room for mid-summer night dreams, and they all opened on to a central foyer, made for comfortable conversation.

I was entranced. Enid grande-damed the parlourmaid a bit, asserted that there was damp in the north walls and jackdaws in the chimneys, but she had a reflective glint in her eye. "My brother has a large family," she stated. "I'm afraid this place is on the small side, y'know."

This annoyed Himself. Back in the car, he said it was *not* too small. "What do you say? We'll buy it."

"It's wonderful," I said nervously, "but are the outgoings and all that all right?"

"Of course not," said Enid. "They're high. What's more, the acreage is much more than you want and the price will be stiff." But she agreed that he should see the agent.

We saw several other places that day, but they simply couldn't compare. One was in a town. "Where is Patrick Street?" Himself called out to a fellow leaning against a shop.

"Well, if you drive fast enough, you'll be out of it soon."

We had the usual lunch in the usual hotel. Same meat, peas, custard, love as much as ever. Himself radiated socia-bility and Enid looked martyred. We drove on, towards

Galway, to see a "Picturesque castle on landscape river, 4 reception, 6 bedrooms, small room suitable for bath. Electricity expected shortly," and stayed right in the car, as the picturesque castle had a picturesque tree growing smack out of the middle of it.

Himself complained that Enid and I kept talking about Beaumont House. "If you like it that much, let's take it. I'll stop the car this minute and phone the agent."

"Easy on," said Enid. "Think it over. All that land would mean a full-time farming operation. Do you want to be bothered?"

"I can always sell off some land."

"Nonsense. Land is value."

"We could move right in, couldn't we?" I said. "No repairs, no painting—it's perfect."

"You'd want a bit of bargaining on the price," Enid continued. "It's bound to be much too high."

"I thought you thought the place was right for us," said Himself, aggrieved.

"I do—if the figure is right."

"Look, the place is on the market at a certain price, and you are either interested in it at that price, or not. Now which is it?"

"In that case, it's out of the question."

"Couldn't we know the price first?" I asked.

"Forget it."

"But——"

"My attitude is, that's the price, take it or leave it."

"That's ridiculous," said Enid.

"What price?" I put in, very confused.

"I don't bargain."

"Well, I can't approve it otherwise," said Enid impatiently.

"All right, skip it."

"Since we've other places to look at," I said hastily, still very much at sea, "let's leave the decision till we've seen them all."

"As you wish."

Enid and I exchanged glances. "I don't get it." I said.

"This is what always happens," she explained in a low voice. "He's very hard to handle. We must be careful. It's definitely the best place yet, but he mustn't be allowed to sail in so impetuously. I can't tell you how many deals he has spoiled, he's so difficult. We must dicker a bit, you know."

"Yes, I know," I whispered back. Then I said very bravely, "Wouldn't you phone the agent tonight, Billy, not to buy it, but to find out a little more?"

"I'll do it my own way," he said, "or not at all."

So we talked resolutely of other things.

On past Galway town, into the really wild country west, to see a house which a famous artist was selling. "This is the area for artists," said Enid. "They used to come to paint character, but now all that's left is scenery."

Scenery? Landscapes, seascapes? Moonscapes, rather. No trees, not even a bush on this land, but a scene on the moon. Rocks, stones, beds where streams used to run, ridged land, petrified. Fields no larger than graves, engulfed by stone fences; blue twilight and white moonlight to add to its unearthly appearance.

Incredibly enough, the artist's house had already been sold. Since the hour was late, we arranged to stay overnight at a cottage which in the summer was a boarding-house. We were obviously welcome, and the daughters of the house served a dinner that had even Enid purring: mutton boiled on the hearth, potatoes bursting out of their jackets, cabbage fit for gods, home-made baked bastable bread and home-made butter. It was gorgeous. We ate by lamplight at the table in the kitchen, which was also the living-room. Doors in all the walls led to clean whitewashed bedrooms. This was Connemara, on the edge of the Gaeltacht, or Gaelic speaking section of western Ireland. Bits and snippets of folk-lore began coming back to me.

An old man in the Gaeltacht telling of an old woman going for a walk and wanting to express the precise time: "She went for a walk when the dew was thinking of falling." To have said "when the dew was falling" would have been inaccurate. This old woman had never left home. One day she got the notion of going up the hill. She dressed in her best clothes and up she went—and she saw just as much land on the other side. "What a big place Ireland is!"

Ten years ago there had been three people in Connemara who had no English, and one of them was an old lady of ninety. How many now? Words of a Gaelic song—"You have taken the east from me, You have taken the west from me, And now, great is my fear, You have taken my God from me." The way the people of the west liked to sing holding the hand of a friend, and the two arms together swinging the beat of the song. Folkways lost elsewhere in Europe were preserved in Ireland, fringe of the continent as it was.

The west was once land's end, remote, isolated, son after father following the same course. In those days, it was a Connaught joke about the emigration to America: "Ah, Boston's only the next parish," but now the joke is a fact. Nine, eight, seven hours from Shannon to New York: Ireland is in the midst of the world today. Farewell, folk-lore.

Enid had no time for this. "Fancy an American mooning about the Irish heritage! Rave away, I'm going to bed."

Himself and I wandered about in the white night for a while. A handful of boys and girls were dancing in a shabby tiny cottage, windows shuttered and muffled.

40

"Lest the priest can see," said Himself. "The music? Radio Luxembourg, doubtless. Ah well, in another year they'll be gone too—to England or possibly Canada. It's hard to get into the States these days."

Nothing else was stirring; the rocks looked more than ever like gravestones; the silence was beyond that of a cemetery.

"Emigration is the blight of the country," I said, echoing what I'd read in Irish newspapers. "I do feel that the young people should stay, don't you?"

"Hell, no. What have they to stay for? The rocks and the sky? If they had the culture of the Eskimo they might survive here—on sharks and blubber—but as it is there isn't enough mud to build a cabin, let alone a farm. This is a great place for the artist with a full belly. He can appreciate the colours, the stone lace walls, built by slaves, the wild horrible beauty. A great place to come from."

"Can't they fish?"

"Fishing equipment costs money."

"But people have managed to live here all through the centuries. Why should they give up now?"

"You're wrong. They were driven here through the centuries, and the fittest survived, eking out an existence, scraping together enough by any method fair or otherwise to pay the passage of one of them to America; and he with a peasant loyalty could be depended on to send an odd dollar and the fare for another. The history of this area is one of plague and famine. Thank God for emigration!"

"Do they go to England now?"

"Mostly. The people from the west always went to America. Boston and New York were actually better known to them than Dublin, or even Galway town. Now virtually only those with relatives there can get over. And even for the prosperous Irish the dollar curtain makes the States more inaccessible than Russia. Our money system is tied to

England's, and England won't allow the sterling for exchange."

"Oh dear, the Irish will only know us then from the movies."

"And from American visitors."

"It makes me nervous. I feel so responsible, and Enid doesn't seem to think much of Americans."

"She has excellent taste."

"Yes. That's what I thought."

"At any rate, it's hard to find a house that she approves of."

"She liked Beaumont House, the one we saw today. So did I."

"That's the first place in three months that she has conceded is possible, and even that she pretends is too small, and at the same time too big. She's very difficult."

"Oh don't say that. She's been marvellous to traipse around with you. You should be grateful. She makes these objections so you won't seem too eager. We won't go wrong if we're guided by her."

"I wasn't born yesterday. Can't I make my own mistakes?"

"It's preferable not to make any mistake."

"I can't tell you how many deals I could have made. After all, we need a house. She discourages even the agents!"

"Do you want her to ask them if they love her as much as ever?"

"What's wrong with that? Never mind," he said darkly, "she has high notions, like a goat in Kerry."

The next day's drive took us through Sligo, a county I admire. It has trees. It also has hills, lakes, a lovely coastline and *memorabilia* of the poet Yeats. The lakes are the most notable, because they are blue, wooded, isleted and just like American lakes. This in contrast to the black lochs near the glen, hidden amid bare mountains, looking suicidal or homicidal, which they are—ever since St. Kevin drowned

42

his would-be seductress in one and got canonised for it. But the Sligo lakes are sapphire gems, sparkling, happy and sunny, and they have the uninhabited appearance of Maine ponds. Wonderfully shaped hills hove over us as we raced northward; they had flat tops like huge mounds, and mysterious symmetry. Glimpses of the Atlantic and intriguing coves and beaches swept past, and finally, near the town of Sligo, we turned into a driveway and up to a house which had that view.

"Exceptional gentleman's residence in famous hunting and sporting area. Accommodations: five reception, six bedrooms, kitchen with gardens to rere (spelled this way in Ireland), water laid on," Himself read from the car. "Come along," said Enid, "easier seen than heard."

The front door boasted a large iron knocker, its design hidden by coats of paint and a bell-pull. Innocently I tugged at this and it came away in my hand.

"My dear girl," said Himself, "one never uses those things. The knocker is the instrument. If that fails, one simply goes round to the back."

He demonstrated, and it brought results, a little old man who was the caretaker. First he showed us the cellar, a series of arched dungeons, which went back to the fourteenth century. The house had been renovated in the days of Queen Anne, but the foundation was unaltered, even to a stone-lined tunnel which led out to a disused well. "The old people used this for escape," he said. "They was wild times, once."

"Rapparees, doubtless," said Himself.

"A secret passage! What fun for the children."

We were then brought directly to the top of the house, up a broad central stairway. Six bedrooms, two with dressing-rooms adjoining. These were every bit as large as the bedrooms. "What's the difference between a bedroom and a dressing-room?" I asked Enid *sotto voce*.

43

"Don't you have them in America? Whatever sort of people are you?" she said in consternation. "The dressing-room is the room where your husband sleeps."

"Oh."

"What did you think it was?"

"A dressing-room."

"Nonsense, the bedroom is your dressing-room. Much more convenient, really; you move him out and then you have all the wardrobes to yourself."

Six bedrooms, two dressing-rooms and one bath. The toilet was, as usual, elsewhere. The bath fittings were of 1900 or thereabouts and so many copper pipes were running around that it looked like a fire station. Enid turned a tap, but no water came out.

"That's the hot," said the caretaker quickly. "The cold runs right enough, ma'am, from the rain tank on the roof."

Downstairs, some beautifully proportioned rooms opened off the hall, a drawing-room with french windows to a garden, a sitting-room, a dining-room, a morning-room, a study. We noticed one door on the landing which had been overlooked. "That must be the ballroom," said Enid.

"Yes, ma'am."

"Let's see it."

"Don't go in there!"

"Have you a ghost locked in?" asked Himself.

"No, but the English people who are selling the house took up the floor, to make floors for the other rooms. If you go in, you'll fall into the kitchen."

"We'd better see that kitchen," said Enid, and sure enough, it was a two-storey room, with an artistically executed ceiling in plaster, and fancy wallpaper all round the upper half. The bottom half was kitchen.

"When do they expect the electricity to come?" asked Himself.

44

"This summer, sir, so they say. Sure, they've been saying the same for the last five years. They have gaslights, now," calling our attention to the bulbs and pulls hanging in the various rooms.

"*So* interesting," said Enid graciously. "My brother really wants to be nearer to Dublin, but we'll let the agent know."

We withdrew to the car. "That place has possibilities," said Himself happily. "Let me figure the outgoings."

They were low.

"I should think the price would be low too," said Enid.

Himself enumerated the advantages: solid house, gardens stocked with every fruit and vegetable possible, a workman's cottage on the property, a view that was really majestic—hills, fields, trees, white strand, ocean. After all, I told myself, we could always nail up that ballroom door, and a two-storey kitchen would at least be different.

"I'll drive straight to the local agent and make a deal," said Himself.

"Now, Billy," said Enid nervously, "this could hardly be farther from Dublin."

"Who cares? Let's go."

"You must be sure to do it right. Don't commit yourself. Find out first what the lowest price would be. Whatever you do, don't let them think that you have lots of American money to spend."

"What do you want me to say—that I'm a pauper?"

"Just don't go on, as you have done, about your recent return from the States. Don't dare mention America. Say the place is too big or too small or too far or too near, or anything, and that you're only interested if it should happen to be a great bargain."

"You'd better do it, so," he said, his jaw setting.

"Very well, I will." We drove to the agent's office in Sligo, and Enid was very speedy. She came out suppressing triumph. "I'm sure it can be had for practically nothing. They asked £10,000 originally, but they're absolutely broke and would take almost any offer."

"You're wonderful, Enid," I enthused.

Himself said nothing.

"Do you want to make an offer?" she asked.

"I'd be ashamed to—that's robbery!"

"Are you mad? Here's a place easily worth £10,000 and you can probably have it for half."

"I don't like to batten off someone else's misfortune."

"But if you don't someone else will."

"I'll offer £10,000 if you like, since you say it's worth it."

"My God! Don't you dare! You're not in America, where money evidently grows on trees."

"£10,000 or nothing."

"Nothing then," she said, getting in the car and slamming the door. "Really, I wash my hands of you." She murmured to me, "He's more dangerous even than I feared. We mustn't leave him out of our sight. My dear, you are a heroine. How have you ever managed him so far."

By this time the speedometer was jerking up to seventy again. I shut my eyes and gritted my teeth. "I should think it's quite obvious I haven't."

One more place beckoned us on, in Donegal. We stopped for lunch at a seaside resort north of Sligo and drove through what continued to be New England-like country, on and on, till the scenery grew rougher and wilder, more like Scotland, mountainous and bare, and the road often cut through empty plateaus growing nothing but heather. We were heading for a 'granite fishing-lodge', but after fifty miles of wilderness, speeding around curves and skidding in the rain, Himself stopped the car. "The hell with it," he said, "if it's going to be this much trouble to get to, I don't want it."

Enid and I were relieved. "We really have enough to

46

think about, with both Beaumont and the Sligo house," I remarked boldly.

"You'll do well to decide between them," said Enid flatly.

Offhandedly he said, "There are still a few others to see, but we can look in on them on the way home."

"I shouldn't bother," said Enid. "Let's find a hotel for the night and start back tomorrow."

Easier said than done. We drove and drove and drove on the one road. Finally a cross-road gave us a choice of direction and we followed it to the right down a steep hill. A large sign said 'Fishing Hotel' and another sign, larger, said 'Licensed'. This seemed to be the only building within miles, an ample, well-kept stone inn overlooking a tumbling river. At the moment it was headquarters for five or six anglers who would have nothing to do with water—water in streams or water in glasses. I doubt if so much as a pretence of fishing occurred, the bar and unadulterated whiskey being the centre and circumference of their activity. Himself loves a convivial atmosphere, even if vicarious, but Enid took a murky view of the whole operation.

When the proprietor, a small red-faced type, came up to us, Enid gazed down at him coldly. "Can you tell us, my good man, if you have overnight accommodations?"

He must have been the local fanatic and evidently took her to be English. "Accommodations? We've had none here since the English sacked us in 1152."

"A likely story," snapped Enid, looking over the empty lounge.

"The English never sacked here. Isn't this the un-conquered west?" said Himself, vibrating charm in one direction and exasperation in the other.

He unbent at this. "Oh, in that case, we'll find room for ye tonight."

47

"What I've endured for the sake of Billy and his houses," muttered Enid. "And now this!"

Matters steadily disimproved. A taciturn waiter took our order for dinner and returned with tea and bread. "That's all there is," he said angrily.

"Nonsense," retorted Enid. "Bring us an omelette. And here, fetch me a decent-sized cup. I couldn't be bothered weighting my wrist with this thimble."

A long wait, then the waiter returned, leading the proprietor. "Are you the one that ordered the omelette?" he asked, glaring at Enid.

"I am."

"Well, you can't have it."

"Why can't I have it?"

"It will spoil the cook."

Himself interceded once more, and the owner eventually consented to our having rashers and eggs. Enid and the waiter were at daggers' points, however. He slammed plates down in front of her and whipped them away unfinished, spilled tea, refused to get sugar, and vanished for a quarter of an hour when she requested more toast.

Finally he appeared. "Don't bother to put it on a plate," she said sweetly. "Why not just slap me in the face with it?"

"You see," said Himself that night, "she's very difficult. We'll never find a place. Three months of it! I'm fed up."

"Look," I said soothingly, "this trip is almost over, and we've found two which will do—Beaumont House and the Sligo house. Don't rush into buying either of them; we'll get the prices and all the facts when we're back in Dublin, and then you can make an offer."

"You're as bad as she is. Do you want me to be weeks haggling with this one and that one?"

"I'm a stranger here, and you're presumably rusty, but

Enid knows the ropes. Please do what she says."

"Three months, and nothing has suited her."

"She doesn't want you to pay more than you have to, that's all."

"Do we need a house or don't we?"

"We do. But remember, 'let the buyer beware'. When you're buying a house, or buying a meal for that matter, it doesn't have to be a social event. It's commercial."

"E-a-u-x!" (A substitute for another word.) "Don't nag me. My way is to have things pleasant. Never mind, I can see you think as she does. Go ahead, the two of you, get your facts, as you say. Just leave me out of it."

We started early the next morning for the long drive back. Himself wanted to stop to see a house about sixty miles northwest of Dublin, but Enid vetoed it.

"Ridiculous. I know all about that place—Barravore it's called—because friends of Noel's had a look at it. Needs all sorts of work. *Protestants*" (significantly) "are selling it—pious ones by the name of Singleton. 'Magnificent gentleman's residence—it hasn't light or plumbing, electricity expected shortly'—ha!—we know what that means. No," she continued firmly, "you won't do better than either Beaumont or Sligo. I'll phone the agents tomorrow and then we can decide between them."

That night we stayed with Enid, she and I endlessly comparing and debating which of the two places would be It. Himself didn't seem to care. The next morning while we were waiting for ten o'clock, the hour at which offices open in Dublin, to phone, he said he had some business to attend to and would be gone till tea-time.

"What is it, I wonder," said Enid half to herself. "You're sure he said to go ahead and get the facts?"

"Yes."

"Whatever it is he's gadding off about, I don't like it."

49

We phoned the agents and wrote down figures and particulars. "I think there might be woodworm at Sligo," Enid would say, "but those gardens alone are worth a fortune."

"Beaumont is so convenient," I'd reply, "only a short drive from Dublin. Did you notice the built-in presses in the bedrooms?" "Did you know the mahogany tallboy is thrown in in the Sligo sale?" And so forth. Sligo had the workman's cottage. Beaumont could be 'set' for a good income. Sligo was a bargain, Beaumont was a find.

"As soon as Billy comes, we'll make up our minds. I do wonder what he had to attend to. I've been with him constantly for the last three months and recently, at least, he hasn't mentioned anything."

Himself came in, a nasty, smug smile on his face.

"What have you done?" cried Enid, psychically.

"Oh, nothing." He paused to light a cigarette, "I just bought a house, that's all."

"You didn't!" I cried in dismay.

"Not the Singleton place?" exclaimed Enid, clutching her throat.

"The very one."

"Oh, Enid," I wailed, "after all our plans!"

"My dear," she said, turning to me, "I knew it. For three months I've worn myself to a thread, on wild goose chases the length and breadth of Ireland, and then he gets away from me for *one day* and buys this ridiculous place. That's Billy. My dear, I feel for you."

"Oh come now, Enid," said Himself, "it isn't that bad."

"You have bought the whitest elephant in Ireland," said Enid with finality. "The only cheerful note I can strike is that perhaps some day, somehow, some other lunatic will come along and buy it from you. Tea?"

50

CHAPTER 4

*

MOVING IN

ENID WAS OH SO RIGHT. Himself drove the children and
me the next day to see Barravore, through country lifted
unaltered out of the eighteenth century—no telephone poles,
no electric poles, and once off the main road, only horse-
drawn carts and donkey butts. All the way, I had to answer
questions from the children.

"Is this Ireland? Is this my Ireland? Are we going to
our new house? Is it in America? Is it near New York?
Are we going to stay there?"

"And me?"

We had just about given up scanning the horizon, looking
for the house, when he said, "Here it is."

"Where?"

"Here." He turned the car toward a hedge that towered
over us, and dimly a driveway was discernible, and then a
gate, overgrown but in use. No house in sight. We went
down a winding drive under sycamore and chestnut trees,
still no house, till suddenly we were at a front door. The
building was hidden somewhere behind a huge hedge and
rock gardens and flower pots and eye-high fences, and just
for a moment we had a glimpse of a certain beauty and
withdrawal. But in a few seconds the Singletons were
ushering us inside, and what with having to make conversation and being shown through the rooms, that was our
last view of the exterior.

The interior was almost as obscure, thanks to the hedge.

51

Four reception rooms, their walls a patchwork of ugly paintings, five family bedrooms. Not one single cupboard. A toilet of a sort was located on the stair landing of all places, presumably so one could descend to the knock on the front door accompanied by the interesting sound of flushing water. A rainwater tank supplied this and the bathroom. There was no 'drainage'. No heat. No hot water. No water in the kitchen. Just a well in the yard and a hand pump. The implications of all this, reaching as they did practically to divorce, escaped me at the time, though a distinct feeling of malaise oozed around. What struck the attention were the hymn books open on the piano, the Bible texts which the Singletons had posted in every available space: "My help cometh from the Lord," "Live each day as it if were thy last," "God is the unseen guest."

We visited the place several times during the next six weeks, at the end of which time we took possession, but never could we see what the outside looked like. We tried from all angles—front drive, rear drive and finally walked out into the fields, but there was not a spot from which one could get a look at the house. The huge trees hid the dimensions of the roof, the dense hedge spoiled the view from close by, and fences and gardens and outbuildings blocked any vantage point from the back. I kept saying, "It's so frustrating, I mean not to *see* it. How can you buy a house you can't see?" But bought it was, and presently, in we were.

During one of our visits the Singletons had said, watching us carefully, that a jackdaw had broken a window. It was very hard to get a glazier, they said. Himself brushed this aside with, "Never mind, I'll attend to it."

Now we were in and the wind blew regularly through the window. "How about it?"

"No, *all* the windows have to be removed," he announced. How one broken pane in one window necessitated the

52

removal of thirty-odd windows may be hard to understand. Don't expect me to explain, because I too find it hard to understand, hard to the point of impossibility. However, Himself saw it all clearly. He had had, in fact, what might be called a Vision of Barravore in which the obscuring hedges and trees were down, new gardens and trees were planted, new drives and concrete yards were laid out, a new façade gave grace to the front, new stucco and paint shimmered in the sunlight, new steps led to a new porch, a new kitchen took the place of outer rooms, and new casement windows opened on new lawns. The Vision included farm buildings across the lane from the house, even going into detail about electric heating in the pigsties and a grain-drier in the loft. But the Vision did not extend itself to one inch of interior. Decoration in the house? Not important. Wall-paper? Something the maid and I could slap up while we were resting ourselves. Paint? Oh don't bother me with trifles.

Fortunately the Vision had included that detail about pig-heating, because electricity became agendum No. 1. At the time power was being rationed, and no new installations were made. How to get it? Himself pulled strings. He knew some very exalted Ones in Dublin, which meant a couple of lunches there, a couple of trips to the county headquarters of the Electricity Supply Board, a letter or two, and then the dam broke and a parade of examining electricians com-menced. (Meanwhile the draught from the broken window went on unregarded.) These visits were great events to us, though it was a bit disconcerting to go over the same ground so often, and I, at least, felt just a touch stale by the third round. But Himself thoroughly enjoyed every minute, and to this day when he flicks on the switches, there is something immodestly deprecating about his gesture, as though he swung that key from the kite-string and personally blew the glass for every bulb.

The formula for us and E.S.B. big-shots went like this. E.S.B. man arrives. Himself has a drink of whiskey with him. They go out and pace off the distance from the electric line four fields away to our house. They have another drink. For over an hour E.S.B. man examines the pig-house and discusses intricate lighting effects there, as though it were the balcony scene in a theatre-in-the-round. Himself is charmed. They have another drink and we all have tea. E.S.B. man then devotes approximately five minutes to electricity within the house and departs, mentioning, with one foot in his car, that he will do all he can to push our job ahead of hundreds of others, but he is just about to be transferred to the west. Next day another E.S.B. man turns up and we do it all again.

But still in a remarkably short time considering that they are attaching up huge areas of Ireland strictly in order of demand, and that from our area, apart from us, there was no demand, and in others people had been waiting for years, we did get wired. The poles and lines did not go up for another two months, but even that was a record. Our neighbour, Lady Crosby, who had had Castlecrosby completely wired five years ago, was still unconnected. Our accomplishment filled her with envy, but she was not prepared to pay main rates for her huge place, so she did not join in. This, after days of inquiry from her and weeks of explanation from the E.S.B., as she was very deaf. Himself agreed to some complicated arrangement by which we have a monthly charge for the line quite apart from whatever we owe for juice so that (I hope I'm throwing this in casually and gaily enough—through gritted teeth) our electricity costs more than what many Americans and all Irishmen pay for rent. Meanwhile we are regarded as mad. "Sure, wouldn't the ould paraffin do them?"

"The electric" raises the whole issue of romanticism and practicality. I used to say that only untouched nature was

54

beautiful, that a view marred by one housetop was not to be compared with a view of unsullied trees, lakes, ferns and such. I privately crossed my best friend's summer place off my list because from the back windows one could glimpse a railway down in the valley, and even when driving along a road I'd never see again, electric poles struck me as a personal affront. Needless to say, I have eaten those words.

When dusk came on that thrilling day when *our* poles were up and *our* line was finally connected with the house wiring, Himself touched a switch and the house was floodlit. Nothing looked more beautiful then than the house and the row of poles marching regularly over the fox covert on the hill and joining the main line at the railway track in the distance. How purposeful the wires, how upright the poles! How enterprising the railway, to be there to begin with! How sacred the box containing the transformer! The whole thing symbolised civilisation, progress, washing-machines, refrigeration, long-playing records, toasters and mixers and electric blankets, Christmas tree lights and TV. . . . Himself saw scientifically warmed pigs, grain-driers, pumps, automatic watering of cattle and feeding of poultry—and, just possibly, ice-cubes. From then on, when out driving, we both would automatically register which property had poles and lines leading to it and which had not, and our game of 'Would you like to live in that house?' took a new turn. Whereas before, the more ruined the ruin, the more we yearned to put it right, now we regretfully but firmly excluded all ruins except those near poles.

But as of the present, an old hardbitten householder, I see everything in a different light. Electricity is not something that one simply *has* to have. O.K. in the States, where it is available for relatively little, but not in Ireland and wherever else it is a luxury. We could do what others here do, namely, wait for Rural Electrification to come through, since the rate for that is cheap, and in the meantime use the good old medieval method of labour-saving—the working class. Skip the washing machine and go to the convent laundry. Skip the 'fridge and the deep-freeze and hire someone who understands brining, smoking, canning and such. Skip the vacuum cleaner and have an extra maid. Battery radio. Gas-driven pump. Short-playing records. Toast done on the stove. Hot-water jugs in bed, and a big boom-chicka-boom for one thing less to do at Christmas. Let an extra man hug the darn pigs or whatever one does to warm them, and take care of the hens. That would leave only lighting, for which the ould paraffin *would* do.

This might seem to put us back on the dinner-by-candle-light school of thought, with nary a wire littering up the countryside, but no. We adore civilisation, or electricity (they seem to be synonymous); it's just that feudalism is cheaper. In fact, as I gingerly operate my washer (which no maid can be let near) I long for the convent laundry which not only washes but dries and irons cleaner, better and with much less wear and tear on linen, machinery and, of course, me. What's more, the convent laundry does not hold a sword over my head, threatening to break down and involve delayed and expensive visits from the repair man in Dublin.

If only I had grasped the fact in time, the convent laundry is the *perfect* system. The modern washer was only invented when, in our American way of life, labour got notions about being paid; then cheap, good laundries were no more. But too late! We have the washing-machine and I am its keeper. But I now quite appreciate Himself's gesture as he flicks on the switch. I shouldn't be surprised if, like the millionaire who offered his guests a choice of champagne or milk from his private herd, he were to make a candle of ten-pound notes and casually light it. He could very easily say, "This, or the electric, whichever you wish. They cost about the same."

However, we were just plain delighted when, a few weeks after our junketings with the E.S.B. VIP's, two honest-to-goodness electricians arrived to wire the house: Mick and Jack. They took up lodgings in town and spent three weeks sawing up floorboards, knocking down plaster and wallpaper, crawling under floors and between walls and generally acting like human flies. They were both small, apparently a qualification for their profession. Jack was an apprentice, only eighteen years old, and he looked much younger. Jimmy asked in fact, "Is Jack a big boy or a little man?" at which Peggy the maid (maid in the occupational sense, only, I might add) laughed uproariously and backed into the scullery, and Jack blushed.

It seemed cruel to let them bring plain bread from their digs and eat it in the shed, so we told them to take their meals in the kitchen. Thus we learned that Jack was a Pioneer, a member of a total-abstinence organisation quite popular with young people. They pledge themselves not to take a drop of liquor (not even, we found out, soup with a spoonful of sherry in it) and Jack, who looked like a little blond angel anyhow, was very scrupulous and solemn. Under the inspiration of having two men, however small and angelic, all to herself at mealtimes, Peggy turned up for work in the sheerest of blouses and gossamer nylons; she eyed Mick furtively and seemed to have to brush past him wherever she went. He remained poker-faced, but seemed grateful for the drink Himself offered him when work was over one day. Not so the Pioneer. He shook his blond curls and reminded us that he could not; he had taken the vow.

"How long ago did you take it?"

"Four years," said the cherub.

"It's a fierce dog that has to be muzzled," Himself said, and Jack blushed with pride.

Meanwhile, in fact literally through all of this, the broken window was causing a gale. Bill made enquiries and was told of a contractor who would take over the job of installing new frames and glass all over the house. Thus we met Fitzgibbon, better known as Fitz, and two days before the electricians left, Fitz and his workmen arrived.

It got to be that there was no room uninhabited by men with axes and crowbars, no corner unresounding with hammer blows. This was supposed to be finished in five weeks—and lasted for almost a year. When the new crew appeared, we felt that we couldn't ask *them* to sit in the shed while the others ate in the kitchen, so the whole gang became our guests for elevenses, dinner, fourses and tea. This did *not* last for almost a year, for reasons to be disclosed. But oh the upheaval, the crises, the noise, the mess, the frustrations, the disappointments, the delays, the tensions of the Fitz régime. It was like an Occupation. Even today, when people remark that we must have been lonely at first, they positively recoil at the violence of our "Oh no!" We get a mark for fortitude instead of one for understatement.

Fitz was a plausible, disarming, round-faced sort. He had a boyish way of shoving his cap up on his head, and he always had time to talk. He and Himself kept strolling off for long conversations, and presently Himself divulged to me that while we were about it, we might as well put in some bathrooms and do a few other odd jobs.

"Fine idea!" said I, delighted to be one up on the pigs.

"In fact," said Himself, "I've got in touch with Darcy, the architect Enid recommended; but until he can get up here I think I'll let Fitz go ahead. He's a great fellow, you know. Worked in the States, had his own business and was really getting ahead. Gave it all up when his parents wanted him back here."

Fitz went over every room in the house, making suggestions. And he said he could do it all for a figure which struck us as a bagatelle.

"Is it possible?" Himself asked.

"Surely," said Fitz.

"Well, you're a better man than I am. By my figures, you'd be losing money."

"I have me own system. I'm doin' several jobs at once, y' see, and when the men are finished here, say, I'll rush them over to one of the other places. That way one outfit o' men can do three jobs and the whole thing becomes very cheap."

Workmen started knocking out walls everywhere at once, which made me uneasy. The children, perpetually under-foot, had a thousand escapes a day from nails, falling roof slates, chunks of concrete, planks, shovels left lying about and the other multitudinous instruments of building. Was this the way everyone went about remodelling? Himself assured me haughtily that it was. "Fitz's doing a damn fine job, or at least trying to, in the face of tough conditions."

"What conditions?"

"At home. He has an American wife *and you know what that can do to a man*."

But every hour unforeseen complications developed, so that even Himself was somewhat daunted, and we began to dread Fitz's cheery, "You're just the man I'm looking for, sir. Would ye like the tank under the rafters? We've measured, and it will fit sideways. Better nor havin' it above the tub."

"You said it wouldn't fit under the rafters."

"I measured it again, skeow-wise. It'll fit."

"It's all one to me, of course. Put it where you think best."

"O.K." Then turning and yelling to the men, "Take that steel beam outa the wall before the concrete sets. He wants it in the attic."

C

Crash! Crash! Thud. Titanic hammering as two bed-room walls came down around gaping holes, and chunks of plaster litter the beds and floors.

A giant named Art was summoned away from knocking down another part of the house and put to sledging out the door and door frames of the old bathroom where the tank was at the moment installed. Then he knocked out the door and door-frame of the bathroom-to-be, a tiny room of cryptic function (probably a walk-in wardrobe, nineteenth-century style). Then he knocked out various posts and walls in the attic. And *then* it was found that the tank was about a foot too big all round to be installed where planned.

"How do you account for that, Fitz?"

"Glory be to God!" (pushing up his cap), "these bloody men can't measure."

"You had better repair the damage immediately."

"We will that, sir. It's scandalous, surely."

Oh, how we wished we had fired Fitz, Art and the others all busy reducing the place to rubble, then and there. But the house was so far gone Himself thought he had better see it through. So, Art was ordered by Fitz to swing the tank out of the window of the room where it was and up to the window of the bathroom. Both windows and window frames were accordingly knocked out, and the tank was lowered from ropes slung from the roof. This involved the breaking of innumerable slates, the destruction of the plaster all the way down the house where the tank was lowered, and the crashing of all windows under the ones in question. The tank was then hoisted to the bathroom, and *then* it was discovered to be too big to fit even there. Fitz deemed it wise to disappear for a couple of days, and eventually Himself bought a new, smaller tank, and the old one conveniently vanished.

All this, needless to say, took weeks, most of which passed

with the workmen sitting around waiting for the tank to be delivered, or yelling the equivalent of 'Tim-ber'! whenever another window fell. There was no sign of them being rushed to another job. In fact there was no sign of any motion at all, never mind rush. We crept about amid débris for days and days, and ate in a hurricane.

"Where's the other ladder?"

"Paddy has it."

"Paddy, come away ower that with the ladder."

"Put one on top nor the other, they don't be high enough."

"They won't make it, I tell you."

"Don't be so fussy. Up with you, Paddy."

"Here, Paddy, catch. Mind that loose slate!"

"Jasus, who done that?"

"Paddy."

This seemed a clear case of discrimination against Paddy, whoever he was, until we learned that nine out of ten of the men were named Paddy. Paddy Bergin and Paddy Mac, Paddy the Plasterer, the College Boy (so called because he always looked brushed and combed and wore a jacket), Paddy the Bubble (supposed to be a carpenter but couldn't read a level, consequently the nickname), Paddy Leavy, Paddy the Plum (plumber), Paddy Rory and Paddy Joe.

The conversations overheard! With no windows and few doors, everything was dreadfully audible, but the men did not seem to realise this. Paddy Rory and the Bubble were perched on the roof of the library unaware that anyone was inside.

"She said I had no 'tick neck'. What's 'tick neck'?"

"Ah sure, Bubble, teck-neek."

"Teck-neek? What's teck-neek?"

"Jasus! Teck-neek is approach. You know, approach."

"Oh. . . . I'll give her a proch, so I will!"

Those workmen! The windows put in upside down, the

windows removed and done over again, the windows through which rain poured, the windows impossible to open, or to close, the windows of varying height. Months gone by while a dozen men stood around watching old Andy, the carpenter, lift a frame into place and then shuffle off with it again to make some adjustment. Months gone by while the workmen plastered the walls around the windows and splatter-dashed any furniture they could spy. Months gone by while they congregated at our house for meals and then, after a decent amount of sociable conversation, departed. By this time Tom Malone had come from the glen to be our 'man', and he was disgusted to the marrow. "Them ones wouldn't work," he reported, "not even to warm themselves."

Months gone by while they laid a concrete yard. The first one was tilted just as Himself ordered, but the mixture was such that Tom inadvertently swept it up with a broom while trying to clean. The second one they laid was hard as a rock all right, but slanted so that it drained toward the house and made a cascade of the steps to the kitchen. That one took weeks to dig up. Months gone by while they made ash of what could have been a lovely black and white bathroom. When the Bubble put up the towel rack at a visible angle, I wept on Himself's shoulder and begged him to send for the guards. "Get those men out of here!"

The architect, who was from Dublin, agreed that Fitz and his crew were beyond the credible. They had dug a soak-hole for sewage and then laid the pipes so that they sloped away from it. They had built a bathroom downstairs too small to hold the fixtures ordered expressly for it. They had put a roof on a porch, through which the rain fell unimpeded. When the water drained out of the hand basin in our bathroom, with happy hooting noises it gurgled up into the bath. If concrete had to be mixed, and it seemingly had to be mixed every day, it was done on the floor of the playpen, or on inlaid linoleum intended for the kitchen, or on the reverse of expensive enamelled wallboard. Every job had to be done over and over again, and then was not done right. We couldn't understand it.

"How can he make any profit on the job with all those men standing idle and so much material wasted?"

Darcy, the architect, couldn't figure it either. Once he said thoughtfully, "There's an American book that this reminds me of. Have you read it? *Mr. Blanding Builds His Dream House*."

"Read it?" said Himself. "I'm beginning to think I wrote it."

The day the bathroom was fitted out with the last of the plumbing, the well went dry. Not just dry for a week or so, as it seemed all local wells did regularly every summer, but permanently, deliberately dry. (Oh, shades of Singleton saying piously, "The well has never failed and never will—not in this area"). So every day Tom went to the County Council well, over a mile away, and filled a barrel with water, and this had to do for everything—cooking, washing, bathing and—er—flushing. Bridie was the maid by then, poor girl, and to her fell the juggling act of washing everything in order of priority, trying to keep all of us and the workmen fed, dishes clean, etc. Meanwhile we sent for an artesian well firm and were told it would be two months before they could come.

The boss of this outfit, when he finally appeared, turned out to be a retired British Army man, brisk and trim, moustache, monocle and all. He was the last person you'd expect to be a water-diviner, but he was. He carried a pendulum of hazelwood and walked with little mincing steps all over our yard. At several points the hazel swayed back and forth, so he asked Himself to mark off which area he preferred. Then within this limited space he moved very slowly and finally came to a spot where the knob really danced. Then he cupped it in his hand till it stopped, let it start to swing again, cupped it again, released it again, concentrating with such intentness you would have thought the earth were a speaking-tube. "You have," he said, straightening up, "a trickle at thirty feet and a weak spring at fifty. And a river at seventy to eighty."

"Give us the river," said Himself. He was thinking, à la Vision, of water for cattle, water for fowl, pigs, even for garden if need be.

"Very well, and you'll have my guarantee, as always. No water, no pay."

All this was very fine, but then it transpired that the drill wouldn't be free for another month. Very well, we waited.

We waited and waited, in fact, for every slightest thing. And the workmen waited too. For days and days, and weeks and weeks, most of them would stand around "with the two hands in the one pockut" as Tom remarked, waiting for some gadget, or for Fitz, or for supplies, or for one of themselves to do something, and he would be waiting for something else. What twisted the dagger in the wound was the fact that we were receiving avalanches of American magazines and would read the ads and the articles describing fittings, or waterproof paints, or plastic sprays, or tiles—all the things we needed and could not get. And they were always pictured as easy to apply oneself. What fools we, to have thought that setting up house here would be the same as in New Jersey!

Himself was less disturbed than I, getting rather a laugh out of the stationary workmen and the general chaos; but even he wished for the days back when loyal followers would flock at the sound of the O'Neill pibroch, or whatever it was. Fitz grew scarcer and scarcer. For weeks he didn't show at all, except early in the morning or after dark, to pay off his

64

men. He always tried to get away without our seeing him. I was not surprised at this stage to overhear Himself describe him to someone as "a well-intentioned chap, I suppose, but no business head. Failed in the States, you know, and had to come back here."

One day I happened to go out of the back door after dinner and saw Paddy Mac and Paddy the College *washing their hands in our drinking cooking everything water*!

"Do you happen to know that we have to use that water to cook with?"

Silence.

"How long has this been going on?"

Silence.

"Where are the other men?"

Silence.

Finally the College Boy muttered, "In the barn."

I marched them out there, and catching the others absolutely open-mouthed with surprise, harangued them like a sergeant-major. Poor Bubble let it fall that they all had been doing all their washing in it for days.

"Oh!"

"Sure, it's no harm, ma'am, it's our own dirt."

"O-oh!"

When I got my breath again I told them that until they learned to use the hand-basin provided for washing, they were not to touch the barrel, and then said that anyone with a glimmer of sense or the slightest knowledge of hygiene should know that drinking water must never never be interfered with. "If one of you had conjunctivitis or trench mouth, say, or anything contagious, we might all catch it. For your own sakes, never never do such a thing again!"

Silence.

That afternoon, Fitz waited on Himself, and informed

him in a very satisfied way that the men had "downed spades" and were walking off the job.

"Thank God," exclaimed Himself. "But why?"

"Because the missus insulted 'em. She told them they had diseases that they didn't even know what they were."

Little by little the story was pieced together, along with the disappointing fact that they were not quitting. Fitz had thrown that in for dramatic effect. Himself said loyally that I was quite right, and Fitz agreed I was too, surely.

But that night Himself put me on the carpet. "Look, you must understand, social diseases are absolutely unmentionable in Ireland."

"But I didn't say anything about social diseases."

"As far as they are concerned, you did. Just what did you say?"

"I said they might have conjunctivitis or trench mouth."

"They're social, aren't they?"

"Well, ye gods, whooping cough is social too, if you want to look at it that way."

"Don't be flippant."

"*Me* flippant? What do you think you're being?"

"Did you accuse them of making passes at you?"

"What?"

"They say you said they were familiar."

"Familiar! I said they might be contagious!"

"All the same to them."

"Oh my God!"

"See here, if you want to live happily in Ireland, you have to watch those things. You're not careful about what you say. At that women's meeting the other night, you said young Mrs. Carthy couldn't canvass because she was going to have a baby."

"Well, she is, isn't she? And how do you **know what I** said?"

"Never mind how I know—they were all talking about it. You should have said, 'She's not feeling so well'."

"But everyone knows she's pregnant. It's due in a couple of weeks. And anyhow she's pregnant every year."

"That's neither here nor there. Your sort of speech is immodest."

"*Oh!*"

"Watch your language in future."

"Why you . . ."

"That's all."

From that day forth, the workmen brought their own food and ate in the shed. It was their way of retaliating.

The drill finally came, the crew camped in a caravan along the back drive, and the machine bored and dug with rhythmical house-shaking thuds. As day went into week and week into month, we quite forgot what they were there for. Thud! Thud! Thud! At one point the mud that came up was black and we had hopes of coal. At another point it was oily and we had hopes of oil. It was really an anticlimax when at eighty-two feet down, it came up water. The drillers bade us a sad farewell, exchanging photographs and gifts with Tom and Bridie, the caravan uprooted itself from the driveway, and now we had nothing to do but wait for the pump.

Himself wanted a special kind of pump—a jet—and after several days learned that there was a firm in Ireland which carried them. As far as I was concerned, the work was now over, and the pump just a sort of footnote to be added—a rather specialised bolt which would hook up the well with the house. I bought four sets of shower curtains (black goldfish and silver lilies on white background) and set out the guest towels and made the children change their underwear every night. After a week of this foolhardy behaviour, I had to hustle them back into the Stone Age again, because the pump company was obviously unwilling to sell us the pump. It seemed that they had never previously installed one—not that that was necessarily fatal, because they assured us any handyman could do it—but their workmen were all tied up. But Himself took it in his stride and said Tom and Paddy Bergin, now Tom's helper, would do it, provided we were supplied with the manufacturers' instructions. And so it was arranged.

In another week the pump arrived, and Tom and Paddy meticulously, inch by inch and step by step, followed the directions. Himself checked and double checked, and even more rapidly than I had hoped the double line of pipe drew nearer in its three-foot trench. Then the pressure tank was attached, the pump lined up, and all that remained was to throw the switch. Celebrating in my own fashion, I was going around the kitchen, humming a little tune and taking stained tea-towels off their hooks and looking about for dish-rags, pot-holders, Bridie's aprons, babies' bibs—all provender for our dazzling unused washing-machine waiting in the corner. Himself threw the switch. Nothing happened. Tom and Paddy tried. Nothing happened. Those two looked bewildered and disgusted, but Himself only laughed.

Next day the pump men arrived in force, examined the installation and declared the work faulty. Himself insisted patiently that it was correct. After several hours of polite deadlock, he said, "The only way I can see to settle it, is for you to re-install the whole thing. If the pump works I'll pay double your bill, but if on the other hand the pump is the trouble, you'll supply a new one and I won't pay you a penny." The proposition was accepted.

For about a week the yard resounded once more with the noise of men pretending to work—they were going to make a good thing out of this and run up the costs. Some of the pipes were strained, they felt, and must be replaced: the trench had to be covered each night with special straw brought from an expensive distance—they made a week's work for six men out of what Tom and Paddy did in one day. Once again the tank was connected, the pump was set up and the supervising engineer threw on the switch. Silence. Even poker-faced Tom couldn't suppress a wink, and Paddy openly beamed. The pump men grumblingly announced that the jet must have been injured in the first installation, and they piled rapidly into their van, bringing the pump with them to test and repair it.

Loud was the revelry in the kitchen that night. The supervisors had made the mistake of discussing modern poetry with Himself in Tom's hearing—that was all he needed to clinch his initial countryman's distrust of 'fellers with book larnin''. "Them chaps can talk the leg off an iron pot, mebbe, but they don't know much about pumps."

"Them ones is all stalk and no spuds," contributed Paddy.

Water or no water, I must admit I had been relieved when the switch did not go on, but as week began to tick away after week again, dreams of piping-hot baths in the black and white bathroom obsessed me. "Look, phone them and say you don't care what kind of a pump they put in—just fix it so we can have water."

"Calm down. The longer they stay away, the more confident I am that the pump is faulty."

Another week went by. I was now at the stage when visions of baths I could have taken and didn't, haunted me the way food rejected in the past haunts a man in prison. The water was so hot, I would muse. Hotter than you could stand it. And I could have had a tub full every night. With bath salts. And a spotless gleaming bathroom, a mat inches thick all over the floor. Snow-white towels, use half a dozen if I liked. And a lovely warm hall and room to step into. . . . Or I would think of baths in literature, from the steamy description in *Little Men*, in which Nat has the first wash of his life in a huge old-fashioned bathroom filled with jugs and basins and tubs and Nurse Hummel, to the one the beautiful old lady gave Curdy in *The Princess and the Goblin*. And even Claudette Colbert's scene in the old film *Cleopatra*.

"Can't you do *something* about the pump?"

"Look, if I interfere now they'll claim I upset our bargain."

"You and your bet! Ridiculous in the first place. I'm beginning to feel like the White Russian refugee who sold her honour for soap."

"She must have been hard up for an excuse."

"Oh you're impossible! Don't *you* ever feel dirty?"

"Just scrape away the crust, girl. We never died of a winter yet." He began to sing,

> "Oh she washed me all over, I remember,
> And after powder-puffing me, you se-e-e,
> She laid me in the cradle near the fender
> In the little shirt my mother made for me."

When I was beginning to think that we must return to America in order to get clean again, one day, unbelievably, the van appeared. The jet pump was whisked out, set up, attached, the switch was thrown, and the steady purr of the motor filled the pump-room. Tom and Paddy looked bleak, the supervisors looked happy, I looked, I'm sure, overjoyed—until I thought of the double payment. Himself's face was long and sad, though he did give me just the shadow of a grin.

The bill, presented with a flourish, was for £213 doubled, or £426. Well, now we had running h. and c. but £426 seemed an awful lot to pay for the pleasure. Conversation between Himself and the men grew technical, and for some reason they had to consult the plate on the pump. "It's rather dark in the pump-room," said Himself. "Would one of you fellows get the plate and bring it up here?"

"Certainly, certainly." He was back in a jiffy. "Here you are."

"This is the plate from the pump you just put in?"

"Absolutely."

"Well, my friends, that's too bad. Because *here* is the plate of the original pump, which I took the precaution of detaching when you removed it for repair."

"Caught," they said cheerfully.

Whereupon all hands had a drink. We didn't pay them a penny; in fact, they considered us in on the plot and used to drop by and regale us with tales of the lengths they were forced to go to make up the loss on other jobs.

We only had one more wait, this time for a plumber, because of a last little adjustment which had to be made before the water could run into the house pipes. Paddy the Plum had gone to England with his greyhounds, in great hopes of making big money. The other local man was famous for never answering calls. We tried him though, and we wrote to every licensed and unlicensed plumber we heard of, but no one ever replied. Then we gave up.

To be delayed *now*, with the apple within our grasp, was to cross the border from insupportable urgency to the numbness of apathy. What did it matter? It would all be the same in a hundred years. Dust unto dust, life is but a dream, and running water a vain illusion. Pah.

Weeks later Paddy the Plum returned broke, disgusted with dogs, and longing for the comfortable feel of copper pipe. He flew to our aid, accompanied by six apologetic-looking hounds. "Ah, them," he said. "They be too expensive to feed, and too good to shoot."

We wouldn't have cared if he had arrived with a pack of Siberian wolves. It took the Plum exactly five minutes to do the needful. Five minutes—and eleven months—but now we had water.

Well. I indulged in a two weeks' mad orgy, bathed twice daily, did the laundry all day every day with the machine, ripping down towels and curtains, seizing all underwear, practically tearing sheets out from under sleeping children, and sweaters off anyone who passed me in the hall—and then the machine broke down. But we pass over that; it belongs to the new era—Maintenance—and I have yet one more detail to go under the heading of Moving In.

Just this. Fitz had cleared out some time before, leaving us in a shambles. Now he sued us, claiming that he was working on a time and materials basis. The contract? "What's that? Ye have nothin' in writin', surely."

CHAPTER 5

*

THE STAFF

THE ADVERTISEMENTS in the *Irish Times* are glorious going, easily the fruitiest reading in the whole paper. Houses, furniture and *objets d'art* up for auction are described with a wealth of imaginative detail. Second-hand articles—trailers, collapsible boats, electric fences, concrete-mixers, tomato-plants, outgrown hunting ponies, a labrador puppy "rescued from the tinkers"—anything at all, might, and does, turn up its in pages. The Employment columns are particularly alluring, because in country houses in Ireland there is always room for one more 'staff' and always occasion for one less. Comings and goings, sudden crises and sylvan epics are forever looming.

At home in the States my family had had a long line of retainers. How we needed them now! We pined for Hermine and Hedwig, for Crystal and Lola, as we did not pine for our best friends. I kept hoping that a retainer-type would turn up, *sans famille*, a paragon of kind heart and efficiency. Each morning, as soon as Willie the Post brought the *Times*, I raced through dozens of 'Respectable farmer's daughter, domesticated, seeks position in Dublin, indoor', and 'Gentlewoman, C. of I., would keep house for one gentleman'. Himself always assured me that I was wasting my time to try and locate anyone for us by that method. "With the house so upset," he said for the first two years, "and we not settled yet, you can't expect a proper servant to come here."

"*We're* here," I pointed out.

"You'll just have to make do with the locals."

The first week we were in Barravore we had no help at all, and I spent the entire seven days in the kitchen. Just that, from dawn till midnight. 'Above stairs' (the term for the master's as against the servants' quarters) went untouched. There was so much to do in the kitchen that I never got out, and incidentally, nothing was done right.

For one thing, it was terribly dark. This was below stairs, a typical basement, monument to an era when servants were little better than slaves. One tiny window lit a very large kitchen; similar windows provided for the adjoining larder and scullery. Outside the windows, as one looked up, was a high bank of earth covered with dank grass; and massed above that was the thick hedge. At noon some light penetrated into the rooms, but the rest of the day, either way, was crepuscular. I don't see how any cook could have managed there, even in the old days unless they went blind, like insects in caves, and operated by radar. Certainly I couldn't.

There were always children's hands and faces to wash, meals to get (Himself insists on six a day), dishes to wash—with hard, hard water—table to scrub and set and clear, laundry to do, floor to sweep, turf to fetch, turf to chop, stove to stoke every ten minutes, water to pump (out in the yard), water to heat, water to throw out, children to throw out, children to bath, ashes and garbage to dump, lamps to light, and so on and on. Unpacking was out of the question; marketing had to be done, but it left the other duties awry. Countrywomen in Ireland do these things every day of their lives and it doesn't take a feather off them, but to me it was the salt mines. Seven days and I was ready to plant the turf axe in the next person who asked for tea.

Meanwhile Himself was trying to locate a maid and a cook. Since this was one of my first experiences of Irish indirection, I was somewhat exasperated. My technique, had I got out of the kitchen, would have been to stop everyone who passed on the road and say "Do you know a maid?" or, "Come and be our cook."

Himself wasted innumerable hours chatting with this one and that one, pressing stout on Paddy Quinn who did our garden, having long roundabout conversations with the labouring classes. Every so often he would come back and attempt to enliven my dull moments with an account of his research. He invariably found me washing up after one meal or another, and in no mood for whimsy.

"Uh-huh," I would say wife-ishly. Or, "Well, well." And, "Obviously, what we need is less sociability and more action."

Once he announced that the sister-in-law of the fellow in the cottage near the church would come over the next morning. She did not. Another time, the grocer said that the nuns would send one of the orphans whom they trained; but when pressed for more details he reported that Sister Gabriel had hooted at the idea. She had no girls ready and a long line of would-be employers. Then we had a pretty girl who lived down the road, but she left to go to England. Then Enid lent us her maid from Dublin to help out, and just as she left a girl walked in and asked if we had a job. Had she been two-headed and coloured blue, I would have grabbed her.

Actually, she *might* have been two-headed and coloured blue, because in the dim light of our kitchen such small details would, of course, pass unnoticed. Sight unseen, so to speak, I engaged her. This was a Saturday, and she was to come on Monday morning. Hardly had she stumbled out of the door, when the sister-in-law of the fellow in the cottage appeared (she had previously been lurking in the bushes, keeping watch.) She said 'mister' had engaged her, last month.

I was peering at her through the gloom, having thought for a moment that this was the same girl who had just walked out. "You're from the cottage near the church?"

"Yes, missus."

"Oh, then there's been some mistake. You were to come to be interviewed last month, but you weren't engaged. And anyhow, you didn't come."

"Well, the factory's shut down now," she said.

"I'm sorry, I've just hired someone else."

She too made her way out. Later on, and by this time it was so thoroughly dark that Himself had descended and lit a simply terrific lamp (which took half an hour, assorted ominous explosive noises, methylated spirits, paraffin oil and a whole tool-kit of wicks, mantles, scissors, pins and heaven knows what before it would start), still another girl arrived. Thanks to the illumination, we could see *her*. She had flowing auburn hair and very bad teeth. Her message was that the first girl (the two-headed one) couldn't come after all, because Lady Crosby was keeping her on for the summer cleaning. But she, Peggy, would come in her place, if I liked. Needless to say, I liked. (This was the Peggy who was later so taken with the electricians).

She went out, and minutes later, sister-in-law from the cottage reappeared.

"Yes?"

"Lady Crosby's keepin' the other girl."

"Indeed."

"Any chance of a job fer me, missus?"

"No. Terribly sorry, but the job is filled."

Eagerly, "I'll work fer less nor that one, missus."

"Sorry."

She went, again. The next day four other girls came by, all primed with the news about Lady Crosby's summer cleaning.

"Action," said Himself sweetly. "You wanted it and you got it."

Peggy was from the North of Ireland, really, but had come to our locality to stay with an aunt. Her friend Nellie, a fellow called Barney and Mrs. Quinn all worked for us in the next three months, but Peggy was the most remarkable. She was aboriginal. She was slovenly, lazy and man-crazy, and the continual presence of men knocked her mind off whatever bearings it might once have had.

When she first came our orange-squeezer was leaking, though it could still be used, so I set it in a soup-plate and showed her how, pouring off the juice into glasses to drink. Every morning after that we got our juice in soup-plates, no matter how I explained and re-explained, no matter that a new squeezer had been supplied, no matter that we called for glasses immediately. She looked at me earnestly when I scolded her, never answered back, but the juice came in soup-plates nonetheless.

She went to every dance within twenty miles and slept more and more during the day (above stairs, while presumably making the beds). At mealtimes we would ring for her to serve us something and find, a half hour later, that she was out in the barn with the workmen. At one point Fitz suggested that if I wanted to leave instructions for her, I should tack them on the ceiling above the workbench.

Apart from activities at which she was prone, so to speak, she developed a couple of other undesirable habits. One was an inclination to eat all of any special treat we had. I tried to keep a tin of milk chocolate biscuits on hand for the children, but I was fighting against overwhelming odds. Peggy ate them by the dozen. Friends said I was mad to leave that sort of thing in the kitchen—one locked them in the 'store', it seemed. What was a store? Anything with a lock. We had nothing with a lock. I moved the tin upstairs and buried it in a drawer in the sitting-room. She located it, apparently within ten minutes. I moved it, she found it, and this went on till as usual she had eaten them all. The same chase went on with sweets which I tried to keep against sudden company. The killing part was that she always denied having eaten so much as a single piece.

Next, little things started disappearing—Bridget's hairbrush, the baby's locket, cigarette lighters, a fountain pen, and finally a valuable gold ring of mine. We began to feel that Peggy would have to go. Then one day she hurt her arm, she said, and of her own accord sent her friend Nellie to take her place.

Nellie, as all the country people let us know, was 'Bad'. She had an illegitimate child, a little boy of four or so. Nellie herself was eighteen. They couldn't trace the father, the story went: too many possibilities to permit of narrowing down. Nellie went to all the dances with Peggy, seemed to have as good a time, and as far as we could make out, was fortunate. Her father had kept both her and the baby, whereas in most cases of this sort, the girl was ostracised and had no place to go except the county home. Here she would be put to hard labour, usually laundry work, for three years, and her child would be taken from her. So Nellie was lucky.

She had a gay and straightforward manner and was a whiz at cleaning. Peggy had brought her over a couple of times before, to help with the work and maybe with the workmen. Like now, Peggy was always complaining about some ache or pain. "Ah, she's always with an arse or an elbow," said Nellie disgustedly. "Look at my sore leg, it's worse nor that."

One of the men (a primitive who later got two girls and his wife pregnant on the same night—it was a court case) remarked that he'd be glad to give her leg a rubbing.

"Thanks," said Nellie tartly. "It's been well rubbed."

Nellie at any rate never disappeared into the workshop at mealtime, and accomplished more cleaning in a few days than Peggy had in months. She had always done the house-work at home and also worked in the fields with her brother. I asked her if she couldn't stay with us instead of Peggy. "I'll ask Mammy," she replied.

In due course she reported that Mammy said no, because Nellie was necessary on the farm and the harvest would be in in a few weeks. But by that time Tom Malone had come and our situation was much improved. As Lady Crosby said after one look at him, "Is he married? Did you say no? Well, you'll have no trouble getting maids from now on." We hadn't.

However, it was now August, while we had moved in May and had suffered along without him all this time. We were in fact anxiously awaiting him, week by week, and had almost given him up for lost when he appeared.

"What happened to you, Tom?" Himself asked.

He had been sick, with the maneeric.

"The maneeric? What's that?"

"Sure, everyone knows the maneeric! It's the faver."

Then he had six teeth to be pulled. "I was two weeks sufferin' an' eight weeks fillin' out forms. Finally I got to the dentist."

"Are you all fixed up?"

"I come into his room, an' he takes out his pliers an' pulls for a couple o' hours till a tooth come out, an' I thought me two big toe-nails went with it. So that's the last I seen o' him."

Then, apparently, Tom had spent a fortnight or so saying goodbye to his friends (always a ceremony in Ireland), and next was off on his motor-cycle to us.

Hardly was he in the door when I received a letter from Lilly, the freckled girl who lived in the glen.

Dear Mrs. O'Neill,

Just a line to let you know I have just left my job this morning. I was absolutely run off my feet. This morning the first salute I got was an insult so we had it hot and heavy I told them what I thought of them and took my coat and left, so here I am back at home again. Tom used to drive the car for them and they didn't get anyone else, so I had to go *fasting* to the station two or three mornings and I had a crash driving visitors to the train and I told them I wouldn't drive again let them pay a driver.

I forgot to tell you the boiler blew up the other night, the wheel went wrong and the English visitor held a match to the batteries and the whole thing blew up, so I don't know what they are going to do they can't carry on without a man.

Mrs. O'Neill, I would like to come and work for you. I wonder would you make a match for me with Tom? I have a couple of hundred pound.

Well cheerio.

Kindest regards,

Lilly.

This threw me into a dither. I already knew from glen gossip that Tom was supposed to be doing a line with a girl named Mary who had once stayed in the glen but now worked in Dublin. Mary was in love with him, anyhow. But apparently that was no obstacle so far as Lilly was concerned. Lilly had been very kind to the children; it would be quite nice to have her in the house, I decided. What to do? I went looking for Himself, letter in hand, and he said, "Leave it to me," and when he had the opportunity made some delicate advance to Tom on Lilly's behalf.

"No soap," Tom said without a moment's hesitation. "If she comes here, I go."

"Well, is there—er—anyone who might come and keep house for us?"

"I might hear of some one," replied Tom cautiously. "Do know of a couple, come to think of it. But not Lilly. I wouldn't have her for practice. Fact is," he added meditatively, "I wouldn't use her for shelter on a freezing night."

The strength of this language startled me, when Himself repeated it with what amounted to tender nostalgia. "Leave it to the glen," he said proudly, "They're a vigorous race there."

"Couldn't he just say 'no'?"

"Have you no soul? Don't you appreciate the elemental emphasis in that? Aren't you the one who wanted folk speech?"

Lilly did not come. Tom opened negotiations with Mary, but she couldn't leave her Dublin post, which involved chauffeuring a rich, insane old lady and her nurse. I gathered that this was regarded as a soft berth, despite the fact that Mary often had to help the nurse control her, and sometimes they were forced to dump the old lady by the roadside and let her caper about a bit to calm down. We had nothing to offer to equal that.

So Tom got in touch with Bridie and she came instead. He brought her one Sunday night—she was on the back of his motor-cycle, and her suitcase was on the front. We all like Bridie, which is fortunate, and what is more fortunate, she likes us. She is tall and skinny and manages to remind you of a little girl. She looks sort of dopey most of the time, a condition induced by practically continuous daydreams; but whenever I recall my days in the dungeon at Barravore, I can only conclude that nature is very resourceful. Bridie's method is to lower her head and charge through the work, and the main things (meals) get done, but unimportant details like floors, furniture and beds remain unswept, un-hoovered and unslung.

Oh well, there is no point listing the back-breaking features of a house like Barravore: there should have been two maids and a cook, and there was only Bridie in a fog. We fell into the habit of telling her everyday to do the daily jobs, and when told three or four times a day, she does them. Of her own accord she is kind to the current baby and refrains from whaling the others.

She is a good cook too, though too addicted to bacon and cabbage. I had to break her of that, as well as of boiling vegetables to mush; and of course she had to learn to make basic American dishes like chop suey, spaghetti and chili *con carne*. But she is really interested in food and reads cookery books at night for pleasure—they have even displaced her firm favourites *The Miracle* and *The Oracle*, two pulp magazines devoted to romances of servant girls who invariably marry the boss, after adventures involving luxury, travel, murder, illegitimate babies and dope. ("He entered the room. 'Who are you'? he said, as his eyes caressed her trembling form and ashen face. She tried to pull her sheer negligée together. She felt her limbs shaking, her heart beat faster and faster. Why was she feeling like this? Why was her heart pounding? Why? Her breath. . . ." etc.) We used to blame the daydreams on *The Miracle*, but they continue in the cookery book era. Apparently you can wander around in a vision of *crêpes suzette* or queen of puddings just as well as of purple passages.

It is quite a comfort, when Bridie passes us glassy-eyed these days, to know that what is going on is more of this order, "Take two cups of sifted flour, one cup of sugar . . ." She sometimes makes the masterpieces she reads about at night, except those in American magazines, the most glamorous of all, because we can't conveniently get the ingredients.

Most of her triumphs come from the Countess Morphy's cookery book. We bought this, originally, when Tom shot a deer, because it had more headings under Venison than any other cookery book in Dublin. By the time we had eaten the deer, Bridie was so accustomed to claret and currant jelly, to say nothing of herbs, garlic, mushrooms, truffles, glazes, brandy and what not, that she was in quite a Cordon Bleu mood and ready to tackle the most complicated dish.

All the while Bridie was breaking in, we were on the look-out for another maid, "one who would fit in." Tom knew of no one else free just then; Himself heard of no one, and none of our friends had any leads. I suggested from time to time that we advertise, but Himself always turned white at the thought. In his mind there seems to be an iron line between domestic help which one acquires through osmosis, and 'proper' staff involving letters, interviews, references, etc.

"You would bring a housemaid into this house?" he asked, aghast. "Aren't things bad enough as they are?"

"Well, the whole idea is to make things easier. A cook, for instance, would free Bridie to do the cleaning, or a house-maid would let her cook."

"You simply don't understand. No cook or housemaid would come here—not in her right mind."

"Well, there's no harm trying. Someone like Bridie."

"Another one like her and we might as well give up alto-gether."

I could see only too well what he meant. Until we were in order we couldn't get help, but then, in order to be in order we had to have help. So I kept on with the Employment columns in the *Irish Times*.

There was a spate of 'middle-aged' girls, which always tickled me. But the middle-aged girls always wanted adults only. I began to read local papers too, and every possible part of them—Situations Vacant, Educational, Houses for Sale, and the all-embracing Personals, getting great value for my misspent time out of items such as these: "Cork-based traveller required" and "Wanted, two rooms to hold fifty people, one on top of the other." Sometimes there were "Cards of Thanks," a column devoted to announcements like this: "Mr. and Mrs. J. O'Dougherty wish to convey their thanks to all who sent good wishes and gifts on the occasion of their Marriage, which they greatly appreciate."

One day a rather unusual item appeared, out of the ordinary run of appeals by and for nannies, governesses and 'generals'. "French boy, eager to learn English, will go as cook-handyman in return." At this point, Bridie and I, still under the heady influence of the Countess Morphy, were struggling our way through sixty or so "absolutely essential" recipes for French sauces. While Bridie was muttering over béchamel, I said something about the French boy. That did it. Her eyes rose to her hairline practically, and she squealed with joy over the idea of getting someone in the house qualified by nationality and training to cope with the Countess.

"Do write him, missus. He could make all them yolks."

"All right," I said, and what's more I did.

Three weeks passed and we had no word. Himself, who thought the whole idea addle-pated, said that undoubtedly the French boy had placed himself elsewhere. Bridie slugged her way through the work as usual and gave up hope for deliverance.

Then one night, when Himself was in Dublin and had not yet returned, there was a knock on the front door. I went to it and saw on the porch three men, one a dark-haired youth wearing a stormcoat and beret. The other two introduced themselves as neighbours and said they had picked up this fellow on the road; he was French and he had our address. It was Jacques. "Madame——" said Jacques, clicking his heels and bowing.

Despite fourteen years of study and several periods of living in France, French is a language I do not speak. I mean the sound to my ears of my own awful accent is too distressing. Any time I have had to utter a few words, as for example to a porter, it was a matter of closing the eyes, clenching the fists, and plunging. Well, here was the plunge swirling around my neck, and I hadn't even jumped or caught my breath. In five minutes of gruesome mono-syllables on my part, and a flow of pure sound from Jacques, it was established that he had come in answer to the letter; that he was not the boy who had written the ad.—a friend had composed it for him—and that he could speak no English. I explained that he was hardly the person for us; but inasmuch as it was pitch dark and there was no trans-portation or lodging, asked him to stay overnight. He accepted with alacrity. When Himself came home and looked in to see this new specimen, he found him already fast asleep in one of the bedrooms below stairs.

"Strange bird," he remarked.

"What do you mean?"

"Likes his comfort. Has a woollen night cap, and six blankets and four pillows."

This was interesting. Bridie said she had given him our one spare pillow and two spare blankets, but he asked for more. "Kept wavin' them in me face. So I gave him me own. And *then*, missus, he takes extry pillows and covers out o' his pack and keeps them all!"

The next morning I told Jacques sternly that he must return Bridie's bedding. He shrugged his shoulders and did so. He was very helpful that first day. He arose early and, using all our eggs, made omelettes for breakfast the equal of which none of us had ever tasted. He informed us that there were 409 ways of cooking eggs and that he knew them all. Could he make mayonnaise, I asked. He thought for some time. "I cannot promise to make one," he said finally, "but I have watched my mother many times. She has always a success."

He went about assembling his utensils, and Bridie combed the hen-house and beat the bushes until she located enough eggs for this undertaking. Jacques donned an apron, transferred the olive oil from our gallon tin to a Waterford cruet which, I admit, was better for pouring, and set to work. After an hour he emerged above, carrying a bowl of perfect sauce. I enthused and he listened gravely, as one quite accustomed to congratulations. "Do you know, Madame," he said with the seriousness of a Kinsey report, "that some women go all through their lives without ever achieving a mayonnaise?"

After all this, when he asked me quite pathetically if he might stay with us, I deserted my better judgment and said "yes". He might have been a great success, too, if we hadn't proceeded to run out of eggs. The second day he was there we got exactly three, which did the children; the next day two; and then none. And it appeared that Jacques couldn't cook with anything but eggs.

Jacques was very finicky, and the mud during that Irish November got him down. Literally, it got everyone else down, too, with lumps of clayey soil sticking to everyone's boots. Every night Tom or Paddy or Bridie (never Jacques) lined up the family shoes for a clean and polish. Bridie being Bridie, half the time she forgot to bring the clean ones upstairs again. That must have been how Jacques came across a pair belonging to Himself. The first I knew was that Jacques no longer made excuses to stay indoors, but instead plunged readily through puddles and muck. He remarked cheerfully, "Monsieur does not care for these shoes, *hein*?"

86

"What's that?"

"These shoes" (pointing to his feet) "are those of Monsieur."

"Oh," I said vaguely, assuming that Himself had presented them to him, "that's fine."

"What possessed you," I later asked, "to give Jacques your shoes? They're miles too big—he has them stuffed with paper."

"I didn't give anyone any shoes. In fact, my own best pair are missing."

Bridie recalled that she had left them in the kitchen hall. Her eyes got big as saucers. "He took them, missus. Jacques. He polished up his own shoes, and wrapped them in a cloth and left them in his room. And then he took the Master's and he wore them. And when he wants to clean the Master's shoes he don't polish them none, he just puts them in the rain barrel."

The boots in question were custom-made and dreadfully expensive. And Himself will never wear clothes that someone else has worn. Futilely, I scolded Jacques. "That was very, very naughty. You must not take things. You must ask first."

He shrugged his shoulders.

Jacques' next bright idea was that, in lieu of cooking, perhaps he could teach French to Jimmy and Bridget. This requires a bit of explanation. Education was our big awful tremendous problem. There were no suitable schools within striking distance of us; as a matter of fact, there were no children. Though Jimmy at four and Bridget at three were not exactly ripe for learning, we had already begun to inquire about governesses, boarding schools (grim thought!) and the P.N.E.U. (Parents' National Educational Union) home-teaching programme. Our friends gave us all sorts of advice, but every man Jack and woman Jill of them warned us against the National School System and compulsory Gaelic. The Gaelic which is taught in the schools is not the same as the traditional language—Himself calls it "Government Gaelic"—and we never found anyone who would give it a thing, from native speakers and school teachers to labourers and 'gentry'.

"But it's their fathers' language and it *has* a cultural value!" I would protest.

"The value is outweighed when so much time is given to it that other subjects suffer."

"Why keep on teaching it then?"

"Oh," said everyone, variously, "it would be the death-blow for any politician who went against it. The people are for it." Well, I ask you! However, one way or another because it was a vital and debatable issue, there was a great deal of talk about Gaelic in our house.

Himself had vague ideas about language in general. Based on his own experience, he thought Gaelic should be a voluntary acquisition and that a child learned more out of hunting or shooting or just rambling through the country than from any subject taught in any school.

My conclusion, after years in drill over languages for which I had no aptitude, was that only Latin was worth the effort. But French, despite the fact that it sometimes seems slightly *passé*, has glamour. I could have resisted French in New York, where glamour goes begging, but sixty miles from Dublin in a house without plumbing or water, it was a different matter. I began to feel as ineffable and culture-conscious as any farm wife. All this 'Madame' business, and the omelettes and the Countess, and the forced conversation with Jacques was beginning to make me fluent. Perhaps he would have the same effect on Jimmy and Bridget. The image of those two lisping their way about the continent in faultless French was irresistible.

Jacques was charmed with the idea of becoming a tutor. He said that he was the oldest of ten and well-used to handling the young. For a day or two all went well. He made Jimmy and Bridget little pipes out of chestnuts and pushed them in the swing and climbed all our trees while they watched. They were amused. I must say I heard very little French, but a great deal of English being taught to Jacques by them. They thought of course that it was just too silly to speak to Mummy in French, so I had a hard time checking on progress.

After a week it did seem to me that their accomplishments were on the odd side. They could say *"Bonjour," "Sais pas,"* *"Mangez!"* and *"Croque-mitaine,"* of all things; they had learned to tie their shoelaces so that the laces went straight across instead of criss-cross, and they had contrived a hundred hiding places to get away from Jacques. Jimmy then refused any more education.

"Daddy, I don't want to go out with Jacques," he wailed to his father.

"And me," put in Bridget very earnestly.

"Why not, Jimmy?"

"We don't want to learn Gaelic!"

After that we didn't know what to do with Jacques. He took to sleeping all the morning and bathing and washing his clothes all the afternoon—in the yard, to the stupefaction of the workmen. Bridie had fits, as her whole supply of hot water would disappear. Jacques seemed well settled down, with the idea of living with us forever, and he probably would have, as Himself cannot, by nature, ask anyone to leave. But Christmas was drawing near, and Jacques announced one day that he was going home to France for the holidays. At this Himself conceded that I might tell him to stay there. It wound up that we had to pay his fare back, but I guess it was worth it to all concerned, to Jimmy and Bridget particularly.

As for me, my hard-won accent and vocabulary slid away little by little, till now, if I should have to address a porter, it would be the same old gulp and plunge. And the Countess Morphy? Bridie has long since reverted to bacon and cabbage, to everyone's great relief.

By this time we had hired Peebles, the long-sought gardener. He walked in out of nowhere, a spry, elderly man, English, ex-Army, and Himself practically fell in love with him. ("Wonderful fellow, knows all there is to know about compost.") He had been a butler, valet or gardener to every lord listed in Debrett, he said, and became an unfailingly fruity source of gossip. None of this meant anything to Himself; what fascinated him was Peebles' use of words. That man relished a language as a drunk does the bottle. He dived into it, swam about, threw it away by the bucketful and left us marvelling by the roadside.

He dug into the garden with equal vim, liming, peating, manuring. He also sowed, planted, transplanted, weeded and so forth. Himself was charmed, lent him money to buy a few acres, instructed me to buy eggs from him, and helped him in every way he could.

But little by little, it seemed to me at least, Peebles did less and less gardening and more and more talking, following Himself around like a cheeping bird, fastening on to Tom when he worked in the yard, holding forth at elevenses till they were stretched to an hour, and thoroughly unsettling everybody. Tom at first regarded him with the good-natured forbearance a big man has for a small one and a younger for an older, but eventually, after months of listening to wordy advice on all subjects, Tom would bolt his tea and clear out, saying pleasantly, "How the hell did we get on before we ever seen you, I wonder?"

Peebles had a married daughter, Dolly, who entered the

picture by falling in love with Tom and lying in wait for him down the bohereen between two of our fields. Dolly had a can-can skirt which she wore summer and winter, and under which her bare white legs gleamed fetchingly as she gathered up her flounces and leapt over gates and hedges—or, perforce, blades of grass. "Dolly is shy," Peebles would say, and she certainly was quick at leaping away, from the presence of males any-how—a startled young thing was the idea. From females, she walked. Dolly's hard-working husband, Benny, was seldom seen.

Peebles was always conveying messages to Tom. "Dolly says why don't you come for a cup of tea on Sunday?" "Dolly says she'll help with the beet, Tom, eh?" "Dolly'll thresh if you like. She can do the work of approximately one and a half men—I have it written in my book." "Will you go out to see Dolly tonight, Tom? Benny has to see the rate collector and Dolly doesn't like being alone."

Dolly was very insistent on coming to 'catch' the turf with Tom on the bog. "No," said Tom to all this, adding pointedly to Peebles, "she can catch Benny's but she can't catch mine."

Himself liked Peebles and was determined to keep on liking him. "I never heard such a flow of language since God was in petticoats." Only once did he admit a setback—the day the refrigerator arrived. There was quite a dis-cussion between Himself and the service man on how to install it and on 'fridges in general. Peebles stopped all work of course in order to hang around and put in his two cents. A few hours later, Himself asked him the name of a shrub he was setting into the hedge.

"Frigidarius electrolarius," said Peebles.

"Say that again."

"Oh, that's just the Latin name, sir," he added hurriedly. "The local appellation might be different, you might say. I'll see if I have it written in my book."

This book was Peebles' great pride and talisman, evidence of his efficiency and ender of all arguments. He carried it about with him and used to read excerpts. "Your hens, madam" (he had taken on their care) "eat two ounces of oats a day, and approximately one and a half cabbage leaves apiece." (He never had statistics on eggs, because there weren't any, except oddly enough on Saturdays and Sundays when Peebles didn't come.) "My own hens," he would continue, "that's the pen of them, a dozen fowl, laid eighty eggs last week and eighty-two the week before."

"Your hens and who else's," asked Tom innocently.

He ignored that. "Now if I do say it myself, Dolly and I know how to get the best out of poultry. In this country, if I may say so, no one knows how to manage. Ignorance, you might say, not efficacient."

"If yer so smart," said Bridie, nettled beyond endurance, "how come yer not rich?"

Peebles said nothing but presently took himself off on his bike, his pockets bulging and the mysterious sack he always carried swaying heavily from the handlebars.

"Poor old Peebles," said Tom, looking after him. "His hens have to eat too."

Himself laughed. "What's the harm? We can spare him a few oats."

"I wouldn't mind the oats, sir, and I wouldn't mind the eggs, but I think it's carrying the thing too far to be selling them back to ye."

"Well, what can we do about it?"

"I'll take care of the hens while I'm restin' meself. That'll keep him away from the eggs, anyway."

Suddenly there was order out of chaos. Buckets appeared under the kitchen counter labelled 'Hens', 'Compost' and 'Trash', and Tom got Bridie to distribute the scraps accordingly. We could have turned off the refrigerator for all the good it did us: if I had future plans for any left-over I had to hide it in the dining-room and do it up secretly for the freezer. Tom was forever boiling potatoes and porridge for the hens; Himself jealously watched every inch of peeling and salad for his compost heap; and it was all Bridie could do to smuggle bits of dinner out to the dogs under her apron.

It seemed to me that even we were expected to hold back at meals so that the buckets could spill over; but I must say the hens and garden picked up enormously. Tom brought in four to five dozen eggs a week ("approximately eight and three-quarters egg a day, if I may say so," he remarked with a grin) and Peebles talked darkly about moving back to England.

Well, in the course of time we had quite a ménage, and even the house improved a bit. Any domestic help at all, after the rush and turmoil of American housekeeping, seemed a dream, nay, a coma, of bliss. But we never reached a stage even slightly resembling a schedule, and the staff was never remote, discreet or silent, as in English novels, with tea in the drawing-room, letter-writing in the morning room, accounts in the office, children in the nursery, a place for everything and everything in its place.

Every so often I'd say, "You know, in a few more months we'll be straightened out," and Himself would reply mildly, "Well, you might as well dream there as in bed."

*

CHAPTER 6

NEIGHBOURS

IRELAND STILL RUNS on lines of old-fashioned hospitality
and friendliness, with rather formal visits to newcomers, but
after one quick glance at Fitz and his crew, those in the
county who came to call drove on out the back drive and
invited us to their houses instead. Very sensible. Apart
from this, we were so occupied with workmen and staff that
our acquaintances were all on the impromptu side.

Of these the most notable was Mike Kinch, who had a
smallholding between us and the river. Mike was a butt of
a man with a bald round face, a comfortable stomach, and
nimble little legs. He early made a deep impression since,
on moving in, almost the first thing we heard were strange
halloos from his field. We could see what was going on—he
was training two cows to pull a plough. We were so green
we didn't appreciate it, but in a farming community where
both cows and ploughing are taken very seriously, this was
absolutely outrageous. It could be passed over only on the
score of lunacy. "Ah, poor Kinch," said the neighbours,
"he do be daft."

But Kinch was impervious—he couldn't afford a horse
and he needed to use his bit of land, and the rest followed in
logical order. Normally animals are very responsive to him,
but this was too much, and the bewildered creatures tended
to separate. "Now, Jessie! Now Daisy!" he bellowed. His

language grew stronger as he danced along behind them, zig-zagging the plough, and obviously headed for disaster. Finally he had to let go, and pegged stones at them in rage, whereupon the cows ran away altogether and hid behind some trees, peeking round the corner at him for all the world like two children. Mike stuttered when angry and we could see him bounce up and down, yelling, "C-c-come away outa there, ye t-t-titty-nosed b-b-bastards, c-c-come outa that this m-minute or I'll p-p-paralyse ye!"

But the next day we were astonished to see the cows again being lassooed and hitched, only this time Mike's daughters were in his plans. Their job was to push the shoulder of each cow and keep them together. All we heard for several days, wafted over a field, was "Lay hard on her, Mary, she's lanin' this way!" or, "Give her a shove, Roseanna, she's pullin' to the right," as one daughter pushed hither and the other heaved on the starboard side.

The fact that Kinch did succeed in ploughing the field earned him no praise. He was regarded as a bad job. Not only was he daft, but he would work only when it suited him and was not above begging for what he needed. The typical 'respectable' country family would starve rather than go 'on the rates' or apply to the Vincent De Paul, but not Mike.

In that way, he was almost in a class with Old Joe, who is a merry-eyed 'travelling man', eccentric in dress (two or three pairs of trousers and two or three jackets on at once, and all of them in flitters) and eccentric in behaviour. People have apparently given up trying to learn the rest of his name, or for that matter anything else about him. They value Old Joe for his good yarns (particularly in the local, I gather, with a frothy pint in front of him and a crowd behind him). Those who have tried to pry get snubbed, and the consensus is: "It's a pity to scuttle him because he's good gas."

Old Joe wanders around from place to place, never doing a day's work, but cadging food and anything else he can, and sleeping out in all weathers. He has been known to remark that when you are thinking about important things you never feel either sunshine or snow too much. Mention weather and he will tell you that no one can ever hope to judge or predict it, only men like himself who have slept out under the stars for the four seasons of the year.

Old Joe hit it off well with Himself—they agree on the pernicious effects of work—and he visited us often. I once asked how he had decided to come to our house the first time. On this day, for some reason, he was wearing a gay flowered bandanna under his hat, and he now scratched it thoughtfully and said, "I came on the heath road, ma'am, and I looked to see which chimney had the fullest column of smoke. For where the fire is generous, the bread is generous too. Then a man at the crossroad told me that Barravore now belonged to Himself, and I knew no one of that name would turn a man away."

Then there was Peter Griffin, who kept a little shop. In about twelve square feet he managed to carry food, clothing, hardware, medicine, stationery, a post office and a phone booth. Through him came the garbled cryptograms that were supposed to be messages and telegrams for us, until the time when we got our own phone (a slight delay of three years). Then his function changed and he became merely a bottleneck. We used to laugh and cry over loved ones phoning from the States—via New York, London and Dublin —only to be drowned out in the last lap by the noise of Peter Griffin's interested breathing as he listened in from the switchboard. (Between Peter and Blessed McQuade and Willie the Post, not a secret could be kept.)

Apart from the church down the road, there were three houses on the lane with Peter. One was a deserted coach-house, converted into a cottage, in which the Carthys lived; and in the other two were the McQuades and the Mac-Andrews. Within sight in one direction was the gatehouse to Ballydown House, and further along a cottage inhabited by a widow with a numerous family; and in the other were we. I thought we were living in the equivalent of wilderness, but Peter put me in my place the very first day.

"How do ye like Ireland, ma'am?" he said, out of politeness. (This was the set greeting for me for a long time. I shook everyone, I'm sure, by giving sincere and therefore rather irregular answers.)

"It's lovely—the countryside is so beautiful and there are no billboards to mar it."

"Do ye think so, now," he said, pleased. "I never thought of it that way."

"Oh, it's marvellous and restful to be away from the rush and tumble of the city," I went on. "Living in the country is a pleasure. Don't you think so?"

"I wouldn't know, ma'am," he replied, "because after all I'm here in the village."

The McQuades were father, mother, three sons who were priests and two daughters who were nuns, a daughter who kept house, two daughters in England and another daughter who worked in Dublin and came home for the week-ends. In the absence of a son at home, their farming was done for them by a distant relative of some sort, one Kevin McQuade, who lived with them and seemed one of the family except that he was very homely while the McQuades were exceptionally good-looking people. But they were all very, very devout, the whole houseful of them. They had almost no friends because the other Catholics were not religious enough to suit them.

The MacAndrews were very, very strict Protestants, caretakers of the C. of I. church. A feud raged. McQuade said MacAndrew's cows muddied their mutual lane; MacAndrew said McQuade did not keep his side of the hedge clipped,

97

McQuade said he would write to the County Council about the mud; MacAndrew sent him an ultimatum about the hedge. And lawyers' letters flew between them thicker than jackdaws.

Mrs. McQuade was a great gossip, with a succession of crossings, blessings, pious aspirations and "Glory be to Gods"; and she had a weird habit of referring to all her children as "poor Eamonn," "poor Nora," "poor Eileen"— at first we thought they were dead. As for McQuade—well, here is a typical conversation.

McQuade (dressed up for his walk to Barravore, a handsome old man swinging a blackthorn stick): "Good morning, sir."

Himself: "Good morning, Mr. McQuade."

"I was thinking, Mr. Neills, what a wonderful name the name 'Jesus' is. The name of Our Lord."

"Yes, indeed."

"Oh, a wonderful name altogether."

"Yes."

"And to think that no other human ever had that name!"

"Good heavens, man, that isn't the case! Thousands of small boys in Mexico, for instance, bear the name Jesus right this minute."

"No! You're codding me." (Looking out from under his eyebrows.)

"No, what I say is true."

"Mr. Neills, you read too much!" And he would turn on his heel and stride away, to sulk over this for several weeks.

But the McQuades couldn't stay away from us for long, since one or another of them made the rounds collecting for all the parish money-making schemes, the weekly silver circles and non-stop raffles, annual drives like "shillin' to buy a brick fer the new church" and "shillin' a head fer yer dead". Unlike most people asking for money, the McQuades

loved their work. They had a trick of bowing as if in benediction, and were very partial to black clothes. The most
cloying of them all, however, was Kevin, commonly known
as the Blessed Man. He was the youngest of his own large
family—"the scrapings of the pot," said Himself pointedly—
one of those short, bow-legged types, and he spoke in a high-
pitched chant.

Early on, Tom had no use for him, because he had some
peculiar curiosity about Tom's affairs and asked and snooped
all he dared. Tom enjoyed devilling him too, as when he
learned that Blessed was courting 'a big farmer's daughter'
who went to the town dances. Tom promptly asked her to
the next one, and made such an impression that she rejected
the Blessed Man's Christmas gift (rosary beads) and sat by
the fire waiting for Tom to ask her again.

We thought Kevin had got his nickname on general
principles, but later Tom on learned the story. It seems the
fellows in these parts gamble on every sporting event they
hear of, and were once holding a post-mortem on a game
that had been a sore disappointment. McQuade, too stingy
to bet, nevertheless had a lot to say. Someone blamed "that
blanking such-and-such so-and-so."

"Oh," put in Kevin, shocked, "you mustn't call him that!
You must say, 'the blessed man'."

"Lucky fer him," added Tom softly, "that them chaps
didn't rip him to pieces like an ould sack, the shally-voiced
straw-fed bastard." Instead, he was known for evermore as
the Blessed Man, or Blessed McQuade.

Actually, we never officially 'met' any of these neighbours
until the night we had the thirty ladies 'to supper'. For,
never mind lack of windows, walls, water and plumbing, we
were emboldened to entertain because of Bridie's gift for
cooking. She rose to these occasions like a trouper and sent
up food that was out of this world.

99

"I love it when ye has company," she generously explained, "no matter what unnatural things ye axe me to make."

But the night that the thirty women came was particularly memorable because it was then that we met the Whytes. It was after the first meeting of the Countrywomen's Association, and I had intended inviting the committee in for tea, but when the time came it seemed a shame not to include the ordinary members too. They all drove or cycled or walked from the schoolhouse to our place, and Himself lit up the drive and doorway and greeted each set of arrivals. The sitting-room, which boasted the only intact windows at the time, was fixed up buffet-style to receive them. Every chair in the house was lined around the wall, but as the ladies filed in, many with enormous backsides, we began to wonder if the sitting accommodations would go round. They kept on coming. I collided with a black-dressed figure on the stairs and wondered who *this* could be—but it was only Bridie, rigged out for the occasion in a spruce uniform with collar and apron that none of us had ever seen. "Pssst," said she. "How many?"

"Over twenty, anyhow."

"Jesus God! I sent Tom fer more cups, but we're gettin' short of water."

"Well, there can't be *many* more of them."

Tom had raced out on his motor-bike and borrowed 'delph' from Messrs. MacAndrew, McQuade, Griffin. Mesdames MacAndrew, McQuade, and Griffin did not bat an eye as they drank tea from their own cups. The masterpiece of the occasion was not the Baked Alaska which we thought would amaze them, but the white layer cakes from American mixes. Six ladies, including Lady Crosby, begged us for the recipe for "the heavenly white sandwich cakes," as they are called. I said Bridie had made them, and she told some of them that

I had. Eventually, caught in our lies, we had to look up a white cake in the cookery book and send the measures on. This was the foundation for my fame as a marvellous cook. Anyhow, they were wedged around the room like sardines, eddying a bit around the chair which Lady Crosby had to herself next to Louise Whyte.

Lady Crosby is large and tweedy, while Louise is small and slim. But no matter how imposing or venerable or nice or pretty or clever or sweet or what-have-you other women may be, they fade beside Louise. Womanlike, I suppose I was struck first by her perfect clothes, elegance being a rare phenomenon in our area, but then almost immediately Louise the person made her impression. She is lovely-looking, of course; not young, but one feels that time has merely dispensed with non-essentials. Her head, for instance, is poised so beautifully it seems a gesture rather than a fact. She combines gentleness, insight and humour, and has a wonderful way of projecting them, so that everyone in her company begins to feel gentle, intelligent and amusing. She turned now and smiled at me. So did Lady Crosby.

"My dear," said Lady Crosby, eyeing the plaster surround to the new windows, "you *have* made great progress."

All the others looked and praised the windows.

Louise Whyte admired the Louise Seize furniture.

All the others ditto. No one appeared to notice the wallpaper in strips, the beplastered floor or the gaps in the wall where the wiring had been inserted. This was not merely etiquette—and I do think Irish people have beautiful manners—but something even more valuable, a casualness about the material world, conspicuous consumption and all that. They drank pots and pots of tea, and ate and ate ice-cream, layer cakes (white, yellow and chocolate), oatmeal cookies, brownies, scones, pound cake, *petits fours*. Bridie beamed with the compliment, as well she might, while they demolished her creations. Then, knock on the door, and Colonel Whyte appeared.

He is the dearest man ever made, but this was our first sight of him, and his height and self-confidence seemed a bit formidable. "I've come for my wife," he said simply.

"Do have some tea with us."

"I'd love to, but I must wash my hands first. I had to change a tyre."

Bridie's face fell. I knew she was thinking, water. Never mind.

"Bridie," I said, as though a river were lapping at the back door, "bring a basin and towel to the bathroom for the Colonel." She gave me an anguished look but obeyed. After his wash, he was led into the sitting-room, and Bridie whispered to me, "Not a drop of water left. He can't have tea."

Himself inadvertently solved that by bringing the Colonel into the library and pouring out whiskey.

"My God, O'Neill," said the Colonel, watching the tumbler fill, "I can't drink that. I need some water."

"Water, certainly." Bell rings. "Water, please."

Bridie came running to me in the sitting-room, where I was chatting with several large women.

"Just tell him you have none."

Back to the men.

"Ah, here's Bridie with the water. What, where's the jug?"

"Isn't airy water."

"No water?"

"Not as much as ter wet a flea."

"Colonel, your health!"

"O'Neill, yours!"

Eventually the ladies hoisted themselves back into their cars or on to their cycles and drove off into the darkness happily calling back, "Thank you!" "Good night!" "God bless!" "God bless!"

To my great pleasure, Louise Whyte stayed on, talking to me beside the fire, while the Colonel and Himself continued to defy the elements in the library, from which occasional roars of laughter penetrated to us. Louise went in once to retrieve her husband, as the hour was by now quite late, but came out saying it was hopeless.

"They seem to have fought against each other during the Trouble," she explained, "and now they're comparing notes on this and that ambush."

Together we sat and looked at the fire.

"Men," she said, sufficiently.

Some time later I tried my luck. But it would have been like taking mother's milk from a baby to interrupt them. Himself was gloriously happy. The Rebellion had been for him the best days of all, and it was a gift of life to meet the Colonel, who knew some engagements as well as he, and who had also found fun in the grimmest times.

"How is it you chaps didn't nip off Major Blank?" the Colonel was asking. "We had word that you were out to get him."

Himself roughly outlined a landscape with his hands. "Now you see," he explained, "two men were waiting to shoot him, and they were hidden *here*, because every morning at 10.5 exactly he came riding along *there*, and this particular morning he didn't come. It was a case of 'I hope nothin' happened to the poor man'!"

"He was transferred," said the Colonel, "just in time, apparently. By the way, O'Neill, you must have known the C.O., who is a dear neighbour of mine in England, General So-and-so?"

"So-and-so? Who later was in charge of such-and-such in the war?"

"That's the one. Did you know him?"

"Know him? Why, Colonel, I captured him."

"Was it you? Outside Dublin? My God, man, you're famous!"

"He had commandeered a farm house, and we surprised the sentries and surrounded the place."

"You walked in on him as he was briefing his staff and said, 'Gentlemen, you are under arrest'."

"My very words. And do you know what he said?"

"No, he didn't tell us that."

"He said, 'No! It can't be. It isn't done!'"

"Was it you who——"

That was the beginning of a very happy friendship. The Whytes braved draughts and dust and called on us regardless of workmen and lack of H_2O, and we visited them frequently, for in addition to being fellow alumni of the Trouble, Himself and the Colonel shared a passionate interest in organic gardening.

"I say, O'Neill," hallooed the Colonel, bursting out of his car and stomping down the path to our yard. "Hello, Tadpole," he added hurriedly to Dorothy, who always bounced with joy when he appeared. "O'Neill, what d'you think of gathering up the manure from the farms round about and composting it? Make great fertiliser, you know. Wide sale for it too, I expect."

"Yes, Colonel, but I don't think the farmers would spare any manure."

"Oh dear, I'm afraid you're quite right. A pity. Make lovely stuff, wouldn't it? One could add the town garbage too."

"The town what? It just goes into the river, you know."

"Does it really? What a loss! Is that so? Perfectly irresponsible of the County Council, I must say. Best organic source you could have, once it's properly treated. Shocking. I shall look into the matter and write a letter to *The Times* immediately."

"But, Colonel, what do you think? I believe we could get the Dublin waste. They offer it for a shilling a lorry load to anyone who will cart it away."

"Do they treat it?"

"Yes, regular sewage disposal plant. Now if we could get a barge and put a load on it——"

"——we could bring it up by canal. What a splendid idea!"

"But how do we charter a barge?"

"We must go down tomorrow and find out."

This was in the air for a week or so, during which the two of them drove to Dublin and over most of the rest of Ireland, poking happily at sewage. Louise Whyte came to tea, shook her head sadly, and repeated, "Men!"

In the course of time she and I had various circum-ferential talks on the subject, neither of us caring to go into it deeply.

"My husband is very creative and full of aptitudes," she would say gloomily. "I hope yours has lots of good business sense."

"Ah yes," I would mutter, thinking of Enid's dire warnings.

In fact, I missed Enid. The bevy of individuality in and out of Barravore called for appreciation, I thought, and I couldn't wait for her to come up. But whenever I proposed a visit, Himself vetoed it. "Look at the state we're in. Wait a bit."

"Goodness, if we adopt that attitude, we'll never see anyone. After all, she's your sister. She'll understand."

"Ha, ha, ha!"

Finally, but reluctantly, he invited her for a week-end and prepared to show her around.

She arrived, looking very smart and bearing gifts. With misgivings flooding in and enthusiasm draining out, I suggested a tour.

"*If* you don't mind," she said brightly, "spare me the locals." She gazed at the gaps in the wall, the paper in strips, the beplastered floor. "Really, I should have thought the work here would be more advanced than this."

"But the local people are so entertaining, Enid!" I urged.

"Yes. I know. Like my charlady. Mmm . . ." she continued, with a brief survey of the other rooms, "I'd have a talk with your contractor, if I were you."

Later in the afternoon the Whytes and Miss Protheroe, who lived in Ballydown House, came to tea. Thank goodness, I thought at least she'll approve of *them*, and to my relief, everything went off splendidly. Bridie made a Hungarian gâteau (out of the Countess Morphy), the sitting-room was remarkably tidy, and conversation did not flag.

When the guests had gone, I gave a satisfied sigh and rejoined Himself and Enid.

"It was a nice party," I said.

"Aye," said Enid. Himself seemed apprehensive.

Enid examined the pattern of the rug with the toe of her shoe. "What religion are the Whytes?" she inquired.

"As a matter of fact, we never asked," said Himself shortly.

"Church of England," I replied innocently, "only here it's called the Church of Ireland, isn't it? Why?"

"I thought so. And Miss Protheroe?"

"Same."

"And the others they were talking about?"

"Same, I suppose."

"Hmmm." She completed the pattern and looked at us. "Tell me," she asked in a tone of pure curiosity, "are there any *more* heathens in the countryside for you to take up with?"

She was equally blunt about the staff. "I'll come again," she said in parting, giving us a sweet and very *final* smile, "when you have your household running efficiently."

CHAPTER 7

*

HIBERNICIS IPSIS HIBERNIORES

BESIDE COMPOST, Himself and the Colonel had in common the fact that each considered the other his nearest neighbour. Lady Crosby and Miss Protheroe also always referred to us as *their* nearest neighbours. This, and all it entailed, was brought home especially one night when the Whytes had a party for us, our first country-in-the-black-of-night excursion, and I remember it well because we forgot to bring along a torch. Ireland is almost a land of the midnight sun; Dublin is as far north as Winnipeg, and so in the summer one can play eighteen holes of golf after supper and read a newspaper outdoors as late as eleven. But in autumn and winter, to reverse Robert Louis Stevenson, it's quite the other way. Day ends at four and when there is no moon darkness descends like a bandage and one can't see an inch ahead.

We had an anxious time wandering around in what we knew was the Colonel's pet garden in search of the footpath. Presently the Colonel was alerted and came out looking for us, guiding us safely past the compost heaps and the herb bed and so on, past perennials and shrubs, and past lawn and flower beds to the front door. He also introduced us to Croesus, Louise's thoroughbred collie, and to what appeared to be a dozen cats. Inside, Louise greeted us in her lovely way and presented the group to us. They were almost all from the other side of town.

"Here you are. These are the O'Neills, our nearest neighbours."

The Whytes did not have electricity, but managed very well with a system that ran on bottled gas. The light was soft and warm, quite bright enough. Ardtown, their house, is uncorrupted Georgian. Plaster decorations of ceiling are just right, and the rooms are perfect in dimension—not too high, low, large or small. The furniture is old and precious and used, and exquisitely arranged flowers are everywhere. We were struck as always by the atmosphere of grace and casual elegance which Louise carries about with her. Pretty Mrs. Collingwood said, "Of course, you're the people in Barravore, where all the wonderful renovation is being done."

"Er—yes," said Himself.

"How nice for Louise and the Colonel to have someone out here at last! Lady Crosby isn't well enough, poor dear, really to count."

Mr. Short meanwhile murmured similar approval to me. "Good to have you here," he said; "no one out this way at all."

Even the Colonel remarked, "Yes, before we came here three years ago, this locality was quite deserted, wasn't it?"

I was trying to figure out who was English and who was Irish. Well-bred people in the country seem to my ear (not a good one) to have the same accent. They look the same, they act the same, they have often gone to the same English schools, they are officers in the same English regiments, they lead almost identical lives (farming, hunting, dining out), and yet the English ones hasten to state that they are not Irish, and at least some of the Irish positively bristle at the suggestion that they might be English. Himself later pointed out that this was what was meant by the expression *Hibernicis ipsis Hiberniores*—English people become "more Irish than the Irish" when they've lived in Ireland for a time.

In America I had always taken an Irish person as Irish and that was that; but here, apparently, the term covered an unsuspected range. The old Irish, Himself explained, included: (1) People like the O'Neills—Catholic, nationally-minded, their land and money lost through resistance to the conquest. (2) People like Lady C.—Catholic, rich, cosmopolitan, and with strong social connections with England (her son was doing his English army service)—they had not resisted. And (3) families who had conformed politically and in religion too, being now Church of Ireland.

"In other words," I replied thoughtfully, "the ones who today are rich, liberal and fashionable are the ones who turned coat in the past."

"Roughly, that's about it. Irreconcilables like the O'Neills of Barna were smashed, and we lost considerable polish in the process, I suppose. Being originally warriors responsible for our clan, the cause of Irish nationalism—a narrow cause if you will—still seems our particular responsibility."

"What about Miss Protheroe?"

"She is Ascendancy. This is the term for people 'planted' here during the Elizabethan, Cromwellian and Restoration periods, who were put in their ascendant position by force rather than through any intrinsic superiority. They're Church of Ireland, big landlords, pro-England."

"Gosh, what a tolerant people the Irish are!"

"Lassie, you don't know the half of it! We even tolerate each other! Some of the foreigners are the best of us, the Scotch-Irish for instance. They were brought into the North in the seventeenth century, mostly, by the Stuarts who sold the land of Ulster from under the feet of the inhabitants to speculators. The speculators recruited for tenants among the Scots crofters. These were Protestant too, of course, but largely nonconformist—Presbyterians and Unitarians."

"Are there any others?"

"Those are the chief ones."

He went on to identify Mrs. Collingwood as from an Anglo-Norman family, in Ireland since the twelfth century. Mr. Short was from the North, Scotch-Irish. Mr. Collingwood, like the Whytes, was from England.

Himself made all this clear without even stopping to think. Tell an Irishman an Irish surname and he can break it down quicker than a notched card. "English people who come from England to Ireland are of course still English, but in a very short time many of them champion Irish causes. Their children, born here, their grandchildren, are completely Irish as a rule. From them our great rebel leaders have come. Even in the old days, in Clan Barna, the chiefs married Englishwomen; and I think it's that strain in us which made us put up such a good fight against the English ever since."

"But what do the Irish think of them all?"

"You mean the people? There's no love lost, I'd say, but it's a case of haves and have-nots. My family and others like us admire and support anyone who claims to be Irish. After all, we were all invaders here at one time or another."

"Does 'more Irish than the Irish' mean more patriotic towards Ireland, then?"

"Not necessarily. It means rather that they identify themselves with us. You'll see."

But I didn't see at all at the time. It was tactless and wrong, but I could not help assuming that people we met socially around Barravore who had an 'English' accent were English. In Dublin one hears beautiful English from all except street-hawkers, practically; but in our part of the country speech does not seem to fall into class lines, though working-class Protestants are conspicuously better speakers than their Catholic opposites.

The country folk are very conscious of their own lack in

this respect, with the result that anyone literate is at a great advantage. It is one of the gulfs which separate the 'gentry' from the 'people', and that division is still very noticeable in Irish life. As you can see, it made us the 'only' neighbours of Lady C. and the Whytes, as though we all lived in an expanse of desert. Actually, of course, the whole countryside between and around us is dotted with cottages, and each cottage is dotty with characters.

In the matter of characters, we began to give them all some stiff competition. Under Himself's influence, the Colonel discovered religion—this in spite of the fact that he had read the lesson in the C. of I. church every Sunday for years. But far from being dogmatic, he did it with the surprised air of a man on new and amazing ground, and Himself had a ready audience for his favourite heresies.

"You don't say, O'Neill! How extraordinary! So that psalm was written by an Egyptian king! I must tell the Canon."

Or, "Tell me, O'Neill, what d'you think of the Book of Job? I never read it before, myself. Terrible tragedy, isn't it?"

"Tragedy me elbow, Colonel, that's a bloody Protestant attitude!"

"You know, O'Neill, you're absolutely right!"

Himself got pained looks from the Canon; it seemed that the Colonel on the preceding Sunday had announced, "I will now read the Gospel according to O'Neill."

On the other hand, under the Colonel's influence, Himself began an all-out attack on the land. He took to sending away to Washington and London for pamphlets, and read furiously for days and nights on all aspects of organic agriculture. Lorry-loads of hideous stuff began to arrive— market refuse, farmyard manure, decaying seaweed, insides of cow's stomachs from the abattoir—the Dublin waste, nicely granulated and de-scented, was by far the pleasantest. We got piles of cards in every mail, beginning, "Your esteemed order has been shipped."

Other cards from the railway station informed us that so many bags of this, crates of that, boxes of seedlings and sacks of plants were waiting to be collected. Peat moss, Russian comfrey, lime, wood-ash, bone-ash and compost heaps of varying architecture began to clutter up the garden, half of them getting mixed into the cement by Paddy Rory, which perhaps accounted for the strange behaviour of our concrete.

Then Himself progressed in his reading up to what was evidently a chapter on the ruinous leaching effect of rain. He thought of his smelly treasures in the garden. Gone were the days of contented gloating; this was a matter calling for immediate action, as, it goes without saying, there was rain every day. Bang went the book, slapped to, and away with Himself in a great rush to find the Colonel. The Colonel happened to be off in one of *his* great rushes, buying hens (bantams, he had heard, were in great demand) but Louise was at home. Himself told her his problem and she suggested getting a gardener. He was charmed with this solution; the only question was, who?

Who indeed? (This was long before Peebles came on the scene.) Louise said that they had been trying to find a herdsman for themselves, as the Colonel wanted to go in for cattle, and they had thought they had one of the locals, but it was so difficult to understand him they weren't quite sure. She was fairly certain that his last remarks had been "No, no, no." In fact, she and the Colonel had been hoping that perhaps Himself could speak to the man and find out what was what.

"Who is it?"

"Michael Kinch."

On inquiry, Himself found the bush telegraph very active.

Everyone knew that the Colonel had made Mike some sort of offer, and there was great consternation when word got round that he had turned it down. "Surely be to God!" exclaimed Peter Griffin. "When would he get a chance like that again?"

Himself went down that evening to a gap in the hedge between our land and Kinch's field. "Tell me now, Mike," he said, "what happened between yourself and Colonel Whyte?"

"Well now, sir," said Mike, tugging at his receding hair-line, "sure I don't rightly know, I can't make out a word he's sayin'. But I won't have it, I tell ye," he added with gathering heat, "not after all these years, I w-won't."

"What won't you have?"

"He w-wants to buy me land, that's what! Like thim English people that was here after the war. That's what they all do be after. They wanted to build a 'summer hotel' down here be the river. Summer hotel! They offy me a fair price too, but I wouldn't have it. Didn't they double it thin! But I wouldn't have no part of it. It isn't the money, ye see, but f-first I'd be sellin' thim the land, and thin they'd be buildin' the hotel, and thin they'd be after me ter grow cabbages for thim, and d-d-damned if I w-w-will!"

"But the Colonel doesn't want you to grow cabbages. He wants you to see after cattle. He doesn't want your land."

"Are ye sure?"

"I am."

"Is it just herdin' thin?"

"Herding, possibly some milking. All your meals there, if you like. Go home when you please."

"Is there cabbages in it?"

"Not a cabbage."

"I'll take it!" cried Kinch, spitting on his palm and shaking hands vigorously with Himself to clinch the bargain.

Strangely enough, the arrangement worked out beautifully. Mike developed a loyal interest in compost, the cattle throve, and the Colonel and Himself instantly set to figuring out details for a project involving cow manure. The newly-acquired bantams were dispersed to the four winds—cooked, sold, given away—and we were awarded the cockerel. The Colonel came speeding up the drive one evening, flung open the door of his car, and out flew, squawking, a handsome little black and white rooster. The children were delighted.

"Hello, Tadpole."

Dorothy bounced.

"Hello, *Mr.* Tadpole!" Jimmy and Bridget responded gleefully.

"I say, O'Neill," said the Colonel, "you'd better have this chap. There are enough scraps" (disapproving glance at me) "from your kitchen to feed five dozen fowl. He's a great compost machine too. Poultry manure is excellent for getting up the heat, you know. Just add some activator and you're well away."

We thanked him enthusiastically, but I was a little uncertain just what we were supposed to do with the cock. Obviously, so far as the Colonel was concerned, he was simply one more cog in the fertilizer works, but cocks had other missions in life, one heard.

Now there is an institution in the Irish countryside known as the Poultry Instructress. She is a bright and attractive young woman, employed by the government to advise the likes of me, and a postcard or phone call brings her to your side. Our Poultry Instructress was named Teresa O'Tuomey, a very pleasant girl, the kind who looks smart no matter what she wears. In Ireland anyone under sixty is a girl and marriageable. I can't imagine what age Teresa really was, but she had the look of having been young a long time, of being established as young, a claim more readily granted because she had a good figure and million-dollar legs. Largely because of her way with clothes (black suit, white blouse, Sybil Connolly coat) she seemed incongruously cosmopolitan.

She was brisk and brief in this first encounter, telling us to put the bantam right in the run with the pullets, since we had no other male bird. She made no mention of the facts of life, but we got the impression that the whole business would be platonic. To the Colonel the rooster was a manure-maker; to Teresa it seemed he was a nice old thing for the hens to have around the house.

The Colonel went home, happy in dreams of organic fertilizer, a man on his way up in the world, switching from chickens to cattle, small compost-producers to big ones. But he and Kinch had hard going sometimes, not with the herd, but with each other; and Himself was constantly appealed to by both of them to serve as interpreter.

"Beggin' yer pardon, sir," Mike would say to the Colonel, "may I have yer prisence?"

"Eh?" the Colonel would reply. "What's that again?" Then, "You'll find it in the tool shed."

"May I *speak* wid ye, colonel," Kinch would repeat wildly, "may I sp-speak wid ye on a subjict?"

"No, you had better get some more from town."

"Y'know, O'Neill," the Colonel would say as he stamped out of his car at Barravore, doors slamming, boots thundering, "I'd be most tremendously grateful if you could come over to my place and make out what Michael is saying. Didn't realise that he spoke only Gaelic. Deuced awkward."

Mike greeted Himself with all sorts of grimaces and eye-liftings, winking behind the Colonel's back as though to say, "Niver mind that one, he's simple!"

"Sure, sir," he exclaimed, "they don't be talkin' like Christians! If I was edycated like they are, not meanin' to be impudint, but if I was edycated, sure wouldn't I talk more clearer nor they do?"

Ultimately they accustomed the ear and got along on their own. The Colonel became so charmed with Mike that he later nominated him for the County Council and campaigned tirelessly on his behalf. He quoted him constantly as a source of wisdom in all matters. Kinch on his part regarded the Whytes as his charges, worried when they stayed out late, and pined when they went on visits to England. He watched the rest of their staff with an eagle eye. "Get rid o' that young one," he'd whisper weightily to Louise. "She do be champagning her hair all day whiniver ye go out." Or, with great jerks of the head and glancings round to be sure of secrecy, "That new chap's no good. Cleverality. He'd b-buy ye and s-sell ye!"

Sometimes Kinch got exasperated with the Whytes themselves. "Go back to the wimmen!" he'd order the Colonel in the course of work with the cattle. And he'd even scold Louise for making pets out of the farm animals. "Sure, ma'am, ye won't let me sell the calf. Ye won't let me sell the ould cow! Wouldn't ye content yerself with Crokus and all thim cats and niver mind the rest?"

But with the addition of Kinch, the Colonel's and Himself's organic efficiency was much improved. They shared lorry-loads of soil-improvers and compost-grown crop seeds, divided a colony of earthworms for experimental purposes (ours froze, his cooked), tried cloches on various vegetables with and without straw covers; and in general settled most of the problems of agriculture.

They were then ready to turn their attention elsewhere, and Himself lent the Colonel a copy of a report by American experts on Irish industry. This had aroused loud controversy. The Irish Government had paid quite a sum to a firm which specialises in analyses of this sort, and the ungrateful experts had virtually reported that there wasn't one single solitary Irish product fit to export.

The government was satisfied, of course. They had standards now and constructive suggestions to wave in front of their industrialists, but to the man in the street this was slander on his country. Himself was pleased with the report. Now, he felt, Irish production would increase and improve, and he was sure that all enlightened folk saw it as he did. Consequently he circulated our copy as widely as he could, first and foremost to the Colonel. The Colonel took it home and read it.

A few days later, zoom! as the Colonel's car tore up our drive; bang! as the door slammed; thunder, as he dashed up the steps and into the hall.

The children came running. "Hello, Mr. Tadpole!"

But he was too preoccupied to notice. "O'Neill, here's your book. I've just finished it. I'd put the bloody thing into the fire if I were you."

"Why, Colonel, didn't you like it?"

"Like it? It's jolly well insulting. Those Americans! Hell melt them! They can't say those things about us."

Himself was delighted and turned to me. "See?" he asked.

I saw. *Hibernicis ipsis Hiberniores.*

*

CHAPTER 8

DISCOVERIES

THE TROUBLE WITH ME, I found, is that I can get used to anything. It worried me. Surely it was a reflection on my bringing up that I didn't do something about it; but I didn't. That first year we had no running water; we lived and ate in one room; we had no cupboards and so left all but immediate wardrobe needs packed; we had beds but no furniture. We washed only lightly and took baths when out visiting. Strangers were all over the house, and we huddled in the overworked sitting-room while laughter ascended from the kitchen and curses descended from the top floor.

But I made a discovery. I couldn't clean the house, because the workmen were in all rooms, or else trunks and crates were. I couldn't do up any of the children's garments because we lacked water, and anyhow they got caked with mud the minute they went outdoors. I couldn't do much cooking, because Bridie didn't like me to. I couldn't sew because we had no place to put the things we already had, never mind new ones. I couldn't weed or tend a garden because we hadn't any yet. I couldn't take or give baths and shampoos because of water shortage. Some days, I couldn't even wash my face. I couldn't entertain, except only the most understanding people. But do you know what I could do? I could bask in leisure.

It was luxuriously wonderful. I suppose we will never

have it again, but it was curiously rewarding while it lasted. We would sit, day and night by the fire, reading insatiably, uninterrupted by phone or bell, untrammelled by guilt over meetings not attended or friends not kept up with, not reading with a purpose but nibbling or gorging, as we wished: American magazines, detective stories, all the latest Penguins, Louise's English novels (a new field, I found), our own old books which we hadn't thought of for decades, farm bulletins, *The Listener, The National Geographic, The Golden Bough*, the early history of Africa, England, Palestine, Iran, Lang's fairy tales, Isherwood, Mari Sandoz, Sean O'Faolain, Robert Graves, Nancy Mitford, Peadar O'Donnell, Fielding, Caesar on the Gauls. Just plain wasteful reading, and what bliss.

The radio might be on for a good deal of it, too; the B.B.C. had hours of uninterrupted concerts. Or, if we wanted, we could have French or Italian or German or what-have-you stations and a brush-up in language. Radio Eireann's plays were another delight, and the Third Programme's debates.

We might sip sherry out of silver goblets through all this, the silver having been unpacked; or Bridie would bring up tea and scones. Or some nights we would whittle marionettes, or weave baskets out of rushes, or write long letters to everyone in America.

We had lots of time for the children too, and used to read stories and sing ballads till we were hoarse, and play records we'd forgotten we owned. It was a lovely feeling there by the fire, warm, slightly grubby, no responsibility, no duties, and all the time in eternity.

There you have it. When we pass a tinker family (mother, father, five children) who have taken up a permanent abode on the back road, living in what looks like an overturned laundry basket, I think, "There go I." Would I have rebelled at that, I wonder, if Himself had led me to an area four-by-four-by-six and said, "This is it?" Or would I, like the tinker lady, have accommodated myself to a congested but warm bed, and all Ireland for the rest of the house? No bothersome kitchen, no insatiable stove, no messy dishes. Meals *al fresco*, *al dente* and *al mano*. She has the last word in simplified housekeeping, anyway.

The Enemy is the standard of living. The higher the standard, the lower the leisure. With no Joneses to keep up with, and nowhere to be conspicuous, we ceased to be consumers except of food and fuel, and often lost track of what day it was. When we got in order, with the stoves and the 'fridge and the washing-machine and vacuum cleaner and all the rest of it, and with going out and having company and engagements in Dublin and meetings and all the rest of that, we were mortals again and hadn't a moment to ourselves.

Another thing I had no trouble getting used to was the food, particularly in that early numb period when sterling didn't seem really to be money, and I never paid attention to what anything cost. Even later, it was misleading, because prices were usually lower than at home, and it was easy to forget that income was lower too. Steak, for instance, choicest steak too, red and white and thick and with a fine flavour. Gorgeous Irish rashers. Turkeys, available only at Christmas time, but marvellous. Geese—ditto—but dreams of tastiness. Pheasant, partridge, pigeon, hare. Venison, at which we were experts. Salmon, poached by Tom and Paddy with a *ga-bolg*, a descendant of the spear used by Cuchulain, with hooks that sprang. Lobsters, prawns, fine fish from the sea, trout from the streams nearby. Fresh herring, which we loved. Caviar, made at home from salmon or herring roes, delicious as beluga. Irish strawberries, with the taste of our wild ones, yet giant size. Victoria plums, sweet as nectar and ambrosia mixed. Wild mushrooms big as saucers. Fresh eggs, home-baked bread, cakes which were lost arts among friends in New York—mocha tarts, cheese-cakes, butter sponges. Home-made ice cream. Each of these in season was my favourite dish.

I had no trouble getting used to not celebrating holidays, either. Old spoilsport, that's me. With the greatest relief I abandoned Fourth of July, Decoration Day, Labour Day, Thanksgiving, Washington and Lincoln, and with the greatest reluctance put up with new ones in their place: Whitsun, August Bank Holiday and various religious holy days (though in this respect Ireland isn't a patch on Italy).

Whether my distrust of these days stems from a solitary childhood when Sundays and holidays meant separation from weekday playmates, or from a crowded parenthood, when a holiday means Make an Effort, I'm not quite sure. Just let them *be* holidays, hangings in space, that's all I ask; don't knock me out of my accustomed round and make me decorate cakes with red, white and blue (or green, white and orange), or arrange picnics, or roast turkeys, or make mutton pie on Michaelmas or pancakes on Shrove Tuesday, or try to keep the young in their best clothes.

If *others* want to celebrate, that's a horse of a different colour. It's *charming* that laboriously disguised 'vizards' still dance and sing from house to house at Hallow'een; and it's *very interesting* that a may tree is a bush carefully decorated— by someone else—with eggshells.

Another discovery—kindness to animals in a new perspective. The English are famous animal-lovers, of course: a dear old lady taking her dog for a walk could almost be a symbol of the Empire. And one felt somehow *because* it was 'English', the Ascendancy had taken over all the organisations for the four-legged. While there undoubtedly was genuine feeling, to be horsy or doggy was also one of the signs of class, with the inference that 'the natives' were callous. The gentry agonised (columns and columns in *The Times*) over aged horses torn from their native pastures and shipped abroad; the people, facing the emigration of their own children, thought concern for humans more in order.

In our area Louise's Croesus was one extreme. The only collie in the memory of local man, he was a public figure. The fact that he was daily brushed, combed, exercised, shopped for, and fed 'stewing steak' was a matter of wonder. Croesus adored the Whytes, but he was an incorrigible rover. It was the usual thing, when driving anywhere in the country, to come upon him padding disdainfully along, and it was then the usual thing to rush to the nearest booth and phone Ardtown.

"Louise, is Croesus missing? We just saw him on the heath road."

"Oh, did you! How marvellous! I've been *so* worried. D'you think he'll get in your car? Otherwise we'll come right over and fetch him."

Sometimes, though, his absence was not a matter of concern. "Spring, you know," Louise would murmur vaguely. Or, "Thank you, but I think he's just out for a ramble."

Needless to say, before we arrived in Barravore, a trail of half-bred collies, like Hansel's and Gretel's pebbles, marked Croesus' favourite routes—the strangest looking creatures, greyhound head and mouselike tail, but in between that unmistakable red bushy fur. Or an apologetic terrier type, low slung, but again red and bushy. Usually, all a dog had in the way of a pedigree was the statement, 'Feeneys beyont have the mother'; but in a short time, as those things go, generations upon generations of part collies appeared, and all by their fur traceable to Croesus. And every so often a puppy turned up which was very like him, "the dead spit o' the grand-da" as the country folk proudly put it.

At the other extreme were the sheepdogs which were owned by most of the local farmers. They worked hard for their keep, which consisted of potatoes, bread and occasional chicken bones, and they were uniformly sweet-tempered, intelligent and short-lived. But if they were treated callously, it was largely due to poverty; certainly sympathy for animals was also to be found, I once had to listen to daily bulletins on Eily Nolan's cow that was "taken quare": "Lookit, her eyes was brighter this morning, missus, an' the faver's lifted; she had a bite to ate, so she did, an' she looks to be aisier in herself." Or Himself would overhear an old fellow on the road say companionably to his donkey, "Stand there now you, an' take a mouthful of air, while I light me pipe." Or Michael Kinch addressing a horse, "Move over here, if ye're so inclined."

Antique furniture. Now there's something easy to grow accustomed to. We saw it in the houses we visited and bought a few pieces ourselves—not that we are knowledgeable by any means, though given a little spare cash under the mattress I think we could get around to it. But right from the start we had furniture on our minds because we had a whole house to fill. Actually, the interior of Barravore, minus the texts, had more or less defied description. It was so familiar somehow, and we couldn't imagine why, until it dawned on us that this was the milieu of Chas. Addams and his cartoons—the same sort of past fol-de-rol, now gone to cobwebs, cracks in the floor and broken windows.

The house really had come down in the world when it fell into the hands of the Singletons, who got it because a Doctor Roche sold it at auction. Doctor Roche drank himself into insolvency but seems to have kept a dashing air unimpaired, because he was still spoken of with admiration. He had a beak of a nose, we are told, which was shining red; otherwise there was never a sign that he lived on the stuff. "Gad," said the Colonel once, quite enviously, "think of the bottles that went into that nose!"

However, despite its latter-day boorgosity, Barravore, like all Irish country houses, seemed to require fine furniture. If you think of it as a farmhouse, luxurious rugs and period pieces sound incongruous; but in the old days the gentry lived in such a setting, and the natives, who were never allowed above stairs, were the ones who got mud on their feet. Nowadays, it is satisfying to note, landowners work like everybody else, though inclined to go in for the better-paying crops, like race-horses or prize steers, and only an elaborate system of shoe-changing keeps the bog off the parquet.

Himself decided early to get a few essential furnishings. "Wardrobes and chests of drawers!" I called after him, as he went off to a series or auctions. The furniture in furniture stores was pretty awful, we thought; the style was thirty years behind by American standards, and it was shoddily made. Auctions were the answer. So off he went and bought a fifteen foot dining table in mahogany—fortunately it came apart in three pieces, each with a pedestal, so we used one third in the dining-room-sitting-room, while the other two were put away with the crates and barrels for future use. He also bought what he thought were chairs to go with it, in the confusion; but it turned out we had become the owners of a ballroom suite, gilded chairs and settee. We put these in the kitchen where they had a Cinderella effect, half at the ball and half in ashes. At first the maid and the workmen were leery of them, but soon they seemed the most natural kitchen equipment possible. Himself then got 'good' chairs from a dealer, Louis Seize we think, delicate but very pretty and sound. He also got a perfectly useless Chinese screen. He did not get any wardrobes, drawers or book-cases.

He was very pleased with his purchases, but I began to feel like Epaminondas' mother, hopefully waiting each day for his return. "Come, come, now don't be in a *hurry*," I would admonish myself as I sorted for the fiftieth time through a pile of children's clothing, looking for matching socks. "Creases again, fancy that," I would say dreamily as I shuffled through Bridget's dresses lying on top of each other at the end of her bed. But there you are again, I am an awful surrenderer to the accomplished fact, and it seemed the simplest thing in the world, presently, to dump the extra clothes in the dining-room-to-be and let them keep wearing what they had on. After all, it wasn't as if they had anywhere to go, except into the concrete-mix.

Conversation, at this period, between Jimmy and Bridget:

Jimmy: "Lend me your safety-pin, Bridget."

Bridget: "No."

Jimmy: "Bridget's a good girl, lend me your safety-pin."

Bridget: "No."

Jimmy: "I need it for my jacket."

Bridget: "No. My pants faw down."

Himself is the type whom, I imagine, quartermasters would court-martial. If you ask him to get you a pound of butter, he will return with six (if he returns at all, because normally he will not have anything to do with housekeeping matters). Ask for a pad of paper, you will receive a ream; and so forth. One day it became clear to him that we *really* needed some article of furniture into which to put clothes. I mean he suddenly understood what I had been talking about all these weeks, and he went right off to Dublin and next day a van-load of furniture arrived. And by van is meant a van to end all vans, a monstrous lorry called a 'pantechnicon', replete with four men expert at moving valuable pieces.

Everyone within five miles was agog—so was I. They unloaded, before my rapidly changing emotions (surprise, joy, admiration, doubt, bewilderment and horror) *twelve* mahogany breakfronts and combination chest-bookcases, one tiny wardrobe, one minuscule chest of drawers, *and* one of those black Chinese cabinets, carved with horrid dragons and inset with gold and shell pictures of cranes, storks, lotuses, which used to ornament Chinese restaurants in Brooklyn when I was a child. "Look, what's this between you and China, anyhow?" I asked him.

Of course none of the pieces fitted in the available wall-space, and the men ended up leaving them dismembered in the dining-room and library-to-be, along with the clothes, the cartons of books, the crates, the trunks, two thirds of the table and the deep-freeze. And later on, at auctions and in Dublin antique shops, we got some smaller chests and side tables.

Another joy, which was gradually worked into the daily round and often overlooked, was the beauty of the country-side. This was on a small scale, wild, natural, untended, yet never raw or simple: like illustrations in fairy-tale books for children. Near us was a field surrounded by a straggly hedge—driving by, it looked like rather rocky pasture. But on foot, what delights! What seemed to be level ground turned out really to be a tiny glen with a babbling brook running between rounded hillocks. Concealed between two of these was the ruin of an ancient building, a monastery very likely, as a small but perfect round-tower rose nearby. The stones were grey and covered with lichens, and the proportions were on child scale, a thrilling place to play. We had two ruined castles nearby, too, with secret passages and steps in their hollow walls, and the remains of moat and portcullis still apparent. Lucky children!

One more thing I grew very attached to—the fire. When we first moved in, this was not the case. There was a fireplace in every room, and fireplaces are lovely and all that, but fifteen of them, each with a nest of jackdaws in its hair and a bed of ashes at its feet, were something else again. Besides, it was summer. Even when the weather grew colder it was hard to take them seriously. Irish people often made conversation about how bright and cosy fires are, while I would think sourly, of course they are, when the alternative is freezing to death. It was a real effort to refrain from asking, "Have you ever seen a radiator?"

But the fact is, they grow on you. Snugged in close to the hearth of a winter night, wind howling and rain streaking the window, the radio bringing music from Madrid or Rome, a pile of books around me, the fire became my pet. When it did well and warmed the room, I felt a sense of accomplishment which no central heating ever supplied. If Himself were around, he took it over. He is a skilled craftsmen with wood, turf or coal and can coax them to leaping flames in a matter of seconds. Heating in Ireland is a matter of self-expression. The warmth, or absence of it, is a sign of your character; and a comfortable room is appreciated, not just taken for granted.

In fact, all the little commonplace comforts came to mean a lot more—a clean well tucked-in sheet, an eiderdown, really hot tea, hot-water bottles in bed, a good stiff drink. Anything that contributed to warmth had an enhanced value, as one darted through draughty halls and cold bedrooms and back to the zone of life around the sitting-room fire. When at first we complained of cold, Himself looked sympathetic and said that soon we'd be acclimatised. When we kept on complaining of cold, he took it as a personal criticism and snapped, "Sure there are lumps in everything. Control your circulation!" But actually, we came to like relative coolness anyway, and even admired the Irish climate, at least in summer and autumn when it only rained half of every day.

Other notes:

A subject of conversation is not 'brought up', but is 'drew down'.

"Sure, it's only codding, and codding is no harm" is the local attitude towards all misdemeanours from counter-feiting to rape.

The few Irish countrywomen who have refrigerators keep one thing in them at a time, and turn them on and off like toasters.

"Mna" on public lavatories does not mean Men. It means Women. And 'Fir' does not mean Women. It means Men.

Some Irish beaches are so strict that there is a set time of day for each sex to bathe. Others are so casual that everyone undresses together on the sand, "naked," Himself explains piously, "as Adam when he was a little boy."

CHAPTER 9

*

MARKET DAY

"Missus," asked peggy, "will ye do a message fer me when ye're goin' to town?"

"Why, of course. What is it?"

"A pair of nylons, please, real sheer."

Queer sort of message, I thought to myself. The next was old Mrs. Carthy from the cottage at the end of the field. "I have a message fer the town, God bless ye, ma'am. I thought maybe ye'd be good enough to bring it out."

"Surely, just write it down."

"Write it? What would I be writin 'fer? It's half a stone of meal, waitin' fer me in Driscoll's."

Wednesday is market day in town, and I was about to go for the first time. What fun, I thought, as I shifted all four gears of our right-hand drive car and sailed out of the gates carefully left open for me. There was a list of things to get from the grocer; the butcher's note consisted of, "See what is good;" the chemist was represented by empty vitamin bottles which were to be replaced; the washing, duly entered in a 'wash book', was headed for the convent laundry.

The three miles into town are very pleasant. The road winds and the country has variety. You go past Griffin's shop, formerly a rectory, and nearby, the Church of Ireland church and the driveway to Miss Protheroe's—shabby gate and gate-house, stone fences overgrown with moss and ivy, and beautiful old trees. Then the widow's cottage, and a half-dozen cottages about half a mile farther on, one at a corner set in a bower of flowers. (There was a mystery about that one. Jane 'the English girl', and her mother lived there, and no one quite understood why they didn't go back to London.) Farm land then on either side, then the gates and driveway to Lady Crosby's. A modern new factory with clean lines and wide expanse of windows. A river, with glens and dells on which cattle graze and wild-flowers grow; and a bridge with a twist on it which I took very slowly, sounding the horn at the turn. Smallholdings next, then cottages, then a row of houses, and behold, the town.

If you've ever seen a picture of an Irish town you'll know what ours is like, because they are all the same. A main street with whited rows of shops, a town hall, a huge church, a post office and twenty-three public houses. Driscoll's is one of these, but which, I did not know. At the first turn an ancient citizen leaning against a wall wagged his head at me, profoundly, in the local greeting. He hopped nimbly to the car as I pulled up. "Can you tell me where is Driscoll's, the grocer?"

"The pub, is it? Just folly the stream of traffic," said he, waving grandly, "just folly along."

The stream of traffic consisted of two dogs, an ass-cart and a morose man on a bicycle. However, such as it was, I followed it, and sure enough, a few yards farther along was Driscoll's double shop, pub to the left, grocery to the right.

Inside was the hushed atmosphere that prevails in all the shops, a charged attentiveness which occurs because shopping is the breath of life here, the only social activity of many of the country people. The smallest transaction has dignity and formality; the slightest word is weighted.

To me, the whole picture seemed unreal—the shops were so tiny, the streets so narrow, the merchandise so unattractive:

like a play on a too-small stage, with fake props and the actors looming too large, because the salespeople all seemed to be acting the rôle of salespeople and to expect the customers to act the rôle of large buyers. Their speeches were timed and their gestures calculated for an audience—you couldn't buy a spool of thread without listening to a speech. You couldn't just ask for a spoon; no, you had to select one from a dusty box and hear a lot of falsehood about its being a masterpiece of industry, far ahead of another (unavailable) brand, and so forth. Himself has the shopkeepers trained to wait on him quickly and cut the talk. They even make this into a piece of theatre and act the epitome of bustle and efficiency; but they look after his departing form wistfully, jostled out of their stride and distracted.

Well, I came in and saw a grey-haired man in a white coat and a grey-haired woman in a blue overall foosthering around—that is, dusting off bottle tops and rearranging tins: Mr. Driscoll and his clerk, Miss Seymour.

"Welcome to Ireland, Mrs. O'Neill," cried Mr. Driscoll in a tone and manner that swept off a plumed hat and bowed low.

"How do you know who I am?"

"Didn't we see you the other day with Himself?"

"Sure, we all know you," said Miss Seymour. "How are the children?" She indicated beaming smiles, a curtsy and a long line of retainers hallooing returning heirs.

"Why, they're fine, thank you——"

"The little lad is a pet, oh he's a pet."

"Tell me," said Mr. Driscoll, "what do you think of Ireland after America?"

"Well, I——"

"My sister was there, and she says it's a wonderful country altogether."

"Well——"

"A wonderful place," he repeated.

"All but the heat," Miss Seymour intoned, raising her eyes to heaven as though heat was something unmentionable.

"My sister met a what-do-you-call-them on the boat going over, a gangster. He was interested in the races over there and she was telling him about the races here. It's a great story, you wouldn't believe it, but my sister bet on a horse at the Curragh and she lost, though she had a marvellous tip to bet on him; but anyhow she lost and when she paid the bookie, her overdraft at the bank was too big and the banker called her in on it. 'It isn't my fault,' she said, 'it's the fault of that damned horse'. 'So it is, so it is', said the banker, 'but what am I to do?' 'What are you to do?' says my sister. 'Why you're to give me a decent tip on the next race'. And what do you know, he did that."

"So she paid back the overdraft?"

"Bless you, no! She went to America."

"Oh. . . . And the gangster?"

"She struck up a great friendship with him, and he took her to all the night-clubs in New York."

"Oh."

"It's a grand country altogether," said Miss Seymour happily.

"Umm. Now I have a list of things we need——"

Mr. Driscoll cried, "Just a minute, Mrs. O'Neill, I'll get your book."

"Book?"

"Sure, to write your order in." He whipped into the back of the store, which was also the first floor of his residence, and came running out with a small lined copybook on which our name was written. Then a duet started, something like this:

"Five pounds of sugar, please."

"Yes, Mrs. O'Neill."

"A box of cornstarch."

"Yes, Mrs. O'Neill."

"Two cans of sardines."

"Yes, Mrs. O'Neill."

"A package of Jello, the purplish one."

"Yes, Mrs. O'Neill."

"Two loaves of bread."

"Yes, Mrs. O'Neill."

"Let me see, what else?"

"Yes, Mrs. O'Neill."

"Box of oatmeal."

"Yes, Mrs. O'Neill."

"Ummm. . . ."

"Yes, Mrs. O'Neill."

"I think that's all."

"Yes, Mrs. O'Neill."

This was written into the book, with the flourish of an invisible quill, as follows: "Half a stone of sugar 5/10, packet of cornflour 2/4, two tins of brisling 3/6, box of jelly black currant 10d, two pans 2/2, bag of flake oats 2/2."

Two women had come into the shop by this time and were standing about in absolute silence, while Miss Seymour plucked this and that off a shelf. When he had finished writing, Mr. Driscoll summoned her with a twitch of his eyebrows, bade me ceremonious farewell and disappeared. The waiting women went on quietly waiting, surrendering Miss Seymour without a murmur. She looked at me as though expecting some direction, and I looked at her wondering what next. Finally she said, "Is that all, madam?" with the greatest diffidence, conjuring up a prostrate supplicant.

"Yes, that's all."

"Should I work for you then, Mrs. O'Neill?"

"Eh?"

"Should I *work* for you?"

I wondered if she were offering to leave Mr. Driscoll and

be our parlourmaid. We were in a servant crisis as usual, and she undoubtedly had heard of it via bush telegraph.

"Work for me?"

"Should I ever take the packets from the shelves and make up a parcel for you?"

Light finally dawned. "Oh yes, will you please, Miss Seymour!" My enthusiasm startled everyone. The women stared at me, but as soon as I noticed, dropped their eyes and looked at the floor. I made for the door.

"Mrs. O'Neill," called Miss Seymour, "the bag? Have you a bag? No? Well, I'll give you a box. Never mind," she said kindly, "I'll work for you now and put your messages in a box."

The street was just a few steps from the square and quite a crowd had gathered there by now. Shops and business do not really start till 10 a.m., which it now was, and the country folk in ass-carts and on bicycles were coming in steadily on all the roads. Stalls were set up, each selling one thing—vegetables or dishes or second-hand furniture or old iron and junk or old hens tied in bundles. The one elaborate stall, which had place of honour in front of the square, was run by Mary from Dublin whose truck was loaded with a variety of produce and who usually undersold the local vendors. She was a scrawny dark little thing with snapping black eyes, lank black hair and a toothy but engaging smile. She wore a shapeless overcoat and an ancient cloche hat. She had about four satellites, men and women, who helped with sales and handed her cups of tea. Mary sold some twenty different kinds of fruit and vegetables and, under the counter, fish. There was always a great congestion around her. She controlled everything with a loud sharp voice and did a marvellous business in very limited space, with cabbages and onions spilled in heaps on the ground, rhubarb leaves mixing with the greens, and donkeys and dogs treading undisturbed amongst them, and the assistants walking on everything with muddy boots as they weaved in and out weighing purchases and handing Mary her tea. Part of the confusion was the lack of any counter or wrapping paper, since customers in Ireland carry shopping bags made of rushes or leather, into which all purchases are poured higgledy-piggledy. Mary saw me immediately and marked me for her own.

"Come over here, deary. Cahbages and tomahtoes!"

She sold me a good assortment of stuff and provided a box to put it in and a man to carry it to the car, and at the same time praised her wares, weighed and sold them to about five others, all of whom were on the 'Mary' and 'deary' basis. She also kept a baleful eye on an old crone in a long black cloak who was handling the vegetables in an impervious way; and she negotiated with a thin, down-at-heels mother of five be-draggled children who were clinging to her skirts and falling in and out of a dilapidated pram. There was an infant, but the four others seemed to be all aged two. The mother and Mary were not on *tutoyer* terms—they bargained, in fact, pretty grimly; but finally the woman bought a codfish and moved away from the stall carrying it by the tail. Mary did not have so much as a piece of newspaper to give her. Nobody but me paid the least attention when the mother made room for the fish next to the baby and pushed off matter-of-factly with the rearranged pram.

The old crone went to shuffle away too, but Mary called after her in her piercing voice, "Honest woman! With the cloak! Come back with the cabbage!" And sure enough, muttering curses, she did. More sales were being made through all this, and Mary continued her chant of "cahbages and tomahtoes, ahpricocks, bahnahnas".

"Bananas?" She caught my glance.

"Ripe bahnahnas."

"They don't look very ripe." (They were small, sick-looking things.)

"Sure, niver mind the green, deary, it's only the outside. I'll peel one for yer."

"No, thank you—don't really——" But it was too late.

She took one up, held it high, and with dramatic gestures peeled four strips till it was half done, neglecting customers and assistants.

"There!" triumphantly. But the banana was unripe and hard as a rock.

"I'm sorry, it's not ripe enough," I said, feeling very embarrassed at the wretched banana which looked so *exposed*, and at the silent crowd watching all this with bated breath.

Mary snorted. "Not ripe, sez she," she drawled to the crowd in a voice that carried for miles. "Not ripe! After me strippin' me bahnahna fer her."

Crushed! I tried to vanish in the hustle and bustle. Over at the old clothes stall another drama was going on. Mag and Lucy, the dealers from Dublin, had dumped the contents of their van on the ground and were busy sorting it out into some kind of order, not visible to the naked eye. Apparently satisfied with their arrangement, they disappeared, and then Mag returned minus coat but with an apronlike affair with two large pockets into which she put respectively coppers and silver. She turned round to the nearest person to her, and in a rich Dublin come-all-ye voice said, "Give us a tie-up, missus, will yer, like a go-od woman?" (She was very fat and short and couldn't manage it herself.)

While she was being tied up, she eyed the inner circle almost sullenly. Then she plunged forward and picked up a brown coat (pleated back and half-belt) and gave it a flourish and then threw it over her shoulder and called, "Luvely co-at! Cum on, give us a start?"

No answer.

"I'll start meself. Cum on six pounds." Giving the coat another shake and holding it out in her hand she called, "Fiver!" It could have been bought brand new in Dublin for that. Just at this moment the Angelus boomed out, and crossing herself with the coat, she looked furtively around the crowd. Not much interest. She called, "Four, wrap it up fer fo-ur," and stood in front of a responsive-looking woman. I saw, with surprise, that it was Jane, the English girl.

Mag: "It's a bargain, miss, not to be repe-ated. Look at the lining of that."

Jane: "The back is nice."

Mag: "The back of it's *gorgeous*. Are yer takin' it, miss?"

Jane: "Not today, thank you."

Mag (raging): "When you see a bargain a-gain you'll snappit." She gave the coat a shake and a fold and threw it into the No Sales Department, a large piece of canvas spread out on the ground. She then made a few straightforward deals—a suit for twenty-five shillings, a coat for fifteen. Then she picked out of the mound a white article, which she shook out and held at arm's length. It was a very large shirt, opened all the way down the front. She moved around with it and took up her stand in front of a poor miserable little woman and, holding the shirt in front of her asked, "Is yer husband big, missus?"

P.M.L.W. (in a sharp Kerry accent): "Mind yer own blidy business!"

Voice from crowd: "That's a wake shirt."

Another voice: "Beg pardin' an' respect fer the dead, but that's a Yank shirt."

Another voice: "That's right, me brother was home from the States an' he had 'em. They have them fastened down the front fer convenience. . . ."

Mag seemed very pleased with this latest bit of information, and holding the shirt out again, called "Luv-ely man's——" (Roars of laughter from the crowd.) Mag again, "I mean luv-ely Yank shirt buttoned through fer conven-ience. . . ."

No response. She began to be a little red and mithered-looking, and pitched the shirt into the No Sales Department disgustedly. A woman came up to her and spoke in a low voice, and she bent down with effort to pull at the clothes in the mound.

"The duck-egg blue? Yes, missus." She dug it out and held it in front of the woman interested in it—a pleated rather fancy dress, pretty well creased and crumpled.

Voice from crowd: "Did you ever see such a yolk?"

Mag: "Yer don't know a good thing when yer see it." To the fascinated woman, "Nice, isn't it, missus?"

F.W. (whispering): "It's grand." (Hesitating.) "How much is it?"

Mag: "What'll yer give me for it?"

F.W. (in a trance, almost): "Can't give much."

Mag: "I'm not hard, make a bargain now. How much will yer give me?"

F.W.: "Seven and six."

Mag (leppin' with anger): "Seven and six. I could have yer taken up fer robbery. I hadter give more an that fer it meself." Straining her neck and looking over the crowd. "Niver a guard around when they're wanted." The unfortunate fascinated duck-egg blue would-be had vanished. The crowd was beginning to thin out, but I noticed that Jane was still there, and so did Mag. She waddled over to her and asked belligerently, "Did yer want somethin', miss?"

Jane replied in her best English accent, "Thank you, I was still looking."

Mag started to say something, but it suddenly began to rain, and Lucy came running up from wherever she had been. "Better start foldin' up."

The drops came down heavily and Jane and I took refuge under a tree. The crowd had vanished as if by magic, and Mag, grabbing up a big bundle of clothes and making for the van, tripped somehow and did a head-on crash on top of the bundle. "Hey, Lucy, give us a hand here for Jeeze sake." Turning her head around she caught sight of Jane and her lips moved convulsively. I couldn't quite catch it but it *looked* like, "You English bitch, buzz off. . . ."

Jane and I buzzed off. This was our first real meeting and later on she drove home with me. The ancient citizen, still leaning against the wall, hailed us as I turned the car back towards Barravore. He came over and I lowered the window.

"Ye're the American?"

"Yes."

"It's a great country?"

"Yes."

"But ye work from dawn till dusk?"

"Well—er—yes."

"Ye're better off here!"

*

CHAPTER 10

THE CONVENT AND THE PRIEST

RELIGIOUS DUTIES REST VERY LIGHTLY on Himself; in fact, it is doubtful if they are on him at all, but rather, floating conveniently a step or so in the rear, out of sight, out of mind. His six excommunications he regards as a panache rather than a fardel sore, and though some of his best friends are priests, he could never never be termed 'defender of the Faith' or 'pillar of the Church' or anything in between. At the same time he is fundamentally a religious and spiritual person, just not an organisation man. Thus it was quite out of character for him, and me along with him, to be pulled into parish politics.

It started with our search for a maid, which brought us to the nuns. They enjoy, so far as we are concerned, a completely mythological reputation as an employment agency. We had high hopes, though, when we called at the convent and asked for Sister Gabriel who was in charge of girls seeking work. The nun who answered our ring wanted to know why we had come and who we were, so we told her. Then she let us into an ugly, terribly clean room, where we sat on shiny hard chairs and looked at photographs of bishops and paintings of saints while she went away. We could hear her heels clattering off in the distance and our own pulses throbbing with about an equal racket as we sat in silence. There is a school attached to the convent and I began to feel overwhelmingly guilty as I sat there, as though waiting for a reprimand for talking in class or being late. I have never been to school with nuns before or since, but in those ten minutes I telescoped a couple of dozen misspent girlhoods. When the returning clatter of footsteps ended these excursions, I became conscious of Himself who was swinging his foot and singing softly:

"A captain bold in Halifax who lived in winter quarters
    Seduced a maid who hanged herself one morning in her
        garters—"

"Bill!" I hissed, just in the nick of time as the door swung open.

It was Reverend Mother whom the nun brought back: a tall, solid woman, her round face in its round coif looking pleased as a child with a forbidden toy. We didn't realise it, but we were great novelties in the community, and Reverend Mother couldn't let slip this unforeseen chance to examine us. Yankees! Pagans! From Sodom, from Gomorrah, from New York!

She greeted us kindly and plunged right in. "You're the new people at Barravore, from America. Tell me, how do ye like Ireland?"

Himself took over. "It's hardly necessary, Reverend Mother, for me to answer that question. After all, I was born and reared here."

"Tell me, did ye go to school here?"

"Oh yes, I did."

"Oh, how fortunate, thanks be to God, because I'm sure your education stood well to you in the benighted countries. Tell me, was it the Christian Brothers?"

"Yes, Mother, the Irish Christian Brothers."

"Wonderful people," said Reverend Mother softly, perhaps tentatively.

"Not people, saints. Altogether removed from the world," casting his eyes to heaven. I began to perceive the drift.

"Yes, yes, indeed. And tell me, have ye any children?"

"Of course, Mother, thanks be to God."

"You are blessed. And of course the girls will be coming to school to us?"

"Well, they're still very young, but when they are bigger where else would they go than to the good nuns?"

Reverend Mother began to purr, poor deceived creature. She and Himself regaled each other with the gamut of banalities. I sank into a fog of embarrassment, out of which I heard phrases like "grand little island", "distant lands", "pagan altogether", "gift of the Faith", "glory be to God!" "only a stepmother would blame me", "woman of the house", "land of saints and scholars", "welcome as the flowers in May". Any time Reverend Mother addressed a question or remark to me, Himself leapt in and replied. My recoiling ears kept rejecting everything he said: it was all I could do to keep from exclaiming, "Who, you?" or, "What, us?" as misrepresentations were piled on thicker and thicker. This was the first time I had seen him with nuns; he was altogether different from the fire-snorting eagle-eyed arguer he is with priests.

But it was worse when Reverend Mother left us happily and Sister Gabriel was brought in. She was thinner, sharper, brisker. The coif on her looked rather whiskery. Then he took the tack that Sister should find us a maid who was an orphan, or a pair of sisters or friends, because we would provide them with a good Catholic home. Did we go to Mass every Sunday? According to him we went daily—early, late and medium. Family rosary? Every night without fail. Sodalities? Children of Mary? CYMA? Just give us time and we would be leading lights in them all. Let a girl stay out late? Never! Our maids were all in bed at half-past seven. Did we let them wear powder and paint? Nothing ever sullied their shiny, soapy faces. Smoke? The vile weed —wouldn't have it within the gates, much less the house. (Himself smokes a packet a day, and gives away another.) Drink? We were all Pioneers, or as good as. Walking out with the lads? "Why, Sister, I wouldn't even let one of my cows look at a bull." Dancing? "I don't worry about that, Sister, I worry about when they stop the dancing."

Sister Gabriel was presently as happy as Reverend Mother, and in a surge of good feeling presented us with a bottle of Lourdes water, rosaries for the whole family and a portfolio of holy pictures. She almost wept at the thought that she had no girls for us now, would not have even one ready to go out for almost a year. She gave us the address of nuns in another town, however, and promised that she'd write on our behalf.

Himself was delighted with himself, but his face fell when Sister Gabriel insisted on taking me off by herself for a tour of the garden. Reverend Mother, it seemed, was waiting to have another little chat with him. Hoist with his own petard.

Sister Gabriel led me down resounding corridors and through double doors, chatting away the while, and I don't think I said anything wrong, by dint of intensive sieving and filtering of all spontaneous replies. We came on a group of nuns in the garden, one of them a dear old body called Sister Winifred, who uttered little cries of joy when she saw me.

"A stranger! Let me see you, child. You're not Irish?"

"No, Sister. American."

"Have you just come? On a visit? No—to live? How exciting. Tell me all about it."

"No, no," said Sister Gabriel. "Mrs. O'Neill hasn't much time."

"You're married! A blessing of God! Have you any children?"

"Three, Sister."

They seemed to be waiting for me to say something else. Finally Sister Gabriel supplied it: "Thank the Lord."

"Thank the Lord," I repeated hurriedly. Meanwhile Sister Winifred took me by the hand and gently turned me around so that she could get a better look at my dress. "My eyes are getting bad," she said, "let me see your necklace."

"Sister!" exclaimed Sister Gabriel, horrified.

"Oh, I know I'm naughty," said Sister Winifred, "but I do love jewellery. And your ring. Ah! Is that all?"

"All I have on now, Sister, but next time I come I'll wear more for you."

"Sister Winifred," said Sister Gabriel sternly, "it's time you were in the chapel."

Sister Winifred winked at me. "Goodbye, child," she said, and scurried away.

"Oh, I like her," I said, but Sister Gabriel looked very annoyed. "She's old, she's doting." And I had the feeling that Sister Winifred would be spanked and sent to bed without supper.

From the garden, the path led to a tiny graveyard where the nuns were buried. Sister Gabriel glanced at me sharply as we stood at the gate. Now what? "Cross yourself," she said. Blushing, I did so. She looked again. What was I supposed to say now? Open sky, green lawns, rose trees in bloom, the quiet river in the distance—I cast on them a desperate eye. From where could deliverance come? *What* should I do? "Say 'God have mercy on the dead,'" she ordered reproachfully, and I could see her readjusting her thoughts on the ideal Catholic home.

"Did you go to convent school?" she asked.

"No"

"Whatever sort of a school was it?"

"Just an ordinary one."

"God help us!" Pause. "Was it in America?"

"Yes."

"Ah!"

By this time I was so upset that I forgot to cross myself even when the Angelus rang, and Sister Gabriel delivered me like a hot brick to Himself and Reverend Mother, who were at the 'perfidious Albion' and 'Yankee dollars' and 'holy Ireland' stage.

But the worst was yet to come. Sister Gabriel saw us to the gate, and Bridget, who had been waiting with Bridie in the car, came running out to greet us. "Ah, the darling little girl," cried Sister. "How old is she?"

"Three," I said. "Say hello to Sister, Bridget."

"No."

"Do you pray to Holy God?" Sister Gabriel asked her, bending down.

"What?" asked Bridget, puzzled, her blue eyes wide.

"She doesn't understand you," explained Himself.

"Of course," said Sister kindly, "she's not yet used to Irish voices." She pulled out a badge of the Sacred Heart and showed it to Bridget. "Let me pin this on you, dear. Here's Holy God."

"No!" cried Bridget. "Take it away!"

Sister was appalled. "My poor little girl! Don't you love our Blessed Lord? There," she said, "kiss Holy God, and He'll mind you," offering her the badge.

"No! No! No!"

"God between us and all harm!" she exclaimed. "Was she baptised?"

"Yes," replied Himself hurriedly, "but it was in New York."

Needless to say, we didn't get a maid. The nuns to whom we were referred sent us on to an orphanage, and the Mother Superior there directed us to nuns in another town, and *they* never answered our letter. Himself blamed me and, after cross-questioning about what happened in the garden, announced that he would have to lead me around like a baby, and I accused him of mealy-mouthed hypocrisy and said it served him right.

"What other way is there to talk to nuns?" he complained with outraged innocence. "You don't expect me to treat them like rational beings, do you?"

"Of course I do. You were sickening."

"My dear girl, when you know as much about Irish nuns as I do, you'll gramachree them too. It's the only possible conversation."

Not long after, the parish priest called on us. I almost didn't know about it, because he asked for Himself and the two of them retired to the sitting-room, hand in glove. When I noticed the strange car and Bridie said, "It's Father Cunningham's," I left the children in the kitchen and raced upstairs.

Even then it had been borne in on me that a priest calling on a house doesn't give a hoot about the wife, social life being by, for and of the men; the reason why I rushed was that 'our' priest at home, a Jesuit, had warned us not to leave books lying about in our usual way once we were in Ireland, and I knew for a fact that on the mantelpiece that very minute were O'Casey's *The Plough and the Stars*, Joyce's *Ulysses* and a book critical of the Catholic hierarchy in America, by Paul Blanshard.

I skidded in on one wheel. Too late! Father Cunningham was in the very act of putting out his cigarette on the marble mantel in full view of Sean, James and Paul. But he didn't seem to notice; he was all smiles at something Himself was saying.

He was a ponderously fat old man, and the smiles seemed to be an unaccustomed strain to his heavy cheeks. I was introduced, and then Himself started signalling that I should get the hell out, and Father Cunningham dismissed me with, "Himself will tell you all about it. We're having a bit of talk about the Countrywomen."

"Holy and blessed Ireland," I muttered to myself. Where else would a wife be put in the category of upstairs maid, to be called back when their masculine lordships were ready for tea, and serious talk was out of the way? And talk about the Countrywomen—who was interested in that, anyhow? Wasn't I the one who was trying to start a guild of the Irish Countrywomen's Association locally? What had Himself to do with it? What had Father Cunningham to do with it either, for that matter?

A great deal, as Himself was finding out, for Father Cunningham was very direct. "What's all this about the I.C.A. your wife is organising here?"

"Ah yes, Father. It will be good to have a bit of sociability around the place, don't you think?"

"No, I do not. Mr. O'Neill, you have been so long away and your wife is a stranger—you're not in touch with all the factors involved as an Irish Catholic would be. You should have come to me about it first."

"Father, that never occurred to either of us."

"For the past twenty years I have struggled to keep such alien organisations out of my parish, and now all my efforts are gone for nought."

"But why, Father? What is there to object to in the I.C.A.?"

Father Cunningham got red and his jowls shook with emotion. "It's a Protestant organisation, founded by Protestants and to this very day controlled by them!" Conspiratorially, "It's not for our own kind."

"But, Father, surely you do not condemn everything founded by Protestants. Where would we be as a nation but for Mitchell, Davis, Tone, Fitzgerald, Parnell and innumerable others?"

"Well, put it that way, Mr. O'Neill, and I must agree with you; but we're free today and have no need for that sort of thing. Look, man, I wouldn't speak this way to you, but Reverend Mother tells me you're one of our own—she was delighted with her little visit with you. Now you take the I.C.A. Teaching women foolishness when the same women would be better occupied on their knees saying the rosary! You know as well as I that women are weak; in former years they called them the instrument of the devil. You'll have them gallivanting out, getting instruction in 'home crafts' and *perhaps other things* from those highbrow Protestants, putting ideas into their heads!"

"What other things?"

Whispering and looking around, "Birth control! Communism!"

"Father, surely you're not serious?"

"Any woman over school-leaving age can be a member. They'll have the young girls there and what they won't teach them! And sometimes men are invited to meetings!"

"Is there anything wrong in that?"

"Mr. O'Neill," said the old priest slowly and earnestly, "I say it from the altar every Sunday: no boy or girl should talk together unless they have the intention of marriage."

"But, Father, that's Jansenism."

"I'm responsible for the morals in this parish, and while I'm here I'll see to it that it's done my way! And God knows it's hard enough. The goings-on around here are shocking, shocking! And you bringing those ideas in here only makes it harder for me."

"But unnatural restraint, Father, finds natural outlet in revolt."

Red face again. "You're talking like a Jesuit."

"Look, Father, young people are the same the world over."

"The ones today are a bad lot. They think of nothing but dances and films."

Himself saw an easy point and said, "Well, that's where the I.C.A. might help. It will give the girls worthwhile activities and a little wholesome fun."

"Fun—with their immortal souls in danger!"

"What do you want done?"

Father Cunningham immediately forgot his concern with souls and became very practical. He stroked his chin and said weightily, "The I.C.A. guild is going through, I'm too late to stop it, so what we must do is make sure that it's controlled by Catholics."

"It's bound to be," replied Himself, startled by this quick change. "Everything is put to a vote, and since there are far more Catholics than Protestants in this area, you can be sure that nothing contrary to the Church will be contemplated."

"But, Mr. O'Neill, our people will not speak up."

"Why?"

"Well, you see, the Protestants are generally better educated and are able to carry themselves in public, and the people recognise that."

"But, Father, is not the Church responsible for education? Is not the National School System in the hands of the clergy? Are you not the manager of every National School in the parish?"

"Yes, yes. But there's been little occasion to teach them public speaking, I can tell you! We teach them their catechism and some Gaelic, and what more do they need? And the parents won't even send the children. They'd rather keep them at home to help with the farm. Oh, they're a bad lot! But we won't go into that, Mr. O'Neill, you're too long away, in you might call it a pagan atmosphere."

"Yes, thank God!"

"Now," said the priest, intent on his plan, "we must see that the majority of women on the committee of this local branch are Catholic, and from them choose the officers. Would your wife take the presidency?"

"No, no, she wouldn't do at all."

Sigh of relief. "Well then, we'll have Mrs. Nugent. She was postmistress here you know, before Griffin, for twenty-five years, and she's very regular in her duties. And I think Mrs. Murphy of the Cross for vice-president—she raised a large family and two of her daughters are in the convent. The treasurer can be a Protestant, I'd say, but I think Miss Doyle, who is very faithful about collecting for the parish lottery, I think she'll be secretary. They're bound to put up Miss Protheroe and Mrs. Whyte, but only two of them won't matter, because Lady Crosby will also be on the committee, of course, and your wife and Mrs. Nugent's niece, and Miss Doyle's sister and Mrs. McQuade and Nora. I must go now and call on Mrs. McQuade and arrange to have the nominations made and seconded. Will you tell your wife about them?"

"I will, Father, but she won't approve, any more than I do."

"Ah, she won't know one name from another. All she has to do is to vote for Mrs. McQuade's nominations. Well, I must rush. Keep the Faith, Mr. O'Neill. Good-bye."

When the politics part of all this was relayed to me, it seemed unbelievable, outrageous, presumptuous, disillusioning, ridiculous and, finally, unimportant. It was just another instance of the kind of thing that forever trips me up in Ireland—the obvious trick, so corny and blatant that one imagines no one does it any more—only, this was the catch, they did! This was country 'cuteness', for which I was always unprepared, though it certainly was an aspect of the same past I had been yearning for.

I had thought, of course, that we could return to a past of our own choosing. In that rosy image, politics, if they entered at all, took the form of forthright democratic town meetings. Kindly pastors consulted their flocks, female as well as male, and talk of women as vessels of iniquity was as much a dead issue as discussion of how many angels could stand on the point of a pin.

But it was at this point that my admiration for the past began to change. Now that I was living in it, I didn't like it at all. Town meetings, were they ever really democratic, I wonder? Women's activities?—Who knows what intrigue, religious and otherwise, might have gone on behind the scenes? So far as I am now concerned, the good old days ain't what they used to be, for when the indiscriminate past rolled down over us, I realised what they could mean— illiteracy, religious schisms, suppression of women, Jansenism and conspiracy.

But Himself was rubbing his hands with glee. He had thoroughly enjoyed the interview. Just what he was always telling everyone about the interference of the Church with the individual. This was a prize example, a vignette to be cherished.

"Keep the Faith," he murmured, "one of our own, our own kind, Irish Catholic—how long is it now since I last heard those?"

"Not since you last spoke with a nun," I said sourly.

*

CHAPTER II

THE COUNTRYWOMEN

FATHER CUNNINGHAM'S list of candidates was elected without a murmur. In October we gathered in the National School, and Miss O'Callaghan, the sweet, efficient organiser from Dublin, made a little speech. I had met her before, in my first enthusiastic visits to Irish Countrywomen's Association headquarters, when the proposal to start a guild was fresh. She said in brief that the foundation of the I.C.A. was the fact that it was non-sectarian and democratic. Hardly had she finished when Father Cunningham 'dropped in'— just to see if the school had been opened up for us, he said. Thus reminded, we all thanked him profusely for permitting us to use the school building. He wanted to take this opportunity to wish us well, he said. We all thanked him profusely for wishing us well. This was a great occasion, he said, a great organisation, a great opportunity for the women of Ireland to show the virtues for which they had long been famous, he said, as against the women of other, more pagan countries. Louise Whyte and I exchanged a look, but we all thanked him profusely for the gentle thought. He raised his hand as though in blessing and departed.

Mrs. McQuade then rose, Trilby-like, and made her nominations in a tense voice, with her eyes tight closed, the ordeal of memorisation being equalled only by the support of faith. Thirty women sat in absolute silence and could not be induced to say anything, yea, nay or ahem, despite Miss O'Callaghan's best efforts. So, in short order, the Ardmanagh Guild of the I.C.A. was established: Mrs. Nugent (R.C.) Pres., Mrs. Murphy (R.C.) Vice-Pres., Miss Doyle (R.C.) Hon Sec., Miss Johnson (Prot.) Hon Treas. Committee: Lady Crosby (R.C.), Miss Protheroe (Prot.), Mrs. Whyte (Prot.), Mrs. McQuade (R.C.), Miss McQuade (R.C.), Mrs. Quinn (R.C.), Mrs. Mahoney (R.C.), Mrs. O'Malley (R.C.) and me.

Everybody being satisfied with this democratic and nonsectarian procedure, Miss O'Callaghan put us through a practice meeting. Business first, then a demonstration of a craft, tea, roll call, social half-hour. Roll call is a device to make every member speak, each answering in turn the same question. Our first roll call was "How would you like to spend a summer evening?"

Mrs. McQuade: "At the rosary, with poor Eileen and poor Eamonn and poor Nora, with the help of God."

Mrs. Nugent: "Havin' tea."

Lady Crosby (deaf): "What's that? Some evening? Are we having another meeting?"

Miss Johnson: "Upholstering a chair."

Bridie: "Dancin'."

Miss Protheroe (near-sighted, in an aside): "Psst! Who asked about summer evenings?"

A large red-haired, red-faced person named Mrs. Dooley: "At the fireplace with me feet up on the mantel."

Other replies ranged from "in bed" (alone, one assumed) to the comparatively sociable "at the films", but it remained for Louise to say devilishly, "Out boating, I think, with a pleasant companion of the opposite sex".

"Ah," sighed little Miss Doyle, "you're putting a longing on me!"

It was soon obvious why roll call had been invented—

apart from the committee, our members did not talk. This way, a few grudging words were squeezed out of each. But they sat at meetings, month after month, patiently waiting to hear something they could understand, something they could flash to each other by bush telegraph from bog to moat, some stray word in their own language, like 'tea', 'bun', 'dance', 'pay', 'free', 'outing'. Nothing else registered.

But once communication had been effected, then they seethed with action, talking—never officially—but before, after and between meetings, in little cliques of their own, quarrelling or combining as the case might be, regrouping after fallings-out, or reassembling into feuds of long standing, but joining for the expression of anonymous opinion. "I heard it through a friend of mine." "It was a girl on the road told me." When put a direct question, of great or little moment, such as, "Do you want to work toward a hall of our own?" or, "Do you want to learn how to make pot-holders out of egg-cosies?" (or perhaps it was egg-cosies out of pot-holders), the standard answer was, "I don't mind," or, "I lave it to yourself, ma'am."

These unmanly evasions dampened my group spirit some-what. I began to question why we had started the I.C.A. anyhow. Louise and I had various talks.

"Think of these barren country lives—the women have absolutely no outlet. There's no sociability of any sort. This will at least supply them with some experience."

"Yes," agreed Louise, "it's too ghastly for them, isn't it? Imagine there never having been an organisation here before, of any sort."

"You'd hardly think it possible to escape one, in this day and age. But here they are, virgin territory. And eager to learn, judging from the crowd."

"It's pretty grim for us, really, and that blasted school-room is so draughty, but at least we *are* doing some good."

But apart from all this, why start anything? Why indeed? Just in typical careless American enthusiasm, in the spirit of countless other beginnings, of mistakes not mattering—just wipe them out and do it again—of a philosophy wasteful of good ideas-at-the-time, of people and occasions. And also because community service is part of the American way of life which I was determinedly lugging around with me like a suitcase. But it was beginning to occur to me that this like everything else, was not going to be an American experience either.

Himself alternated between amusement and exasperation. "For God's sake, girl, will you ever take a tumble to yourself? How often have I told you that these people have been tightly bred for generations to diddle the Ascendancy. By their very nature they can't be democratic. They can't differentiate between you and Louise and that same Ascendancy. As sure as God made little apples, when you least expect it, you'll find yourselves made fools of."

"Nonsense! They'll welcome being treated in a really democratic way."

But there *was* the matter of class distinction. Most of the members said 'dis' for 'this' and 'dat' for 'that' (possible Irish origin of the so-called Brooklyn accent?) and they also said 'fetheration' for 'federation'. Some of them obviously didn't know what a federation was. We expected that Mrs. Nugent would take hold and make everything clear; after all, she was their elected leader. But the vote signified nothing. Mrs. Nugent was as silent as the ordinary members; she could only giggle and leave it to the secretary to conduct the meetings. Never having seen a meeting before, most of the members took this as normal. No one minded in the least, except, of course, Louise and me.

"It doesn't seem quite believable, does it?" she would whisper, as Mrs. Nugent and Miss Doyle rushed through our business, blindly charging towards the moment when, as

F

Miss Doyle always described it, "the meeting terminated".

"They'll learn," I would mutter, and interrupt the proceedings to explain, as matter-of-factly as possible, that a discussion, or a vote, or a resolution, as the case might be, had to occur at that point.

Absolute silence.

But in electing Mrs. Nugent and the others and going through the motions of holding meetings, the group had in no way endorsed her. They had merely followed directions from above, as conveyed through Mrs. McQuade. Above alone knew what they thought of it all at this early stage. The I.C.A. was as unknown to them as darkest Africa—more unknown, since they had seen movies of Africa. Probably it represented to them just something going on, an activity to which, in the vacuum of their existence, they were irresistibly drawn.

It was a scent, a stimulus; they wouldn't miss it. They would sit in silence as they had for generations and hold tight, and eventually, whatever bit of excitement might occur, they'd be in on it. Meanwhile they were doing what the priest said, they were on the side of the angels and enjoying themselves to boot, a rare coincidence; and to cap it, 'the county' was in it for their edification and amusement. Miss Nugent was of no interest to them. She was not part of their game. Their deference, as from time long past, was to Lady Crosby. Louise was English and therefore in *that* category. I was a novelty and chief comic relief.

Unfortunately, Lady Crosby only came to meetings when duty impelled her, about twice a year. So there was a slight shift, and Miss Protheroe was given the ranking position, even being called "the Lady Protheroe" by the older members, almost all of whom had been employed by her or her mother, the original 'Lady Protheroe', at one time or other.

Figures like Miss Protheroe and her mother are stereotypes

in Ireland. In former years, when Ballydown supported a staff of forty, they had been in the centre of things in the county. Paintings of the family, done at various times in childhood and youth, hung about the halls there. There was one of Mrs. Protheroe as Diana, with a coronet and a dominating look, and several of her with her children, for she had had another daughter who died. The girls had indeed been lovely—tall, slender, fair and submissive. Their mother had ruled them, the house and the countryside with an iron hand. No one was good enough for them; they were shipped off to visit English cousins, Swedish cousins, Austrian cousins, and then the money began to run out, and presently it was too late.

The daughter died; the father died; the good furniture was auctioned off; Mrs. Protheroe and Miss Charlotte were reduced to a single woman in the house; rooms were closed up, carpets removed. Miss Protheroe had to take over the responsibility of the estate, for Mrs. Protheroe, ageing now, and lame and embittered, washed her hands of her circumstances. She pretended all was as ever, and occupied herself with supervising a succession of erring gardeners, and with criticising Charlotte. Sometimes she limped in to tea at Ballydown, but invitations elsewhere were refused. She liked to call herself a recluse, and her conversation was exclusively about "the olden days." But Miss Protheroe, as the locals said, "moved with the times." She was over-burdened with decisions and anxieties: the farm, the crops, the cattle, the workmen, the machinery, the house, the car and, pervading it all, the taxes. Life had forced her to become realistic, and she half envied her mother's romantic view. Mrs. Protheroe played the lady of the gardens, but Miss Protheroe daily drove to town, an act of manifest courage on the one hand and manifest danger on the other, for she was very near-sighted, and sold vegetables to the shop-keepers—at hard prices too. She had had to learn how to get along with people, and how to deal firmly with them. Naturally, Miss Protheroe was on the I.C.A. committee, and naturally, Mrs. Protheroe did not join.

As it turned out, Miss Charlotte was well rewarded for her membership in the I.C.A. For one thing, some of the women ordered vegetables, and for another—a consummation long hoped for and long despaired of—electricity was brought to the area! Lady Crosby's *idée fixe* for the last five years had been to get the rural current to Castlecrosby. She immediately had Ardmanagh Guild send a letter to the E.S.B. —it was the secretary's first act—requesting that it be supplied at an early date. Miracle of miracles, such is the prestige of organisation that work started within a month, this after a previous history of false promises, reneges, alarms and rumours which nothing short of an epic could chronicle. Miss Protheroe was overjoyed, for Ballydown had been wired in anticipation some twenty years ago. In return for all this she was willing, when her turn came, to have the I.C.A. committee meet in the old office-room there, dismissing her mother's objections as impractical.

"You needn't worry, Mama. I shan't let them into the drawing-room."

"I hope not! Think of the talk as it is!"

Actually, she was quite right. It was a feather in the cap of all the ladies to be invited to 'the Lady Protheroe's'. The distinction between drawing-room and office didn't occur to them, and the fact that there was no longer a butler, or carpets, or furniture, or heat, didn't matter. This was the grade, and they had made it.

Beer and skittles such as committee meetings at Ballydown, at Ardtown and Barravore kept the I.C.A. afloat during its first year, because none of the officers had a glimmer of what to do.

"You really must thank the visiting speaker," Louise would prompt into Mrs. Nugent's ear.

"I can't, I can't!"

"But you must, you know."

"I'll be better able for it after me tea."

But after tea she would sigh comfortably and forget all about it.

There were other obstacles too. On the occasions when Lady Crosby did attend, being deaf she brought up issues already settled and wanted them voted on again, and the committee grew hoarse shouting explanations. And Miss Protheroe, who could not see across a room, always called the ladies by the wrong names. And Miss Doyle was accused of being bossy. And Elsie Johnson, the Protestant treasurer, always referred to 'we' and 'you', underlining the great divide.

The members were happily enough engaged in making hideous painted glass trays, firescreens, spool candlesticks, knitted vests and anything else demonstrated at meetings, but Mrs. Nugent doubtless reflected the common opinion when she summed up the year's progress to the organiser from Dublin.

Miss Callaghan, to help her out, sketched in quickly the achievements of other guilds—money raised, halls built, works of charity, strides in education, markets organised, etc., etc. "And what did Ardmanagh Guild accomplish in this past year?" she asked.

Proudly Mrs. Nugent replied, "The committee had a meetin' at Ballydown House!"

Then there was the matter of cleanliness. Headquarters encouraged demonstrations and talks on housekeeping, dietetics, child care, nursing the sick and so forth. Our ladies listened politely and went right on frying steak, feeding babies with tea, and treating cuts with cobwebs, flies and all.

When I once asked what powder or soap was the best for washing dishes, everyone looked perfectly blank, and finally Bridie giggled and said, "You're the only one I ever seen usin' anythin' but water, missus."

But our biggest effort came when our guild was asked to take part in a county-wide Clean Milk Campaign. We were to choose a member to enter the contest for the best milker. Mrs. Dooley, who ran her dairy single-handed (her husband was a big farmer and she was a big farmer's wife), was selected by unanimous vote, and beforehand she demonstrated her skill for the committee on one of the Whytes' cows. She did the job speedily and well, and finished up by sticking her hand in the pail and making the sign of the cross in milk on the cow's udder.

"Oh dear," suggested Louise bravely, aware that this was an old custom. "Do you think, Mrs. Dooley, that you could do that in some other way? You know how judges are these days with all this pernickety hygiene. Do you think you could squirt some milk into your hand and use that instead?"

Mrs. Dooley thought about it for awhile and then was struck with inspiration. "I will," she said, "I will! That's a grand touch altogether. It will make it different than all them others, so it will."

When the day of the contest arrived, Louise and I and most of the committee drove miles to the county seat to watch it. Mrs. Dooley was the only woman entrant. The five other contestants, men, were representatives of just a few of the agricultural organisations which harry the Irish farmer. The six of them were lined up next to their respective beasts in a shining clean barn. The cows were washed and brushed, the milk utensils were boiled and polished, the milkers were combed and capped and scoured and enveloped in spotless white smocks. Mrs. Dooley had even washed up to the elbows with antiseptic soap.

"All set?" asked the judge, the County Agricultural Officer.

"Right!" sang out Mrs. Dooley, squaring her shoulders, and forgetful of the pernickety ideas of judges and hygiene, she spat on her hands, rubbed them together, and began.

"But at least," Louise and I told each other, "we have developed in her one member who will talk." The milking defeat, ascribed by some of the ladies to the clannishness of men, and by others to what they called "the Protestant cross", didn't wilt her in the least. Her clouds of glory still trailed and from then on she didn't hesitate to speak: not during the business meeting—that goes without saying—but in the period afterward optimistically alluded to as "the social half-hour", which stretched far, far into the night.

The ladies, very interested in the Coronation, which Louise had seen in England, asked her about it at one meeting. She said briefly that she had thought it a wonderful pageant. The fact that films of the Coronation were not shown in Ireland, because of anti-English feeling in some quarters, made this a ticklish subject.

"I'll bet it was smashing," said Miss Doyle admiringly.

"There's only one bunch that can get away with crowns," said Mrs. Dooley, "and that's the British monarchy, I'll say that for them. That young woman they have over there, she has a head for a crown, so she has."

"It's a good job the President here don't have to wear one," she continued. "The ould feller ud faint with fright if he saw a ten-pound crown bein' landed down on him."

Another pet topic was 'the electric' for which the houses were now being wired and fixtures and appliances bought. Miss Protheroe was quite transfigured with joy; Mrs. Dooley had her own opinions.

"Did you get wired up yet?" someone asked her.

"We did."

"Now you'll be buying an electric cooker and an iron and a washing machine——" This was to get a rise out of her.

"We're hard set to get machinery for outside, never mind it inside. The woman who can't wash a shirt and a shift and the others without a machine is no woman at all, so she's not, and I wouldn't give her house room, so I wouldn't. There's some," (did her eye rest for a moment on young Mrs. Carthy, a notoriously bad housekeeper?) "that ought to be in a home, under supervision. I'd electrocute them with a toe in the rear. Washing machines, sez she!"

Mrs. Dooley was great gas, the members said.

Miss Doyle seemed to get on their nerves; they resented her businesslike manner and its constant reminder that she had a town job at big money. "Ah, she's up a needle. She has her nose in the air." Miss Doyle looked as though she hoped for something from life. She was small, quite pretty, though no longer young; she admired Louise's clothes enormously. The ladies were 'agin'' her.

On the other hand, they got on well with Elsie Johnson, despite the fact that she was a Protestant. "Sure, the Johnsons are almost Catholics," they explained. Did they mean that they lived in a concrete bungalow on their exceedingly prosperous farm, while other Protestants in our locality favoured ancient cottages with muck in the yards up to their ankles? No, for mucky yards were fairly non-sectarian. They meant that Elsie was one of *them* despite her allusions to *us*. She too spoke the language of tea and outing. She was a small olive-skinned girl, brisk and swift in her movements and speech, like a saucy but very competent bird. She was a great worker, a rock of dependability when any tea or supper had to be organised, and she was the best of all at knitting, crocheting, cooking, sewing, any kind of making.

None of them, to my surprise, had much use for the

McQuades. "Ah, they're too holy fer the rest of us, they'll be in heaven before they die." But Mrs. McQuade and Nora did not stay the course long. Early on, they proposed that we should run a 'social' and give the proceeds to Father Cunningham 'in lieu of rent' for the National School. This seemed fair enough; the social was advertised and held, members donated cakes and those who came played whist, and a profit of five pounds was presented to the priest. Shortly after, a cottage close by became vacant and it was suggested that the I.C.A. should rent it (rent was two shillings a week, a typical figure for country dwellings) as then we'd be more comfortable and under no obligation for the National School.

Mrs. McQuade incoherently opposed this, for unexpressed reasons; it was felt that Father Cunningham would be annoyed at losing the five pounds each year. When it became known that the cottage in question was owned by the Church of Ireland, Mrs. McQuade had hysterics. "Pay rent to the Protestant Church! God between us and harm!" She took to her bed. The rift in the lute, the Protestant-Catholic issue, was beginning to tell.

We did not take the cottage because eventually the majority of members indicated that they also did not approve, after allowing Louise to spend hours of time and trouble examining the place, getting estimates for repairs, and haggling with Canon Smith over the price. After weeks of "I don't mind," and "I leave it to yourself," they passed the word along so that it reached the committee and us seventh-hand: "So-and-so told such-and-such that this one was speakin' to that one, and she heard it from a girl on the road—they don't want to rent a Protestant house."

Mrs. McQuade and Nora came to no more meetings. Perhaps, as in the case of Cæsar's wife, the mere suspicion of scandal was too much for them; or perhaps they were getting back at Himself because, via Father Cunningham, they regarded the I.C.A. as his instigation. During this period an incident had occurred in Danny's, the butcher. Himself went in one morning and found the shop full and Blessed McQuade asking for "a pound and a quarter" of steak. Blessed knew how to stretch a penny.

"Now, Danny, give me good weight," he was saying, "and I'll pray for you."

Himself called out, "Have you the meat for my dogs, Danny?"

"Yes, Mr. O'Neill, I have. I'll parcel it up for you."

"Thanks, Danny. I'll have the two of them pray for you too."

Shortly after this, the McQuades resigned.

When elections came round again in October, Louise was ill in bed with flu, which every year keeps her indoors for at least two months. And thanks to the imminent arrival of Sally, I too had been absent for several meetings; the canons of modesty so decreed, and I was more than willing to conform. Even at best Louise and I dreaded the schoolhouse and the bundling-up necessary to attend—several layers of woollen underwear, two pairs of woollen stockings, fur-lined boots, tweed suit with two sweaters, ancient fur coat, scarf around neck, second scarf around head, fur gloves. In any case, we agreed, it would simply be another democratic non-sectarian vote for the same officers and committee, so neither of us gave the meeting a second thought.

The next morning Miss Doyle called on me to say, "Mrs. Whyte was elected president. Will you tell her, please?"

Successive flashes came over me. Joy! This was incredible; a Protestant and an Englishwoman to boot! The women really had learned to admire and appreciate Louise. Progress! They wanted her to represent them, and they wanted a real guild, with business run correctly and a gracious president to guide them. How wonderful, this was what we had worked for. At the same time, I was terribly afraid that Louise would say "no". The Colonel had urged her to resign altogether because of the strain on her health and the usurpation of her time. And now she was sick.

"You mean to say that you didn't ask her before nominating her?"

"No."

"Then two of you had better go round and implore her to accept. She's not well, the draughts in that building are very bad for her, and now that the Colonel's taken on the Antiquarian Society, she won't have much time."

They duly waited on Louise, and though she put up a good fight, in the end she did succumb. But the Colonel made them promise first that she would be excused from winter meetings and from any exertion, such as looking over cottages which the group had no intention of renting, and that they would immediately take steps to find another meeting place. Yes, yes, yes, of course.

And at the next meeting, full of reform, they voted to start a building fund.

*

CHAPTER 12

A DANCE AND A SOCIAL

ORGANISATIONS THESE DAYS ARE SUCH that it doesn't matter whether you've joined the Old Men's Chess Club or the Young Ladies' Archery Society, there is absolutely no differentiation; don't think you'll move a pawn or bend a bow, you'll be spending your time in either case raising funds. In the Irish countryside, the regimentation in this direction is complete; there is only one way, tried and true, to make a bit of money, and that is to hold a dance.

Dances are the one social outlet, and neither cold nor rain nor sleet, nor priests threatening hellfire, nor doctors threatening TB, nor employers threatening the sack, nor fiancés threatening the jilt can keep Irish girls from going to every dance within bicycle reach. They normally begin at ten and continue till three, with a couple of hours added at either end for going and coming; and sometimes there are two or three a week. The young men attend in crowds, after spending the evening in the local as usual, not infrequently going to the dance for the sake of the sobering effect of the supper. There is almost always at least one disorder, from rushing the gate to assault and battery. Giving a dance is not a carefree social function. The sponsoring group embarks on a commercial enterprise in which responsibility for order and breakage looms large, and the work involved is a *little* short of building the pyramids with kindergarten blocks.

For the Countrywomen, there was, first, the matter of getting the orchestra, then of setting the date, the place, the price, and the question of whether to serve supper included, or extra. Since all of these are indefinites, it was hard at one, two or six meetings to get anything in black and white. The orchestra was the key issue; and generated desperate emotions. There were unsuspected numbers of local bands, each with its following and its foes. Feelers had to be sent out into the public to determine which was the most popular at the moment, and I.C.A. social half-hours raged with the partisan battles. Joe O'Mara's faction lobbied against Malachy Mulhall's, while adherents of the Fitzpatrick band and various other runners-up were reduced to relative silence. Finally the O'Mara party won, and Miss Doyle was instructed to book them. Several meetings later she reported that they were engaged every Friday and Sunday night for the next two years. (These are the best dance nights; Saturday is given over to polishing shoes and otherwise preparing for Sunday and the effort of getting up in time for Mass.)

O'Mara was making the impressive charge of forty pounds a night; Mulhall, on the other hand, could give us a Friday night two months ahead and would only charge thirty. So, another meeting was called and this was agreed on. Elsie Johnson then rushed off on a tour of nearby hamlets where halls were available. After complications which involved swapping nights with a fellow who showed films and promising the mineral water concession to the local shop, one of them was hired. Needless to say, none of the halls contained water supply, electricity or heating. Minor matters such as posters, advertisements in the local papers, sandwich-making and the baking of cakes by members were duly worked out; a squad to decorate the hall was sworn in, and lo, the day of the dance dawned.

Really, the labour made it more like a work-out for the scene-shifters' union than a dance, carting as we did tanks, barrels and pails of water, paraffin stoves, gas stoves, buckets, huge kettles, pots, tables and towels, cups, saucers, plates, spoons, sugar, milk and tea, all tracked down, negotiated and borrowed for the occasion by Elsie Johnson, who, it seemed, owned and operated all the Protestant dances, tea-stalls and picnics within miles. Having the excuse of the new baby, I did relatively little, but Himself and Tom fetched and carried all afternoon. With her other hand, Elsie made hundreds of sandwiches and buttered dozens of scones. Without her inside knowledge and previous experience, we would have been defeated on every front; but this way all went like clockwork.

Louise worked morning and afternoon in the decorating division. The hall, the size of a small gymnasium and equally bare, was full of trash from the last dance. As none of the promised members turned up, Louise and her maid, Lil, swept, mopped, aired and then, with their last gasp, festooned. Bridie and I made cakes all day, having rashly agreed to eight and being, alas, famous for them, or so the ladies craftily made out. By the time the dance started, Louise and I were exhausted; Bridie and Lil were fresh as daisies.

Elsie and two faithful workers had the food situation well in hand; and when most of the Countrywomen arrived, blandly ignoring the duties they had failed in, the entire membership sat down to a good tea in the supper room, leaving the paying guests fringed round the empty dance floor. It was difficult indeed to pry the ladies loose from the supper—only the danger of having to assist Elsie finally made them move. By this time it was past eleven and the orchestra now arrived—fashionably late, one supposed. They proceeded at once to make up in volume what they had lost in time, and the result was perfectly shattering to ears, nerves and conversation.

The girls, of whom there was a crowd by now, sat at one end of the hall, attired in anything from house dresses to rather amazing home-made 'dance frocks', all of the lightest materials. That they didn't immediately die of pneumonia is testimony to man's—or rather woman's—ability to adapt to environment. They sat shivering at the far end and sporadically, in self-preservation, danced with each other.

At the other end of the hall were the young men, fewer, smaller, warmer, staring into space. Himself does not dance; neither does the Colonel. Tom was 'on the door', seeing that hopelessly unruly people did not get in and that everyone paid, so he could not be pressed into setting an example. The girls gyrated around, doing steps wonderful to behold; the boys sat in silence. Suddenly there was a great accession of male customers—the pubs had closed.

Feeling strength in numbers, doubtless, a few of the bolder or affianced now danced with the ladies of their choice. Some Countrywomen stepped out with their husbands. But there was still a mass huddle at each end of the hall. Could it be Malachy Mulhall's music, I wondered? It was oh so ample, but, despite the announcing of waltzes, quick-steps, even the wicked hokey-pokey which (Bridie said) the priest at home had forbidden, all the numbers sounded fast and jumpy and looked exactly the same. Surely something was wrong?

But we did have a male dancer on our side—Michael Kinch. Very courtly, he waltzed with Louise, and then to my trepidation, approached me. It was a great relief when all he asked was, "Are you idle, missus?"

Idle? Perhaps Louise wanted me to do something, or I was due in Elsie Johnson's department. "Why, er—what do you mean, Michael?"

"Ain't I sayin' it, ma'am? Are you *idle*?"

"Well, er—yes."

He took me by the arm and led me toward the floor. Delayed light! I felt exactly the same linguistic and social dismay that I had ages ago, at a midwestern university, when someone asked me, "Are you organised?"

"Oh! No, thank you, Michael. I don't dance."

Just then the Danish engineer of the town's chief industry appeared at the door with his wife. They flinched a little, but smiled and walked gamely up to us. Fanfare. "The next number will be a tango," called out Malachy.

"I like much the tango," said the Danish lady, "but my husband do not dance."

"Oh Michael! Here's a lady who's *very* idle." And he gallantly led her off.

Back she came after perhaps four bars. "I cannot dance this Irish tango. The rhythmo is different."

Well, that's two of us, I thought. Actually, it was blissful to be *not* dancing and in such good company, accounted for otherwise, one of the workers, not expected to scintillate. Much better than to sit lonely on the sidelines, trying to put the mind on Other Things and not to notice the smug glances and phoney behaviour of ladies who *had* partners! I felt full of sympathy for the girls who were merely butter-flies, and ostentatiously sliced a cake or two. Louise, dis-tressed at the bouquet, nay, bank, of wallflowers, went up to a few youths and courageously said, "Wouldn't you like to dance? May I introduce you to a charming partner?" Floored by this unheard of procedure, they allowed them-selves to be presented to Bridie, Lil and their companions. A little more mixing of the two factions ensured, a Paul Jones helped, and things began to loosen up. Bang, bang, bang, went the drum, te-tum, te-tum—perhaps the idea was that the noise would brainwash resistance out of them.

There was some excitement at the door; two girls wanted

to go out and return later, but this was forbidden. There was a rule at all dances that men could go and come, but not ladies. Once in, you stayed in, or else paid a second admission. How unfair, I thought: another trifling instance of the double standard.

"What would respectable girls be thinking of, to leave a dance!" exclaimed Elsie who had darted out of the supper room for a breather.

"Whatever the men are thinking of when they leave," I retorted.

"Why, Mrs. O'Neill! Not *that*!" she cried.

Elsie was in her element. She was undoubtedly born with a tea kettle in one hand and some minced ham in the other, her manifest destiny being to organise suppers. "It's a good crowd," she said with satisfaction, looking them over "More than *we* had at our last."

From midnight on, it being no longer Friday, supper was served, and by two o'clock the affair was a great success. The hall was by then very warm indeed, and the dancers could hardly find space on the floor. The men, bolder now, walked over to the girls and actually asked them to dance, and by gum, Mike's invitation was standard. Shuffling his feet with embarrassment, the boy would say, "Are you idle, miss?"

Reply, with lowered eyes: "I don't mind."

"Come on, then."

The I.C.A. ladies sat around the sides, stuffed to the eyes with their own confectionery and laughing uproariously. Drunks tried to come in and were repulsed by Tom. Other crowds were let in cheap, since there was no more supper. During it all, the same old rhythmo beat its way through waltzes, fox-trots, mambos, cha-chas, rock-and-roll, chewing them all into one monotonous ear-splitting hash. Then, at three o'clock, the party was over, and the happy company dispersed into the freezing countryside, there to navigate, chiefly by bicycle, through the moonless night to their respective hedges, ditches and hearths.

Elsie and contingent were still gamely washing-up at four o'clock. We did not get to bed till daylight, returning stranded ladies and articles to their homes. Louise was ill for several days after with a horrid cough; but all was worth it— a net profit of forty pounds.

In the next months, by dint of raffles, jumble sales, outright gifts, whist and beetle drives, we accumulated a little more. By the time summer came again, everyone would be pleased to relax for a few months, one would have thought; but no, the members wanted an excursion. If an outing by a stretch of the rules could be called educational, half of the funds for it might come from the treasury. Since a good lot voted aye, that was it. Louise and I put the I.C.A. out of our minds for the summer, and let the excursionists attend to their own details.

One evening a girl rang the doorbell to tell me there was a special meeting for those going on the excursion. "Well, I'm not. Thanks just the same for notifying me, but I won't attend." Similar answer from Louise. We didn't learn, except by chance and at the eleventh hour, that at the meeting they had voted that the entire cost of the excursion should come out of funds. They had already engaged a bus and paid the fee.

"How could Elsie Johnson have given them the money?"

"I saw it in her eye," said Louise darkly. "After we made that money at the dance, she immediately flew about saying, 'And now, how shall we spend it?' "

"But she was the delegate to summer school, and everything. She *knew* better."

Elsie, called to account, blushed but held that the others had 'overruled' her.

"How could they overrule you when they were breaking a rule?"

Mrs. Nugent said something about lovely jam tarts. Miss Doyle said she hadn't even known of the meeting. No one else said a word, as always, except forthright Mrs. Dooley. "It was my idea. What's wrong with spendin' the money that way?"

"It's forbidden in the by-laws," said Louise.

"By-laws? We can do without them, so we can."

"No," I said, "you can't. Not if you want to belong to the I.C.A. If you just want to be the Ardmanagh Social Club, that's different, you can do as you please."

"We asked for money from members and friends for our building fund," explained Louise. "It's misrepresentation to use it for any other purpose."

"Well, the money's paid for the bus already," said Elsie. "What should we do?"

"Go, of course."

"Yes," I said bitterly, thinking of Louise slaving in the hall and me baking cakes all day, "these ladies never get a day at a beach and a ride in a bus. No one would want to deprive any one of you of that."

As a result of my remark, Mrs. Dooley withdrew, saying she didn't need any bus to bring her anywhere, she had her own van, and she huffed out of the meeting. But everyone else went and had a fine time, unburdened with conscience or their own purses.

They spent the *whole* of our hard-earned funds on their excursion. Louise and I told each other that we would throw in the sponge if it ever happened again.

"They were really very naughty indeed," Louise said.

"They just don't understand that they can't make the rules. It specifically says in the constitution that nothing of that sort should arise."

"Of course, the poor dears don't really know what is and what isn't done," said Louise kindly.

"I shouldn't have thought Elsie Johnson would have let them."

"She worked so hard at the dance, she probably felt that the money was hers. And she wanted the excursion as much as they."

"What slays me is their taking the tips out of funds too—such ducal ones at that, a pound to each of the men. Wouldn't you think *that* at least could have come out of their own pockets?"

"Well, the whole idea is to educate; they'll know next time."

Louise, bred in the tradition of Women's Institutes and good causes, was less disturbed than I. She was used to exhorting, cajoling and setting an example. But as an egalitarian I was unwilling to look at my fellows as naughty children, and consequently was beset with a much more subtle and difficult form of *noblesse oblige*, which was strained now in the effort to communicate with these as women and peers.

After all, I was the local American, and the basic message of my country is: give the opportunity, and any man can flower. To withdraw frankness and *laisser-faire* and substitute superiority and firmness, seemed to misrepresent my national philosophy.

Not, however, theirs. Our ladies giggled like schoolgirls and Louise's earnest little speech fell right off their well-padded backs. They swore they would never do it again, but it seemed to me they had a gleam of triumph in their downcast eyes. My own pep-talk to them was very silly. It might be summed up: "Are you mice or are you women? Women of the world, arise! Don't you want to be mistresses of your fates? Don't you want to be responsible citizens?" Their answer, clearly, was: "No. Not if we can have free excursions, lemonade, jam tarts, paddles in the sea, by being irresponsible."

Another season, another dance, other sales of work, jumbles, raffles—the usual, in short. Another spring, another excursion. This time we kept a watchful eye on proceedings, and it was iron-clad that those going were to pay all the expenses. Under these circumstances, somehow, the same bus fare was reduced from thirty-five to seventeen pounds, the tip from two pounds to ten shillings. Elsie arranged it all, and was very pleased with her efforts.

The only matter left unfinished was a second social for the National School, 'in lieu of rent', and Miss Doyle undertook to run it. Like the first one, this social was to be held in the schoolhouse, music for dancing—instead of whist—being donated by a talented local quartette, and members supplying food. The whole idea was to keep expenses to a minimum. Admission was a shilling and by invitation, as the school was too small to hold a crowd.

Neither the Whytes nor we went to the social, but first doubts hit us when our invitations came—engraved. The rest followed with depressing consistency. High-priced posters advertised the event; the band was given ten pounds; food was catered from the confectioners in town at the cost of another twenty pounds, even though we members sent home-made cakes. Handsome prizes were awarded; and when all was reckoned up, we had a deficit of twenty-five pounds. A further five pounds then had to be illegally voted, to make it up to the priest, who was innocently expecting the profits.

"Blast them," I snapped angrily to Louise. "They've done it again!"

"Oh, it couldn't have been deliberate," she protested,

shocked. "You don't really think they were trying to take advantage?"

But recalling Himself's words, I said grimly, "I do."

Elsie Johnson, this time safely on the side of the sheep, added to our pain by describing the waste of food that went on, sandwiches thrown on the floor and trampled, cakes bitten into and pitched aside, and instead of using the members' contributions and any uneaten lots being returned to the bakery (a standing arrangement), the bakery stuff was grabbed first, and the donations were given away afterwards to friends of those in charge. Elsie blamed it all on Miss Doyle. Hearing this, Miss Doyle wept—she had only wanted everything 'nice', she said. "How did I know they were going to go on like that? It was the ones on the teas!"

"Ah," nodded Elsie privately to Louise and me, "you can be sure they gave away our cakes to their friends."

Miss Doyle had to account to more than the treasurer. Mrs. Dooley came up, a week after, and asked for the return of her pudding, "seein' as how it wasn't needed fer the party".

"The pudding's been disposed of," replied Miss Doyle.

" 'Disposed of', sez she. An' what is that, may I ask?"

"What was left after the party was divided up among the participating helpers."

"Niver mind the lawdy-da airs, I want me puddin'. Who has it?"

At the next committee meeting, this was put to us. It turned out that it had been given to young Mrs. Carthy. Mrs. Murphy volunteered to drop down to her and ask for it back. But as luck would have it, she found only Mrs. Carthy's husband at home, leaning on the garden wall. "That I.C.A. is a wonderful institution. Lookit the grand prize me wife won at the last social, the finest puddin' we ever eat. 'Twas gone in no time, down to the last crumb. Sure, ye've a great organisation there."

So the committee empowered the treasurer to go out and buy a pudding to give to Mrs. Dooley. "Very well," said Elsie, "but I don't approve. When *we* give a social, nothing like this comes up. What if all the members asked to have their contributions back. There's precious little in the bank as it is."

"Ah yes, how true," murmured Louise, "but fortunately our members who are pillars of strength, like you, Miss Johnson, those who never fail us, do not feel like that. You will be tactful, won't you, Miss Johnson? Do bring it to her house, if you can, so as to avoid any unpleasantness. We shouldn't want the Carthys to know, should we?"

But Elsie Johnson was a strong-minded girl, and her whole being was affronted by the insult to the injured treasury and the fact that this time *they* had had all the fun. At the next meeting, after the business, the roll call, the tea, the demonstration, the chit-chat, Elsie suddenly rose. She reached into her bottomless rush carry-all and stood up, addressing the chair. "Yes," said Louise, unsuspectingly nodding to her. "Ladies, I believe our treasurer has something else to say."

Elsie waited, as always, for complete silence before she spoke. "It has come to the attention of the committee," she said, "that there were complaints over food donations to the last social. So as to avoid any bad feeling, the committee authorised the purchase of a plum pudding to replace one—er—lost. Here, Mrs. Dooley, this is for you."

"Oh, Miss Johnson," rebuked Louise, in her gentle way, "not here!"

"For me, is it," bellowed Mrs. Dooley, drowning out Louise. "Are ye tryin' to shame me?"

"It's you shamin' me," put in young Mrs. Carthy, tearfully.

"What have you to do with it?" roared Mrs. Dooley.

"We eat your puddin', but it was give to us."

"I gave it to her, I'm not afraid to admit it," cried Miss Doyle in a high, thin voice.

"Ladies, ladies!" from Louise.

"Sure, no one's accusin' anyone," put in Mrs. Murphy.

"Do ye hear any of the rest of us claimin' for our cakes?"

"Who was on the teas that night?"

"Didn't all of us take home some left-over?" said Eily Nolan.

"What are ye tryin' to make me out?" shouted Mrs. Dooley.

"Quiet, quiet," someone yelled, but it was a free-for-all. The only voice that could be heard was Lady Crosby, asking, "Oh, I say, are they settling the date for the next dance?"

"Ladies, ladies," cried Louise, but no one could have possibly heard her.

"Take it, Mrs. Dooley," chirped Elsie Johnson briskly. "It's been bought out of the treasury for the express purpose of you. Now take it."

"Do ye think me family is waitin' on ye to have a puddin'? Think again," shouted Mrs. Dooley, and with a mighty heave she threw the pudding out of the window.

"Ladies!"

Bedlam. Young Mrs. Carthy was in tears. Mrs. Dooley was hitching up her skirt and spitting on her hands. Elsie was pink with anger and perhaps with fright. Louise's rappings on the desk for order merely added a staccato note to the symphony.

"It's destructed altogether," exclaimed someone in a hushed voice.

"It's gone and good riddance," said Elsie loudly, ruffling her feathers.

"Let it rot!" cried Mrs. Dooley. "I wouldn't touch that puddin' with a ten-foot pole."

"Thank God we've seen the end of it," shrilled Miss Doyle.

"Ladies! Ladies! We must have order," gasped Louise, rapping fiercely. "This matter was highly irregular, and I'm sure we all agree it was most regrettable. We'll consider the whole unfortunate business closed. The meeting is adjourned."

Just then, in walked the Colonel, having come to call for his wife at the appointed hour. Smiling pleasantly, hat in hand, he was carrying something.

"I say," he said to the sudden silence, "I just happened to stumble over this in the yard. One of you must have dropped it." And helpfully he held out the pudding.

The upshot of it was that I brought the pudding to Dublin as our contribution to a national I.C.A. sale of work. The Colonel had made Louise resign, pleading ill health, and as it turned out, this was my last call to headquarters. Recent events had taken the wind out of my sails and practically vacuumed off the sails too. But the *coup de grâce* to the American clubwoman in Ireland now came, all unconsciously, from one of the I.C.A. executives in Dublin.

She was telling me about the brand new headquarters building, the gift of a philanthropic American foundation. The director of it had recently visited Ireland, and everyone was charmed with him. "I wish you could have met him," she said sincerely. "He's so fascinating, so scholarly, so well-bred, so cultured, so generous, so thoughtful, so modest, so educated—in fact, he's the most un-American American you'd ever meet."

Some time later I overheard Bridie and Eily Nolan discussing the fact that Louise and I no longer came to meetings of the now flourishing Ardmanagh Guild.

"Ah, poor Mrs. Neills," said Eily. "That does be how it is. Or-gan-eye-sations take a lot of time."

*

CHAPTER 13

EDUCATION

WE HADN'T THOUGHT MUCH in advance about education. The nearest school, we assumed, would be the logical place. Himself had benign memories of his first lessons in the National School in the glen. A wonderful master named Pat O'Connell had presided, drunk as a lord a good deal of the time, but obviously the kind of born teacher everyone wishes for his children. To this day, Himself chuckles when he tells how Pat, in a science class, demonstrated distillation from treacle and drank the product, informing his students that it was water. In fact, he kept a glass of water underneath the rostrum for any curious scholar to sample, and if this had blighting effects on possible future chemists, they didn't seem to mind.

Another time there was a great to-do over one of the village concerts which Pat was forever organising. He'd go round the desks pointing his stick for the scale, "Do", sang one, "Re", another, "Mi", "Fa", and so on, and on this basis Pat would say, "You can sing," "You can't," and pick his team accordingly. The elect would mount the stage at the concert and thunder 'A Nation Once Again'. The walking-stick was part of Pat, and when at the same concert he undertook to recite 'Fontenoy', he used it as a rifle.

> " 'Push on, my household cavalry!' King Louis
> madly cried.

181

> To death they rush, but rude their shock, not
>   unavenged they died.
> On through the camp the column trod—King
>   Louis turns his rein.
> 'Not yet, my liege,' Saxe interposed, 'the Irish
>   troops remain!'
> 'Fix bayonets!' "

(He went through the motions.)

> " 'Charge!' "

And carried away by fervour of patriotism, plus other fervours, he charged right off the stage and into the lap of the parish priest.

Himself also recalls Friday in childhood as a day of deprivation: no rashers for breakfast, merely fish for lunch, and it was a regular thing for all children to be put to bed at tea-time. The last was explained by Mary, the nurse, "Wisha, Friday is the night for the ghosts and the goblins."

"Sure," says Himself, laughing now, "it was another kind of spirits altogether."

Tucked into bed, yet wakeful, the children could presently hear a thick voice surprisingly like Pat's issuing forth from the square in front of the barracks where the Crown police were billeted: "The best man of ye come out and fight! Up Sinn Fein! God save Ireland! Afraid, are ye? The whole bloody lot of ye come out and fight!"—Pat's weekly challenge to the enemy.

Naturally, after such a liberal education, Himself thought school didn't really matter very much. The main thing was for children to be independent and free. Rebellion against authority, he uttered autobiographically, was the key to progress.

This was not my country; it was up to him, really, to cope with the situation. In New York I could do it blindfolded. I sighed to think of the expertise in that direction going to waste over here. But he did not cope. He did not even speak. All he said was that wherever else the children were going, they were not going to the convent school in town. This, of course, after his honeymoon with Reverend Mother.

But when I broached the subject of the local National School to friends, visitors, anyone, all and sundry were aghast at the thought of our children going there. At first this upset my notions of democracy, but in the course of the development of the I.C.A., I saw their point. Since our meetings were held in the school (two rooms), we became very familiar with the inky forms on which the scholars perched, the vicious draughts that chased each other through the windows and out of the door, the inadequate turf fires, and the dreary visual education aids on the walls. Holy pictures everywhere—all right. Crumbling maps and cut-outs in Gaelic—very well.

But, symbol of ignorance and shopkeeping (or 'shoneenism') was the large diagram which had the place of honour along the longest wall, and which, incidentally, I've seen in almost every schoolroom I've entered; and thanks to regional I.C.A. meetings, I've entered many. This boasted large, clear, newly printed images of a steak, a glass of milk, vegetables, fruit, bread and butter, and then the information in sign language that a box of certain sweets was the equivalent in nourishment of all of these. I wondered how much this one thing accounted for the depraved diet and the passion for sweets among the Irish, and for the wretched teeth you see in the young people.

To go on with the black inventory. The children were caned with a thick heavy stick. There was no water nearer than half a mile, and no sanitation. Father Cunningham held the turf allowance down—in January the school had no fuel at all, in February, just imagine! it closed, as the entire student body had the flu. Scabies was a common ailment; fleas were taken for granted.

But what cemented our repugnance to the National School was our growing acquaintance with its scholars. To have our young beaten was a horrible prospect, but it was better than to have them conform. Perhaps a Pat O'Connell could have transfigured the school, but to us it seemed that the combination of rote teaching and government Gaelic ended all learning. The children resisted by going into a dive and shuffling off any processes involving thought and, judging from the local graduates whom we came to know, they surfaced unencumbered by knowledge of Gaelic, English, reading, writing, scripture, spelling or history. They had come a long way from both St. Patrick and Oisin.

What to do? Louise most diffidently mentioned that there was an excellent National School fifteen miles away. The teacher was famous for her way with children, almost all of whom went on to preparatory schools and ultimately to universities. The rub was, the school was Protestant.

If Louise was diffident, I practically cringed as I offered the idea to Himself. "Er, would you, I mean only for a little while? They're getting older and they should see some other children occasionally, and soon they'll be ready for real lessons."

"No. Haven't I enough trouble as it is? Do you want Father Cunningham on our necks?"

"B-but——"

"*No.*"

One evening the Whytes came over with visitors from England, the Fowlers. Conversation fell on the O'Neill treasure in the glen, and the Fowlers voted themselves in on a search party. "Very well so," said Himself, "but if we find it we'd have to turn it in to the government."

"Must we?" asked Mr. Fowler.

"Well, perhaps we could go to Spain with the gold—they like gold there still."

"Couldn't we go to America?"

"Certainly, that's it, we'll go to America."

"No," said the Colonel, "I don't want to go. I like it here."

Louise and Mrs. Fowler laughed at him, and Louise mentioned that while she and the Colonel adored life in Ireland, we were finding terrific problems in such matters as education.

"Oh," said Mrs. Fowler, "do you want my advice? I love giving it. Do say you want it."

"Of course," said Louise. "Your children are the same age."

"Tell me all," I begged.

Mrs. Fowler did. She lived in the country in England, much as we did in Ireland, with about the same staff, but she had a governess. "Not a proper governess, you know," she said, "they're very grand creatures, but a nursery governess. That's what you must get."

She didn't have to twist my arm very long. This is her nursery governess's schedule:

Up; the children dressed and washed for breakfast at 8.00 a.m.

After breakfast, upstairs to make children's and own beds and tidy rooms.

9.30 start lessons.

11.00 break for orange juice, tea for governess.

12.30 lessons stop. Children play in the garden till 1.00 p.m., get ready their books or jig-saw puzzles for rest hour.

1.00 lunch with governess in schoolroom.

Children rest till 3.00, while governess does ironing and mending.

3.00 up, dress, go for a walk until 4.30.

Tea next, governess serves it in the schoolroom.

After tea, children brought to mother in drawing-room. Children are all spick and span for this visit. Mother reads or plays with them.

6.00 bathed and put to bed by governess, in bed by 7.00.

At night she cleans their shoes, mends and knits. She uses the schoolroom as her sitting-room, likes to be alone in the evening, usually listens to the wireless.

This governess was Montessori-trained. She had a day off each week, three weeks holiday in the summer, and her wages were £175 a year.

It's hard to express what this information did to me. Never mind getting such a paragon, just knowing that she existed was enough. I felt like pinching myself to see if it was true; was I actually hearing this? Late of New York park benches, of improvised discipline in the sandpile, of four-hour schedules, of endless laundries and moppings, of grim feeding-sessions, of spanks and screams, of milk on the shoulder and baby food in the hair—this blessing was going to happen to *me*? I vaulted towards dizzy heights of anticipation.

Mrs. Fowler wrote out an ad. which we inserted in several English papers, and she told me about Mrs. Boucher in London, the famous agency through which apparently most of England and Ireland are staffed. She also told me about P.N.E.U., the English equivalent of the Calvert system in America, but intended more specifically for children in the outposts of the Commonwealth where there are no schools.

Shortly afterward we joined the Parents' National Educational Union, and found it had an inspirational, back-to-Nature, nineteenth-century philosophy. It was an irresistible reminder of Emerson, Alcott, Thoreau, Christian Science and other uplifting American institutions, with an equally irresistible tone of far-flung empire, *noblesse oblige* and stiff upper lip. Wordsworth is the P.N.E.U. poet, Victoria its typical monarch. The founder of the philosophy was a remarkable woman named Charlotte Mason, who developed her methods primarily for *parents* as teachers. It is used by teachers in ordinary schools, too. (P.N.E.U. schools abound in England today, and there are even a few in Ireland, but, alas, at a distance from us.)

The usual practice of P.N.E.U., however, is in the home schoolroom, with mother or governess in charge, and texts, examinations and advice supplied from London headquarters. The idea was for us to get a young woman imbued with Charlotte Mason ideals; or if that failed, to get one trained otherwise (Froebel or Montessori) and imbue her ourselves.

We advertised in the P.N.E.U. magazine, and the London office promised to look hard for us; but months passed without a suitable applicant. From Mrs. Boucher's came sheaves of notices about young women who had been governesses everywhere from Bangkok to the Canaries, but the ones we liked had always found posts by the time our letters reached them. Finally, and doubtfully, I travelled to Dublin to register with an agency there, womanned or manned, by a formidable type named Miss Kavanagh. A flight of dark metal-rimmed stairs led down to her basement office. She deduced that I was Irish-American and gave me the treatment accordingly.

"We belong to the noble Irish race," she trumpeted, her mannish voice throbbing and her monocle flashing. "When the rest of the world was living in caves and tearing the flesh raw from savage beasts, we were a nation of saints and scholars, of art, music, song, poetreh!"

"Yes, I know. But I'm not Irish."

"When I was a slip of a girl," she continued in deep bass, "blushing through my teens, down in the County Kildare, the beautiful county where Bridget opened her cloak, I dedicated my life to St. Bridget. Do you think I work for material gain? That will be a registration fee of ten shillings, thank you. No! I work for Bridget, for Banba, for dark Rosaleen, for Kathleen ni Houlihan! These," she continued more calmly, with the manner of one kindly giving secret information, "are names for Ireland."

"Yes, I know."

"Your family is a great one in the history of the Gaelic race. The O'Neills defeated the Danes at the mighty battle of Clontarf, when the strand ran red with——"

"It's my husband's family. I'm American. And anyhow at the time of the battle of Clontarf, these O'Neills *were* Danes."

"——the strand ran red with blood, but the great Gaels of Ireland drove out the intruder and the wine of victory coursed through their noble veins. Ancestors of mine were there—we are the élite of the Irish—and other ancestors defeated the Protestants at the Boyne and struck a hero's blow for the Emerald Isle."

"But the Boyne wasn't that clear-cut, you'll recall. More Catholics fought on the Orange side than for James, and vice versa."

"Oh really. I see that you know Irish history."

"Just a little. From my husband."

"My family were the Kings of Leinster. They were earls by decree of George III, you know. My grandfather came from Scotland, but he received the holy gift of the Faith and became Catholic (thanks be to God!) like the great O'Neill family. You'll want a Catholic governess of course."

"Oh no, it doesn't matter to us, just as long as we have a really good one."

"You are Catholics, I presume?"

"My husband describes himself as a non-denominational pagan."

"Indeed! No, you must have a Catholic. It would not be right to let the children be under a Protestant. Now, I have a lovely girl in mind for you. She's just out of the convent."

I could practically hear Himself saying no to that one, and rose to go.

"We really wanted more of a choice," I said.

"You'll hear from me, you'll hear from me," she said. "It's always so interesting to meet Irish-Americans. What a wonderful country it must be! And think of the great Irishmen who have played such an important part in American history, sons that the Island of Saints can be proud of, men like O'Dwyer and McCarthy. How beautiful to be coming back to the land of your fathers, an exiled Celt returning to Erin!"

"I'm not Irish," I said desperately, "and what's more, I can prove it."

"Goodbye, goodbye!" she called, waving her handkerchief as though she were strumming a harp.

We put ads in the Irish papers, we answered ads, we drove hither and yon interviewing. P.N.E.U. interviewed in London for us. Total result, nil. Governesses we had already turned down started reappearing in our mail, which we took as a sign that the bottom of the barrel had been scraped. Then we got a succinct letter from Mrs. Boucher's: "We should advise you not to stand out for a governess who has had training or previous experience, as long as she is willing to go to Ireland."

Slowly it dawned that the beautiful dream, the life polite, was not for me. We were on the wrong island. Sixty miles from Dublin did not appeal to the kind of person we wanted; and as we didn't want young things just out of school, or old bodies who expected breakfast in bed, that about did it.

The gap was filled, or enlarged, by two governesses acquired through unorthodox channels. The first, a Spanish girl, was recommended by a 'friend', in superlative terms. It turned out that Fernanda hated children, ate with her nose in her plate and her spoon in her cup, insisted that in Spain it was bad manners to say please or thank you, asked the price of everything and tried to sell smuggled jewellery to our guests when our backs were turned. She sat next to the wireless in the evening, it is true, but not to the one in the schoolroom, because Madrid was too faint on it. She crouched on the floor next to the one in our sitting-room and yelled "*Olé*" all night while we endeavoured to read or talk. Clad in tight-fitting black slacks and vermilion coat, she took the children walking, singing the while toreador songs in a voice like a bull.

We used to see the locals clustered in groups watching her, their mouths hanging open. Nothing like Fernanda has hit the Irish countryside before or since. I brought her down to Dublin on her days off and she bellowed unmelodic Spanish folksongs into my ear all the way in. So it was with almost unbelieving relief that we parted with her, when she got a job singing at a theatre in Liverpool. Like Jacques, she had refused to teach the children her language (they all do this, I'm told) but eagerly learned English from us.

The only survival we have from her is "Comez la cortethe", or whatever. It's supposed to mean "Eat the crusts". She and I conversed in French or what passed for it, but the 'th' 's were spreading like funguth all over our vocabulary by the time she left. Himthelf marked the Thpanish off hith good bookth. "Ha!" he'd say bitterly, "courtethy, politeneth— the thingth for which Thpain is famouth! God pretherve uth from any more!" "*Olé*," I added absent-mindedly.

Next we took on a very nice Irish girl "with a perfect accent". She kept the children tidy, trained the baby, was pleasant and well groomed; but she could not teach. She hadn't the warmth nor, alas, the information. She lasted for a season; but then we had to let her go.

After some months enhoused with his children, all happily letting off steam now that there was no one to ride herd, Himself was visibly nervous. "Shut up!" he'd scream at Jimmy, in a voice that could be heard in London. "Didn't I tell you not to talk so loudly?" "For Christ's sake," he'd growl, snarling at Bridget, "when will you learn manners?"

The fights, tears, hysterical giggles and piercing yells, which mothers get conditioned to accepting, like the rain or the heat, make fathers—at least Irish fathers, or at least *this* Irish father—act like prima donnas. "How dare you spank your sister!" "What do you mean by hitting your brother with a stick?" But to our lone wolves, appealing to blood ties was about as useful as expecting the Jews and the Arabs to settle their differences in a Christian spirit.

Himself could develop none of that deafness which is the mother's natural protection against insanity. The merest shriek would get his instant attention. "Keep quiet," he'd roar, "God damn it, keep quiet." Then, "Anne, what sort of a mother are you? See after this child, he's cut his finger off." Of course, as any female reader will know, this would mean that Jimmy had scraped his thumb on the wall and that not so much as one drop of blood was in evidence. Alarums were his speciality. A chorus might be raised in the yard, right under his nose, and I swear he'd leap into the car and fetch me back from having tea with Louise, declaiming that Bridget and Dorothy had burst each other's jugular veins and that it was due to sheer maternal neglect. By the time we got home, all would be happily playing cowboys in the barn, with no sign of carnage whatsoever. This would set Himself back not one whit. With great dignity, he would glower at everyone and stalk into the house.

"How long do they keep them during the day in that school you spoke of?" he asked very offhandedly, one night.

"Till three or three-thirty, I think," said I, carefully not showing any emotion.

"Be about four before they were back here, what with the trip. Hmmm. Fifteen miles. Tom and I could take turns driving them in—you, too, of course. Isn't it about time a term began?"

"I'll run over tomorrow and find out."

Irish schools run on three terms, roughly from September to Christmas, from early January to Easter, and from after Easter to the end of July. Schools in the country alter these bounds to suit farming needs, sometimes keeping on in August and closing in September so that children can help with the harvest. Since I am unable in Ireland to distinguish between town and country, I wondered on which side of the invisible border this school would fall. Fortunately for us, as it was now September, it was a town school.

The teacher was a tidy, kindly, strict little body of indeterminate age. She had the improbable name of Miss De Bate, and she was absolutely delighted to have three new scholars. Like many Protestant schools, the roll here was low. If it fell below twelve, the authorities had the right to close the school. With our children to swell the ranks, she had eleven, close enough to skin through, she said. There were no bothersome questions about where we lived or what church we went to; Miss De Bate just wrote down names and address and told me to bring them along. The building consisted of one large classroom in one wing, and Miss De Bate's living quarters in the other. No insidious diagram on these walls—just maps, travel posters and a print of the Parthenon. There was an indoor lavatory, and a fenced-in green field to play in. Students were aged three to twelve; and Miss De Bate handled them all simultaneously. "We all help each other," was the only clue I could ever get as to her method.

Dorothy, by far the youngest, brought home excited comments on the other girls' dresses—pronounced 'drepses'. She was hardly out of diapers herself, but became immediately clothes-conscious. School was for her a glorious opportunity to wear swishy American petticoats and a *very* tight belt, and all two of the little boys admired her.

"I'm going to mawwy Dermot," she told the Colonel.

"Why, Tadpole?"

"Dermot's a sweetie boy. I'm not going to mawwy Philip —he pulls my skirp."

Jimmy also had romantic adventures. He proposed to the little Danish girl. "Ulla, will you marry me?"

"No."

"Why?"

"I am bigger than you."

"But I will grow up."

"I will still be bigger."

Jimmy and Bridget reported every day bits and snatches of knowledge; addition was done to some rigmarole about "you put the dogs in there and take the horses down to here" (tens and hundreds, I think); classes were divided by marching periods; they danced 'The Grand Old Duke of York'— Bridget loved that; and while the bigger children had history the little ones were allowed to listen, so that we got garbled accounts of a son who killed his father in a car (Cuchulan and Ferdid at a ford); and whenever he misspelled a word in English, Jimmy insisted that it was Irish. Discipline was enforced with a ruler, but Miss De Bate was their favourite person, so that seemed to be all right. "Teacher says that teachers who slap are the best teachers," explained Bridget, "because they really *want* their children to learn."

Miss De Bate was very keen on songs, and so were our young ones. Himself was warmed to hear that they were taught by the same old do-re-mi-fa-sol system. They'd hardly been in school a week before they had a brand new repertoire, which temporarily erased 'Casey Jones' and 'The Cow-boy's Lament'. One day they earnestly shrilled their latest acquisition for Himself:

"The busy indus-tri-ous little bee . . ."

"My God," exclaimed Himself, turning to me in horror, "if they go around singing that, everyone will know they go to a Protestant school!"

"Well, I'm sure it's not a secret, or won't be for long."

"Now, children," he said briskly, "that was a lovely song, but beware of industrious bees. They sting. Beware of in-dustry altogether, it stifles the soul. Boorgose. You just tell Miss De Bate this, Bridget," he continued pontifically. "Con-sider the lilies of the field, they toil not, neither do they spin."

That night, contrary to custom, in fact diametrically oppo-site to custom, he gathered them around him in their night-clothes, airily dismissing me from my usual job of reading a fairy-tale. Presently childish trebles raked the air with 'I Won't Work for a Living':

"Some people work for fun,
    They say it's all sunshine and gain,
    But if I can't get sunshine without any work
    I'd rather stay out in the rain."

"There," he said in a satisfied way, "now go and sing that to Miss De Bate."

With only the baby at home, hammering down walls and baying to the dogs, the quiet was almost unendurable. I squandered my newly gained leisure by going down to Dublin a lot and experimenting with cooking while at home, tossing off little things like beef Stroganoff and caviare made from herring roes (gorgeous). Himself spent his time thinking up arguments for the inevitable showdown with Father Cunningham. Neither of us could understand why that black sedan had not shown up.

One day it did. Tom spotted it from the field and hallooed to Bridie. Bridie took one look and ran hot-speed up to me. I put down the recipe file and went looking wildly for Himself. "The priest is calling!"

Mad scurry, but by the time the doorbell rang we were all in our proper places, mine being a spot out of sight on the top landing. Himself went to the door.

"Come in, Father," I heard, and as the footsteps approached tried to silence my chattering teeth. They came briefly into view, Himself and—a new priest! A plump, chuckling, youngish man.

"Oh," Himself stammered foolishly, "I-I th-thought you were Father Cunningham."

"Father Cunningham was transferred, a month ago," said he, grinning. "I can see you're well up on parish affairs. I'm Father Kelly."

"Come in, come in and sit down, Father. I'm afraid I'm rather low in stock. I have Irish, Scotch and Bourbon."

"A little Bourbon if you please."

"Well now, Father, there's no use in talking about the weather, there's no use talking about the crops, so get it off your chest."

"Well, Mr. O'Neill, of course——" But at this point Himself shut the door and I heard no more.

A good hour later the door opened again and they both came out. "Oh dear," the priest was saying apologetically, "the trouble is, I'm so dreadfully tolerant."

"Fine, Father, you see my point, then?"

"Yes, I do, but you won't tell anyone, will you? I do understand, but I can't let it go, you know. You couldn't see your way to coming back to us?"

"Not except on my conditions, Father."

"Dear oh dear. Look, my son," he said, his face brightening up, "we'll talk no more about it. I'll pray for you all, and we'll trust to God to make it come right."

"Thank you, Father."

Hardly had the front door closed behind him when I was down. "Quick, tell me, what did he say?"

"Oh, nothing." Himself sounded rather disappointed. "He didn't argue. He isn't interested in the school. He took the line that where the children go is my affair."

"How marvellous, what a relief! What did he want then —money I suppose?"

"No, not a penny."

"What then?"

"What he wants is that I should come back to the fold. He said they'd ignore the excommunications. I said far from ignoring them, the Church should publicly apologise for them. If they did, I might consider coming back. He said they couldn't. That's all."

"He sounded a darling. I heard the end. Aren't we lucky to have him instead of Father Cunningham!"

"Hmmm," said Himself. "Don't go overboard. They all have their plans, you know, priests."

The Church of Ireland ministers also had their plans, and one day in December the children came home from school filled with news. "School is closing."

"You mean, the term is over."

"No, Mummy, no more school after Christmas. The Thorntons are going to Canada and the Canon says school must close."

This was confirmed by Miss De Bate, who looked grief-stricken but stoic. "Yes, we're losing the Thornton children, three of them, and that puts us down to eight, and Canon Smith feels that we must give up. After all these years."

"What will you do?"

"I don't quite know. I'll stay on for a while. No, I wouldn't be a governess," she said, reading my mind, "but a private school post might turn up."

Everyone felt grim, but I most of all. The pearl of teachers, found only to be lost! And what was to happen to our children and their newly-won knowledge of A to Zed and I to 9?

But Christmas was imminent, and we put all other preoccupations out of our minds. We suffer, by the way, from November birthdays, which exhaust our ideas and pockets so that in the few weeks before Christmas we are likely to be listless and easily annoyed. Just a few days before, we suddenly feel like parents again, and then there's a frantic rush to make cakes and biscuits, find and decorate a tree, find and roast a goose, fill stockings and sing carols. Caught in this whirl, we have no time for visits or conversation, and only become Christianly again some time after New Year.

Old Joe called in January, looking strangely normal in a new coat, and contributed to our returning goodwill with an account of his travels. He had been in the next county, it seems, and one day in one of his regular towns he learned to his surprise that Father Cunningham was priest there now. It was cold, and he was wondering where his next bite was coming from, when he found himself opposite the presbytery and thought perhaps Father Cunningham might be glad to see a familiar face, what with Christmas coming on and all that. No harm trying, he thought, so over with him to the hall door and hesitatingly he pushed the bell. "The door was opened by a nasty bit of work in the shape of a young woman," said Joe, "who looked at me as if I was something the dog brought home. 'Well, what do you want?' said she."

"Want to see Father Cunningham."

"You can't see the priest, he's resting."

"Don't tell lies, young woman. I'm after seein' him pass through." This was correct, and Father Cunningham heard the remark and came heavily to the door, looking cross and unapproachable as usual.

"Well, what is it?"

"A little help if you please, Father. It's very cold."

"It's a little help I want myself. Where do you think I get it? I haven't a second shirt to my back, strange though it may sound to you. Why don't you find a job for yourself?"

"It's too late to be changing me mind about them things now," said Old Joe. "Good day, Father, and sorry for troublin' you."

"Be Jasus," Old Joe continued to us, "I walked all the ways from there to the town here without a bit o' luck. Finally, didn't I find meself outside the priest's house here? Might as well be killed for a sheep as a lamb, so I rang the bell. Dacent-lookin' housekeeper came to the door, so I touched me cap an' said, 'A little help if you please, ma'am. It's very cold today.' "

"Yes, indeed it is. Have you no topcoat?"

"No, ma'am," and then remembering Father Cunningham's chant, he added, "And I haven't a second shirt to me back."

"That's terrible," she said. "Come in. Wait here now, and I'll see what I can do."

A few minutes later, Father Kelly appeared, carrying a very nice warm topcoat. "Here you are," he said, and he himself helped Old Joe into it. Then he handed him a parcel and two shillings.

"That will keep you going for a while," he said. "Now go round to the kitchen and ask Mary to give you a plate of supper."

Thoroughly warmed and well fed, Old Joe took his leave with thanks. He was very curious to know what the parcel contained, so he got off quickly round a corner and opened it up and found therein *two new warm winter shirts*.

"No!" we breathed, but the story was not yet over. "What did you do, Joe?"

"I folded up one o' them and rammed it in me pocket, and I made a parcel o' the second one, and back with me the whole blasted road to Father Cunningham. Took me two days. He didn't recognise me in me new topcoat, so he opened the door himself.

" 'Here you are, Father,' I said, and I give the parcel a thrust at him. 'Here's a shirt for you. I'm after gettin' two. You can't say I let you down, but that's more than I can say for you. A dacent priest I know of gave me the coat I'm wearin' and two bob and a plate of meat and *no mention of jobs*. Good day, Father.'

"And I left him," said Old Joe, "with the ground cut from under him."

CHAPTER 14

*

MORE EDUCATION

OLD JOE WASN'T THE ONLY one to mark the difference between Father Cunningham and Father Kelly. It was well discussed all over the countryside. The change had far-reaching effects (a maypole for summer dances; the wedding, previously forbidden, of a pair of second cousins who had meanwhile accumulated several children), but we were back to our same old problem.

"Well," I said to Himself, when the Easter term was beginning, "what do we do about school now?"

"School?"

"You know, lessons."

"Ah well, if it's lessons, there's no problem at all. Don't bother your head about it."

"What do you mean?"

"Just what I said, no problem. You're going to teach them."

"Me?"

"You. You have the P.N.E.U. books. You have the degrees. All you have to do is read it up and get to work."

The fact that I had neither the experience nor the temperament for teaching was brushed aside—a few hours with the P.N.E.U. philosophy would presumably fix all that. This was a challenge, he went on, a wonderful opportunity. Surely every mother would welcome the chance to be her

children's teacher? And he would fit up a room in the basement for us. My continued objections were met with pained
surprise: "Don't you want to learn the best methods of
raising children?"

"But I'm not as good a parent as I know how to be
already!"

"What a ridiculous idea! You're a wonderful mother. Do
you ever neglect them? Never. Do you ever ignore a stubbed
toe? Never. I'll see after that room right away. Maybe
Tom could nail up a bench." And off he strolled, happy, I
knew perfectly well, in the thought of mornings by himself at
the sitting-room fire, undisturbed, unexerted, uninvolved.

The 'anybody can do anything' and 'do it yourself' attitude
is an intoxicating one, I have always thought, but I have also
always thought certain fields were exempt, like surgery and
child care. My children *did* learn from me, but any credit is
due to P.N.E.U. and the textbooks: I was merely a thrilled
observer of the process. They really do work, those silly
symbols mankind has cooked up to represent ideas. The
readers we used are miracles of non-obvious engineering,
contrived so that all sounds and combinations are presented
in logical order, while the child is conscious only of the story
told. The incredible is true, namely, that children *do* learn—
I mean they really do comprehend and you can practically
hear their minds ticking. In short, education is wonderful.
We were quite converted to it.

We finally sat down one morning in a completed schoolroom. The chimney cleaned, a cosy fire burned on the
hearth. A big table (the third third) stretched in front of our
three chairs, theirs straight and posture-conscious, mine a
huge soft winged thing bought when we were anticipating
a governess. ("You must get her a nice chair to sit in at
night, with a high back to keep out draughts.") Maps lined
the walls, courtesy of the *National Geographic*, except for one

faded old roll which featured the world in 1906 and photographs of reigning monarchs—Teddy Roosevelt headed one side and the Tsar of all the Russias another. We tacked up Michelangelo and Giotto reproductions in the blank spaces too small for maps.

Before us we had scarlet-covered exercise books, dozens of sharpened pencils and erasers, a carton full of textbooks on various subjects, a vase of flowers, and our readers. We had a blackboard, chalk, crayons, drawing-paper, paints and brushes, two easels, a tin full of clay, a radio and gramophone, our library of folk-song records, a bookcase full of folk-tales and folk-songs, hollow blocks, building blocks, meccano sets, old car-assembly kits, a globe, a star map and flash cards. Also, I was sitting on *Home Education*, the P.N.E.U. Bible, more or less as an amulet.

Thanks to the months with Miss De Bate, the children knew their A B C and numbers, but it fell to me to teach them to read and write. *Home Education* quoted John Wesley's mother, who had taught each of her children to read at the age of five. "One day was allowed the child wherein to learn its letters, and each of them did in that time know all its letters, great and small, except Molly and Nancy, who were a day and a half before they knew them perfectly, for which I thought them very dull."

Onward and upward! Nothing for it but to sail in. School was from 9.30 to 12.30. Our schedule called for several subjects, and I added more, not being able to resist them, so the programme as envisioned was something like this: reading, spelling, writing, numbers, history, world we live in, nature study, drawing, Bible, singing in Latin and French, dictation, history of art, story-telling. In short order, in fact immediately, this programme was dispensed with.

Dorothy was also dispensed with—forcibly ejected, howling, and the door bolted. After all, she had the baby to play with by then. I marvelled how Miss De Bate had put up with her, for it seemed pointless to try and teach someone who couldn't count and who said 'drep' for dress and 'cope' for coat.

This left us with two scholars and one subject, on which we exhausted ourselves each morning. Elevenses recuperated us somewhat, so we briefly tried one other subject, and the rest of the school-day was given to dessert in the form of being read to, or painting, or working with the hands. Fortunately our texts were all co-ordinated, so we ran into no difficulties skipping from the number book to the readers. Eventually we did work in dictation and art and word-study. Possibly with the Wesley family in mind I assumed that the more one expected the more one got.

"What are the vowels, Jimmy?"

"A, e, i, o, u."

"And how do we pronounce them, Bridget?"

"Anh, eh, ih, ah, uh."

"So if you hear 'anh' as in 'cat', what is it?"

(You can almost see the wheels turning as 'anh' is translated back into 'a'.)

"A"—triumphantly.

"Good girl! Now write 'a' for Mummy, and write 'cat'."

"Jimmy, if you hear 'eh' as in 'hen', what is it? Write hen. Now both of you write hen, ten, cat, bat, sob, tub, bit, bet, but——"

"But why don't we say 'bit', Mummy, when we write 'b-i-t-e'?"

"Er——" (quick consultation with handbook) "because an 'e' at the end makes the vowels long again, the way they are in the alphabet."

"A, e, i, o, u?"

"Yes. So with an 'e' at the end, the 'ih' in 'bit' becomes 'i' and we have 'bite'. Now put an 'e' on the end of hid—what do you get, Jimmy?"

"Hide."

"Put an 'e' at the end of 'hat', Bridget."

"Hate."

"My, what accomplished children you are. Clever, wise, witty. I adore you."

I grew adept at creating sentences like "Kate is the name of the horse with the mane", or "I hate a cane you can bend", and adjusting to the un-American vocabulary we had to use—words like 'sweep' 'soot' 'tinsmith' 'whilst' 'entrained' 'tube'—an odd first lot for ex-New Yorkers. Of course it didn't always go well.

"Jimmy, will you kindly spell 'dictation'?"

"I can't, I can't."

"If you can spell 'station' you can spell 'dictation.' 'Station'."

"I can't!"

"Did or did not Old Lob and Mr. Grumps go to the police station?"

"They"—sniffle—"did."

"Well, if they did, by gum you can spell it. You had it in the book!"

Mrs. Wesley wrote, "Samuel learned the alphabet in a few hours . . . and as soon as he knew the letters, began at the first chapter of Genesis. . . . Easter fell low that year, and by Whitsuntide he could read a chapter very well. . . . I cannot remember to have told him the same word twice."

This, alas, cut no ice with Jimmy. But he did recall 'station' and was prodded into 'dictation', made to close his eyes and write each letter in the air, pronouncing it as he did, and then to write it in his book. Bridget always did what he did, so the two of them knew it thereafter. Numbers never presented any problems—they simply raced through three texts. I felt uneasy about this; surely it was a little un-refined, a little boorgose? Gipsies, for example, while grossly illiterate not to mention all the other things, have a great facility with figures. What would Himself think?

I needn't have worried. Himself, snoring peacefully by the sitting-room fire, couldn't have cared less if they had been studying to be pickpockets.

Two terms of this and there might have been more, but one morning a letter came from Miss De Bate. She was going as headmistress to a small private school not too far from us, and she wondered if we'd care to come and look it over—Rathcastle Hall.

The name rang a bell with Himself. "Of course! That's the Freyke place. I heard Brigadier Freyke was running a school there. Well, well." This was the kind of thing that appealed to him, because in the old days Hugh O'Neill, the father of Fergus, had sacked Rathcastle, and it served them jolly well anachronistically right, because the Freykes in Elizabeth's time invaded Barna country and slew an O'Neill of importance, who was subsequently buried in a cave under a cairn.

"Oh dear," I said, "you don't think it's dangerous to send a new generation of O'Neills there?"

"Notatall. Ha ha. What a pity! So the Freykes are running a school."

He seemed to regard this as a great step down in the world. I felt like asking him what he thought I had been doing; but instead we put on impressive clothes (that is, took clean gloves, and Himself wore for once the trousers that went with his coat) and drove the ten miles or so over to Rathcastle.

It was an historic demesne. Massive gates, no longer, un-fortunately, opened by the lodge-keeper; a drive across spacious pastures, where horses played under huge shade trees. Vast, vast house, complete with colonnaded wings. Gardens, fountains and lake behind; mountains in the distance. But our practised eyes noted the moss growing between carved stone blocks, the tendrils of ivy creeping through the walls, the—was it, could it be?—incipient tree beginning so forebodingly on one of the roofs. Five poodles appeared from the gardens to yap at us. I eschewed the bell pull, we pushed a bell, and in the ten minutes or so that elapsed before a wheezing fat cook arrived from the nether depths to let us in, Himself sized it all up.

"I see it all," he said. "Poor old Freyke. The Land Commission took over the place—only a few acres of this are still his. The rates must be gigantic. Yet it's an ideal location for a school. I see it all."

He had worked up a great sympathy for them, standing there. Down to their last guinea, last butler, last cook and last hunters, no longer able to entertain or dine out, these survivors of the Ascendancy were staking their all on the school. Thus I was startled when I met Mrs. Freyke to find her dressed in a little print that could only be called smashing. She certainly didn't look like a woman who spent her days with nothing but poodles for company.

They were a striking couple. Brigadier Freyke was tall and erect with bright blue eyes and clipped English accent. He was also very energetic and kind, and so indeed was she. We were shown through the place—an exhausting trip—the bedrooms (most of the children boarded there), the classrooms, the dining-room created out of a billiard room, the chapel, the library, the galleries filled with paintings and sculpture, the basement full of gymnastic apparatus, the gun-room, the sitting-rooms, the bathrooms, the offices, the stables and the walled gardens containing acres of vegetables, the playing fields, summer-houses, etc., etc. We had come during the holiday, so both staff and students were away, but besides

Miss De Bate, there were five teachers, and there were twenty boarding pupils and ten by the day (age-range, six to sixteen, girls principally, but boys of six to ten allowed). Each boarder brought her own horse and her dog; riding, I gathered, was the chief subject. Any old person could teach Latin or chemistry, but Brigadier and Mrs. Freyke took the riding classes. A school holiday was declared whenever there was a hunt. The school was registered from Belfast instead of Dublin, and we noticed that its stationery read "Rathcastle Hall, the Royal County" (a name that went out, presumably, with the Trouble).

"Well, what do you make of it?" I asked Himself when we got home.

"It's a bit of old England, all right," he said, "but it won't do the children any harm. Be an experience for them, and after all, that's what education really is."

Off they went. Every morning Himself or Tom drove them; every evening they called for them. I went to Dublin twice a week and Bridie and I spent my leisure experimenting with caragean (a dark-purple seaweed) in cooking. Reports started coming in from Rathcastle Hall. Miss De Bate was now known as Batesy. The students were to the last girl classically named: Sylvia, Penelope, Claudia, Julia, Barbara, Olivia, Lydia, Augusta, Hermione, Virginia. The boys inclined to be named David and Ian. Even the six-year-olds got something fearful called 'detention' if they were bad; and the most tremendous swapping of personal possessions went on at all levels.

But the main, the key thing was, "you mustn't tell". "It isn't done, Mummy. Even if *you* ask me, I mustn't tell." Hmmm. Scholastically, all was well. One of the teachers had lived in France, so in due course a French song was learned, called 'Cantois pour' according to Bridget, which baffled me for some time. Bridget and Dorothy adored

207

dancing in 'frocks' and slippers imported from London, and all three did well at riding, wearing, among less chi-chi haberdashery such as my old jodphurs, expensive crash caps of black velvet. Despite my best efforts, we learned little more than this about what went on at Rathcastle.

But between terms, two of the Freykes' own children (it was around their governess that the school had started) came to spend the day and play with ours and one of them did something naughty.

"You mustn't," I said. "What will we Americans think of Irish children?"

"Oh, I'm not Irish," he replied aghast, "I'm English."

It explained a lot. Intimations and nuances of this sort fluttered down to us like shot-puts. There was the fact, for instance, that the Freykes frequently went away, *mère et père*, that is, to London, except when it was the season to be in France, in which case they were at Deauville. There was the fact that the oldest Freyke boy was at Harrow, and the school kept the Harrow terms, which meant more holiday than study, it sometimes seemed. There were the casual assumptions in conversation when we had tea with the Freykes: the natives, servants and rates on the one hand, and hunting, the old regiment and the Conservative Party on the other. They seemed to be only dimly aware of Irish questions and politics.

"Y'know," Brigadier Freyke said sadly, "I was Resident Magistrate here and my father before me, and his father before him, and then one day, somewhere along in the twenties I think it was, I—er—I found I wasn't Magistrate any more! Deuced awkward, y'know. No notice about it at all. The—er—the local railway porter was sitting on the bench in my place! The bloody fellow hadn't even studied law, any more than I had! I was later told, y'know, that there was a chap in Dublin behind it, some chap with a queer sort of name, foreign name y'know, what was it now, dash it all, what was it—can't seem to recall——"

"De Valera?"

"That's it, that's it! How extraordinary of you to remember! What a remarkable memory you must have!" He eyed Himself with profound admiration.

Then he continued, "Yes, he was the one at the back of it. But he must have been in with the natives, y'know. And of course I needn't tell you what the natives are like around here—worse than in India."

"Good heavens, Freyke," said Himself, laughing, "I'm a native myself."

This set him back a bit. "My word, O'Neill, so you are!" He gazed sorrowfully at Himself, pulling on his moustache. And then suddenly he brightened. "But how you have improved!"

At the end of the year a school concert was held. On that afternoon, all available parents and friends were assembled on folding chairs in the library at Rathcastle, facing the windows where a stage had been erected and curtains were strung. The library's ceiling had been imported from Italy centuries ago, the story of Mercury and Argos in sepia; and along with the ancient decorative books, the huge nineteenth-century globe and the draped doors, it made a properly academic atmosphere. Programmes, carefully lettered by the big girls, were passed around.

The first number was 'Jack and the Beanstalk' by the youngest ones, in which Jimmy had the part of announcer, bowing from the middle with great aplomb. Bridget was a fairy and Dorothy was an ogre's child, roaring expertly, as well she might. There followed songs and piano-playing by big girls. Recitations then, Shakespearian and Tennysonian. A main event next—a Latin play. For this the curtains were with great difficulty pulled apart and girls in bed sheets and wreaths declaimed *"Quam fortes senatores sunt!"* Oh, the familiar heroic nobility of the patricians, the familiar long sentences, leaving one out of breath, the tonelessness, the effort for expression.

I felt quite sentimental—just like Latin plays in my old school. It was all very reassuring and comfortable and reminiscent, even to the fact that every time the scenes were shifted there were searing, tearing noises. But on the whole, the production was a great success; and Miss De Bate, blushing, and panting from her backstage exertions, was brought out for a triumphant bow.

Finally, after renditions of 'Ecossaise', 'Two Studies' and similar pieces on the piano, the little ones were led forward once more to sing a French song. That's how I discovered that what they had been carolling at home for the last year was 'Quand trois poules'. But the big moment, for me, was yet to come. It was last, when, the concert over, everybody was asked to rise for the national anthem. To my amazement, for after all this *was* Ireland, the assembled company sang, 'God Save the Queen'.

I cast one glance at Himself, who had solemnly rolled his eyes heavenward and was singing with the rest, and thought I had done him an injustice. He really was interested in his children's education. Freedom, independence, rebellion against authority—and he had come to this.

CHAPTER 15

*

TURKEYS

THE LONGER WE KNEW JANE, the English girl, the
more we admired her. She was a little thing, quite
fragile, but she prided herself on doing as much as any of the
cottage folk, and of course without a man in the household,
she had to. She gardened, cared for pigs and hens, footed
turf and even planted and dug 'main crops', i.e., potatoes, in
space in a field allowed them by a neighbour. She did all
these things, not in the least heroically, complaining some of
the time and laughing the rest of the time, but she did them,
and made possible her and her mother's maintaining themselves on the tiny pension the father had left.

Mrs. Cobley was Irish, but Mr. Cobley had been a soldier
in the British Army in the old days. They met when he was
stationed at a camp in the north, married and moved to
London. Then, during World War II, he and Jane's brother
were killed, and Jane, who was an air-raid warden, was
buried alive for five days in the collapse of a building. She
had a breakdown soon after being rescued, and finally Mrs.
Cobley was told that the only hope would be to get her to
some quiet place. So they returned to Mrs. Cobley's old
cottage in Ireland where the country air and Mrs. Cobley's
faith and care brought Jane around.

They really had the book thrown at them, Jane and her
mother; and yet gentler, sweeter, more gallant people you'd

seldom find. Jane loved to say, "When I came to Ireland ten years ago I weighed only five stone and was flat on a stretcher —and see me now!" For she was rosy and healthy and looked like a girl in her teens.

But the scars were still there. After one visit to us while the workmen were in operation, she refused to come again till they were finished. "Your house looks as though it's been bombed," she said flatly, mincing no words. We often called at the cottage instead, and it became quite a fixture to drop in for Mrs. Cobley's lovely welcome and the ever-present cup of tea.

Mrs. Cobley was unique. She stood, for me, for the old-fashioned Irish country person, a wonderful type which has almost vanished. She spoke impeccable English without a touch of a brogue, and once mentioned her surprise when none of her friends in England recognised her as Irish. "I speak as I always have, and as my family did in the old days. We were taught to speak correctly. I remember my dear father saying, 'Georgina! Repeat what you said, and say it properly,' and I would reply, 'Yes, sir,' and I would say the thing most carefully, because otherwise I should be switched about the legs until I danced."

She was the father and mother of hospitality, as they say, and you'd think that she and Jane had invented tidiness too —they made an art of it. Never, no matter at what unheard of hour we dropped in, was the little kitchen-sitting-room one molecule out of order, and this in spite of the fact that they cooked, ate and entertained there. Their cottage was a joy to the eye and to the spirit: outside, a bower of flowers; inside, the cosy open hearth, its crane and tripods black with pitch and polish, and the rest of it gleaming white, hearth-stoned twice a day.

This white background, along with the orange colour of the flames from the burning turf and the black of the turf itself, were carried over in the pattern of the furniture covers and draperies that Jane had made, and in the 'delph' on the ancient black dresser. The curtains were always freshly starched and laundered, the furniture polished to a warm glow, there were always flowers at the windows and a kettle singing over the fire.

Time had estranged Mrs. Cobley from the Ireland she knew, and Jane was 'the English girl', a foreigner; but, aliens though they might be considered, they had re-created a beauty long gone by. Himself found in their house the only bit of the cottage Ireland that he recalled, and I the only bit of the past which lived up to expectations. I also found Jane a source of adventure.

One bitter day in early March, the north-easterly wind seemed to be strong enough to blow the car off the road as I drove in from town. Halfway along, I came upon Jane trudging back with her market bag and week's provisions. She was 'starved with the cold' and climbed into the seat next to me with thanksgiving. By the time we reached her home she was only about half warmed up, so she asked me in for the usual cup of tea. As we walked up to the door we noticed a turkey sitting down in the yard.

Once inside, Mrs. Cobley bustled over us like a nanny, set the water to boil, cut bread, laid the table and presently handed each of us a welcome steaming cup of tea. Jane was fairly well thawed out by now. I remarked, "What's wrong with the turkey sitting down outside?"

Jane said, "I don't know. One of the locals, a nice old body named Rose Brennan, used to take care of the turkeys for us, so I know very little about them."

"But Rose died last year," added Mrs. Cobley.

"Yes. But what *is* wrong with the bird?" asked Jane.

"She has been like that for some time now," replied Mrs. Cobley. "Did you not notice her before?"

"No," said Jane, yawning luxuriously.

"She has to go," said Mrs. Cobley.

"She what?" asked Jane.

"She will have to be taken."

"Make up your mind, Mother. First she has to go, then she has to be taken. Who takes her?"

Mrs. Cobley sent an embarrassed glance at me. I stared into the fire. Mrs. Cobley started to say something and then sighed. "Poor Rose, how I miss her!"

"Ha!" snorted Jane. "How I miss London! But when does the turkey go, anyway?"

"She really ought to be taken today. If she is left much longer she won't be inclined."

"Inclined for what?"

"Oh," groaned Mrs. Cobley, exasperated, "she won't hatch."

Jane stood up. "How do I take her? I gather it's my job."

"I'm afraid you will have to carry her."

"How about taking Mrs. Farrell's pram?"

Mrs. Cobley was horrified. "You can't take her in a pram! Wheeling it all round the crossroads!"

"How do other people take turkeys? Tell me where I have to go; come on, let's get this over."

"I'm afraid you will have to take her to Mrs. Howard."

"Good God! A two-miler each way?"

"How I miss Rose! Yes, I know it's a long way. I never had to worry when she was around."

"You didn't worry much when you decided to keep two this year. How's the other one shaping? I may as well take the two together while I'm on the go."

"She hasn't started pouting yet. You are very sarcastic."

"What for God's sake is pouting?"

"Oh, I can't go into that now."

"What do I say on arrival with the turkey?"

"Just call Mrs. Howard, or her daughter, Mrs. Butler, and say, 'I've come with the turkey, please.' "

This made Jane angry again. "I'm going to cut across, and after a two-mile stretch with the wind in my teeth and a turkey tucked under my arm, I'd say it would be sticking out that I'd come!"

"I'll go myself."

"You know you have no intention of going. Now come on, where's this turkey."

"I must tie her legs."

"Good God, why?"

"You don't want her to get away, do you? And I do wish you would not keep using God's name in vain."

"In vain? It's a good job for you, Mother, that you won't be at this journey's end."

"Look, Jane," I put in at this point, "I'll have time to bring you there, wherever it is."

"Now!" exclaimed Mrs. Cobley, delighted. "Off you go!"

We got Jane and the excited turkey into the car. Mrs. Cobley had tied the bird's legs together, and was very particular that Jane should hold her in just such a position. "Tell me how to get there," I said, as we started.

"Just stay off the main roads," muttered Jane. "All the windows here have eyes."

After a rather wide detour on back lanes, we came to a big farmhouse and parked the car. Two enormous turkey cocks charged out the gate and made for us, and I was really afraid to leave Jane alone. The cocks were fanning their tails and making horrible throaty noises. I took a quick look at the hen under Jane's arm, poor thing, and became quite attached to her for a moment; but she ungratefully seemed to be enjoying the commotion.

"Dirty brutes!" cried Jane, whirling round to dodge the cocks.

"What should we do!" I cried. They are frightening creatures, you know, even at a distance. Here they were practically on top of us, pecking at us and flying up to get at the female.

"Stand still. Otherwise they'll fight and probably take it out of the hen later. Mrs. How-ar-d!"

In a few moments two sturdy women appeared, dressed in burlap aprons and wearing muddy high boots. Mrs. Howard took the hen while her daughter shooed off the cocks. Somehow or other, without a word being said, we had formed a procession which two small boys now joined, and which wended its way towards a shed with the two turkey cocks in full pursuit. Oh happy, happy wedding day! Those women don't lose much time. Mrs. Butler toed one turkey cock flying and then turned on the small boys. "Be off in ower that, the pair a yous!" Then turning to me, she said, "Kids do be very well up, these days."

"Up!" snorted Mrs. Howard, "they're up as a glass of stout!"

The boys hovered around the outskirts of the shed, but the rest of us went in. There, Mrs. Howard squatted on the ground with the hen, legs astride her, waiting for the cock. Mrs. Butler also bent down judiciously. "I think we should've left her a while."

"No, comin' in the car like that Miss Cobley held her so's she's all set."

"I what?" asked Jane.

"She's in position. You done well."

"Oh. Thank you."

"I dunno," persisted Mrs. Butler.

"Look! . . . There now, they know better nor us."

Excitedly, "Watch out!"

Jane and I were trying hard to look at nothing at all, but the other two were right in the fray. Mrs. Butler called over her shoulder to us, "Bend down; ye're supposed to watch, too, so ye know."

"Oh, thank you just the same, but I'll take your word for it."

"No, Miss Cobley, your mammy'll want to know."

Jane went over and obediently bent down, and I did too, meeting Mrs. Butler's head coming up, which collided with my nose. "Ow!"

That freed me from attendance, I thought, so I retired to a corner, thus blocking the view of the two small boys who were peering in through a crack.

Great thrashings around of wings and purry cackles. The women, bent double, seemed to be getting in the way.

"D'ye know what ye're lookin' for, Miss Cobley?" giggled Mrs. Butler.

"Haven't the faintest."

Snickers.

Then, turning to me, "Sure *ye* do, *missus*."

"Certainly not! As a matter of fact, I *must* be going. Will you make it home all right, Jane?"

A muffled "Yes", came from Jane's upside-down head, so off I went.

When I next saw Jane, I asked her, "Well, how was it?"

"Awful! The works."

"The women didn't seem a bit prudish when it came to practical business, did they?"

"Prudish! *I* was innocent when I entered that place, but you couldn't tell me anything about turkeys now. Filthy things!"

"How horrid!"

"It was simply vile."

"Tsch."

"And upside-down too!"

After it, they had made Jane stop for tea, which turned out

to be bad luck, because she had the walk back with the turkey tucked underneath her arm just at dusk when the men were leaving the bog. She said she tried to figure out a by-road but by that time they had caught sight of her and she didn't dare retreat, but scuttled past as quickly as she could, pretending not to see them and not to mind anything, whereupon the catcalls started:

"Where did ye bag that turkey?"

"Isn't she very conceited? Wouldn't even look the side we were!"

"Isn't she bad-minded?"

Then a few whistles and "Happy Christmas!" (this in March). Because turkeys are sold only at Christmas-time and bring excellent prices.

She met Eily Nolan; in fact I gather she practically bumped into her.

"Ye've wind in your sails today, Jane."

"I just knocked across the bog men."

"I heard the great hee-haw laugh. C'mon in and have a rest. Lawsey, Jane, yer mammy's a terrible woman to have ye at that job; sure no one carries a turkey around. Not in the daylight any time. Why didn't ye borrow the ass and cart?"

Jane explained that I had brought her over, a fact which Eily seemed to relish particularly. At any rate, at the next meeting of the Countrywomen, several of the women greeted me with knowing smiles, and one told Louise Whyte I was a great turkey woman. Another, an ancient toothless creature, called out, "Seen the prices?" and cackled away in merriment.

This was all very baffling until one market day I met Eily in town and innocently greeted her, "How are you, Eily?"

"Well, lookit, Mrs. Neills, I have a turkey down on thirty eggs this week, and very cagey she's sitting too, but, Mother of God, didn't I put one down a fortnight ago on twenty-five, and she was as good as ye like, but a rat gone in on her."

"Oh my."

"A rat gone in on her."

"What a pity."

"A rat gone in on her. And didn't she riz!"

"Ah."

"She riz."

"Oh."

"She riz. Well, lookit, I didn't know which end of me was up, I scoured the country and only fer old Minnie Tracy givin' me two old cluckin' hens, an' hard set she was to give 'em because the insurance man was bringin' her a clutch o' duck eggs that her daughter was after sendin' only she couldn't get them to the place, don't ye know, but the insurance man said if she could get 'em to Griffin's shop he'd bring 'em the rest o' the way——"

"Ah yes."

"He'd bring 'em along, so she was hard pressed, so she was, but she give me the two old hens just the same. And only fer her, I would've had a right drop, and all me lovely little turkeys gone!"

"How did you know you had lovely little turkeys, Eily?"

"Lawsey, Mrs. Neills, ye're a gift! Didn't I test them half-time and they all birded? Isn't that what had me in the faver? But sure, ye're the great turkey woman yerself, sure ye are, don't be coddin' me! Happy Christmas, Mrs. Neills!"

So now I am an impostor in the confraternity of the knowledgeable. But for that bump on the nose I might really know.

CHAPTER 16

*

MRS. PROTHEROE'S PARTY

IT WAS SPRING AGAIN. The wild flowers in the fields around Barravore were a constant invitation to ramble, and our regular walk along the tree-shaded side path to Bally-down House was transformed with huge bright violets, blue-eyed grass, yellow cowslips and dandelions. Ballydown looked enchanting, the big red house viewing the heath, its slipping columns and decaying porches masked with cherry and apple trees in bloom. One could almost see the grass in the act of growing, and the flowers in the gardens were burst-ing with colour and fragrance. Nature waved away the flaws of time.

It was on days like this that I found I was quite willing to live in Ireland, when it wasn't raining, and there was the promise of warm weather ahead. We had nature walks, and I thought of how there had been woodlands around New York when I was a child, and weren't any more; and how nice it was that our children could have a taste of unregi-mented 'country' within two minutes of their home. The intoxicating warm scent of spring was as effective as ever, I suppose, and Barravore, with the land ploughed and sown and the house running smoothly, seemed a fair enough haven.

This feeling, though recurrent, was not enduring. Bridie would jar me by reverting to the traditional way of coping with recipes (adding a half-pound or so of butter and three or four more eggs to the measures, in the unshakable conviction that all women who write cookery books are on the stingy side); or Himself, probably reacting to spring in his own way, would urge the children out of the house at all hours and, when, they complained of cold or damp, grow very impatient. "Conduct yourself!" he'd cry. "What are you, a little hothouse flower? A little sugar plum, to melt in the rain? Control your circulation."

"I never heard anything so silly in my life," I'd protest.

"They're warm," he'd reply. "Why wouldn't they be? Look at me."

"Yes, but look at me," waving blue fingers at my indoor garb, which even in spring consisted of everything I owned large enough to go on top of everything else.

"Ah," he'd say, disgusted, "there's always lumps in it."

But when those occasional exquisite afternoons came, they were like unexpected mollifying gifts, packaged in sunlight and bright blue ribbon. On one of them, Miss Protheroe had us to tea, along with the Whytes. From the drawing-room we could look across the fields to Ardtown, the Whytes' house.

"You've planted potatoes, I see," said Himself to the Colonel.

"Do you think they pay?" asked Miss Protheroe.

"We just put them in the narrow field," the Colonel said. "It was Michael's idea. We're really going in for calves, you know. Michael and I have knocked down two of the old outhouses to make a calf nursery."

"Too ghastly," said Louise. "Think of the muck."

"Oh, I shall cart it all away for compost."

"You haven't so far."

"Only because the guinea hens are laying on the compost heap."

"I do hope you'll move it before the Antiquarian Society meeting."

The Antiquarian Society was enjoying new life, now that the Whytes had taken it on, and all of us in the Colonel's orbit were members of it. Himself, though new in the ranks, was a rising star. The Protheroes, however, had not joined.

"Did you say meeting?" asked Miss Protheroe.

"Yes, in just three weeks, very short notice I'm afraid. Lady Agatha asked if we'd care to arrange it. This time she'd like a large crowd, and really we don't know how Ardtown will hold very many."

"Charlotte," said Louise, "I've just had an idea. Seeing Ballydown look so delicious has just put it into my head. Do forgive me if you don't approve, but do you think we could possibly borrow your house for that night?"

"Why—I don't quite know—er—I don't know why not. I must ask Mama."

"Will you? How terribly kind of you. We would bring everything needed, of course, and perhaps we could borrow your staff, and you and your mother and I might together make out a list of people to invite——"

"We should love it, I'm sure."

It was the idea of inviting that won them. Mrs. Protheroe and Miss Charlotte were thrilled at the thought of a party for Lady Agatha. They welcomed their rare chances to show off the drawing-rooms at Ballydown, and Louise let them feel that it would be their party and their guests. They had loved the social world in what Mrs. Protheroe called "the olden days", and they hadn't had a gathering of this size for at least thirty years, for the cruel and unmentionable reason that they couldn't afford it. Now, here on a platter, an occasion was handed to them. They were to be in society once more and at no cost to themselves. It was too good to be true.

It took them days to compile the list for invitations. Louise was tearing her hair, as time was so short at best. The Antiquarian Society members in the neighbourhood were included of course, and any potential members or interested people were to be asked. The difficulty lay in the Protheroe list. Miss Protheroe was kind-heartedly inclined to propose anyone. Mrs. Protheroe censored her daughter's suggestions with a large black pencil.

Her feelings were very fine about who was worthy and who was not. She noted with gratification that some of her nominees were already Antiquarian Society people; this showed that the Society was the right sort. For the rest she included all 'the county', and she unearthed ancient address books and directories to locate Lord and Lady Carport, and the Hon. Mrs. Lalique, from sixty miles away; the Countess of Skrene, Sir John Uniack. Baron and Baroness de Moller were thought to be dead, but she wasn't quite sure. Anyhow, this seemed a small consideration.

Finally, after hours of weighing one thing against another, a selection was made, and she wrote out the cards in her spidery hand, "to meet Lady Agatha", having rather forgotten the Antiquarian Society aspect of the occasion. The envelopes were carefully addressed, and Louise sighed with relief when eventually they were mailed. At least everyone was free now to attend to the other preparations.

For Louise and the Colonel, these were enormous. Two weeks ahead of time, they and Michael started trucking carloads of apparatus to Ballydown. Dozens of paraffin lamps to supplement the lighting arrangements, gas heaters, oil heaters, bottle-gas stoves and hot-plates, buckets of coal for the fires, bags of turf, dishes, cups and saucers, spoons, boxes of tea and sugar; and first, last and all the way—water, for the supply at Ballydown was mysterious. Chairs were hired from town and, talk of the countryside! a Dublin bakery was to cater.

Meanwhile a great flurry had been occurring at Bally-

223

down. Reduced as they were, the Protheroes had only three rooms furnished as in the old days, a huge glass-panelled salon with an Aubusson carpet and, opening off from it, the drawing-room and a dining-room which had its own minstrels' gallery. The rest of the vast halls on the first floor were without so much as a stick of furniture. Paraffin light had been kind to all this; one had got the impression of lighted warm rooms just ahead and the rest obscured in darkness. If anyone wished to go upstairs, Miss Protheroe would disappear into the shadows and summon Mrs. Delaney, their 'staff', who would lead the way with a lamp up the broad beautiful steps and through broad, uncarpeted halls to the appointed door. Somehow, this experience was extremely luxurious.

Now, however, the long-awaited electric showed up all sorts of inadequacies. Mrs. Protheroe, cane in hand, daily did a survey of the reception rooms, and grew increasingly tense and upset. "The carpet is a disgrace," she said, pointing, "and there's a hole right next to the Italian chair in the drawing-room. We must do something about it."

"Perhaps we can move the chair."

"Oh no! You know perfectly well that that set can't be moved—it will fall apart. Where is the little table—you know, the one with the bronze legs that I had in my sitting-room?"

"Good heavens, Mama, I'm sure that was sold long ago."

"You have such a mania for selling things, Charlotte. You see, if we had only kept it, how useful it would be!"

"You have such a mania for hanging on to things, Mama! You haven't seen that table for thirty years."

"Well, we must find something to put over the hole. And we shall need a few standing lamps in here. And screens. And ash-trays. And a hearth-rug there."

She went from room to room, ticking off items. Long dormant memories stirred. Mrs. Delaney was sent for and dispatched on messages undreamed of; windows were washed; ceilings were broomed. Louise got long lists of 'requirements'. Porcelain figures and silver snuff-boxes were unlocked from a secret hoard in Mrs. Protheroe's bedroom and carefully placed for best effect downstairs. She thought of nothing else but the party, and even, in honour of the great occasion, forced Miss Charlotte to accompany her to Dublin, and—unheard of extravagance!—new draperies for the salon were actually bought. A special trip was made in the ancient Prefect, and swathes of material assembled. Consultations, decisions, changes of mind: boldly the order was sent off, and the draperies arrived in time for the party, were hung in fact that very day. Green and rose brocade shone at the windows, to replace the shredded and tattered rose velvet (which was thriftily re-erected in Miss Protheroe's bedroom.)

On that same trip to Dublin, Mrs. Protheroe insisted on buying herself a gown, threatening to have a tantrum when her daughter timidly opposed her. The best shops in Grafton Street were invaded; sales girls were summoned and dismissed; the old lady's hauteur was tremendous—nothing suited her, except, alas, the most expensive; and with Miss Protheroe reduced to babbling like a distraught hen, it was the most expensive that was bought.

Mrs. Protheroe was triumphant. She visited the corsetière; she made an appointment with the hairdresser. At one time she had been beautiful; now she began to look rather eerily smart, and she glowed with excitement.

She was busy in toilful ways too. Miss Protheroe bought plaster and attempted to fill in cracks in the walls, and her mother, her head flung back and her eyes shining, directed the hanging of paintings over the worst of them "Charlotte!" she would cry, gesturing with her cane, "fetch the one of me in red. No! Not that one! Well, what if I *did* point to it, you know very well the one I mean!" She wore Mrs. Delaney out mounting ladders and trying the pictures at different heights: she could hardly do this herself and Charlotte, of course, had no 'eye'. Lonergan, the current gardener, was allowed to enter the rooms to hammer, under her supervision, the undersides of various couches and chairs where springs and linings were hanging exposed. She had him shift furniture so that the bad side of each piece was adroitly hidden; she rearranged the knick-knacks in the cabinet— three solitary chess-men in ivory, a broken Chinese jade, a cloisonné clock that didn't work. Flowers were lopped wholesale from the gardens and arranged with extravagant abundance. Finally she saw to it that the drawing-rooms were meticulously dusted and swept. All was in readiness.

On the evening itself, the Whytes and Lady Agatha and her secretary came over early, but they were followed promptly by various Antiquarian Society members and guests. Mrs. Protheroe, looking really splendid, chatted with Lady Agatha while Louise and the Colonel checked on last minute arrangements and found to their horror that Miss Protheroe had not lit the fires early as promised. The Colonel struggled to get a blaze going in each of the rooms. Miss Protheroe greeted the new arrivals, of whom there were a great many. "I do think," said Louise, coming up to Lady Agatha, "that we can begin very soon."

"Very well," she replied, "I'll just gather up my notes."

"How can we begin," asked Mrs. Protheroe coldly, "when no one has come yet?"

"Oh, there's quite a crowd," said Louise.

"I see no one." (Acidly.)

"Others will be along presently, doubtless."

"These—er—persons—who are here, who are they?"

"Members and guests."

"And those two?"

"The new dispensary doctor and the county agricultural agent."

"Really! And that one?"

"It's the Crosby gardener. Lady Crosby had to regret, but she asked if she might send him. He's very interested in the raths on her land, and she expects that he will learn a lot. Mrs. MacDonald sent her steward too, and Mr. Toynes brought his bee-keeper."

"Charlotte!" called Mrs. Protheroe in a strangled voice, and hobbled out of the room.

Miss Protheroe clucked distractedly, "Excuse me, I must see after Mama," and trotted along after her. Very soon she returned. "I'm terribly sorry," she said to the Whytes, "but I find it will be quite impossible to have the meeting in the drawing-rooms. The old billiard room will have to do."

This was one of the shrouded unseen chambers which had not been used for several generations. It was bare, unfurnished, all dinginess, not to say dirt. "How can we possibly meet in there?" asked the Colonel angrily.

"You must have your man move some chairs. Lonergan is lighting a fire."

"But no fire will light, Charlotte," said Louise frantically. "Surely you can see it's out of the question!"

"There'll be no trouble about that," Miss Protheroe asserted.

"Yes there will, you know there will!"

"It'll light good enough, ma'am," put in Lonergan, "unless there does be foul air in the chimeny."

"Of course there must be foul air. And anyhow, it would not be warm in time. People are shivering and turning blue as it is."

"This is outrageous," exclaimed the Colonel. "We cannot be responsible."

But before the guests could be directed there, clouds and

clouds of black smoke, as from the mouth of hell, belched forth from the room. Jackdaws' nests, the accumulation of centuries, crashed down. The grate broke. Miss Protheroe dashed hither and yon helplessly. The Colonel, Himself and some more alert members stamped out lumps of flaming débris and opened the windows.

Louise said icily to Miss Protheroe, "I am so sorry, but we shall have to have the meeting as originally planned, after all," and invited the guests into the drawing-room. Mrs. Protheroe was discovered there; possibly she had had some idea of barring the door, but she fell back and retired to a chair by the fire, glaring as the Colonel hastily piled on coal. The room was abysmally cold.

Still, Lady Agatha, an undaunted speaker, gave a fascinating talk on ring-forts, shivering only slightly. Of no mean calibre, she. Around the frigid room, members and guests huddled together for warmth. The celebrated Protheroe Italian sofa, ready to break at a whisper, supported three figures wrapped in fur coats and travelling rugs. Miss Protheroe listened with one nervous eye on it, and the other on her mother. The old lady was white—with cold, one assumed. A wretched group in the far corner fell to blowing on their fingers in desperation.

At refreshment time, though, as always, there was a thaw-out. Everyone made his way to the buffet, except Mrs. Protheroe, who, breathing heavily and leaning on her cane, stood rigidly in place to receive the as yet unarrived guests. Unaware of any mishap, most of the company chatted and drank tea in the usual gossipy way. The new dispensary doctor, O'Hara, and his wife joined the Society then and there. Several other prospective members bought literature. Lady Agatha's secretary was busy explaining and giving change. Miss Protheroe poured tea and Mrs. Delaney and Louise's Lil offered plates of sausage rolls and sandwiches.

The atmosphere seemed very normal. Louise and I, however, went over to Mrs. Protheroe. "Won't you have tea?" Louise urged with real concern.

"Not yet. It's quite early," the old lady replied in a strained voice.

"I rather imagine everyone is here," said Louise gently.

Mrs. Protheroe paled. "Have you heard who is coming?"

"There was no R.S.V.P., you know, so I can't be sure," replied Louise reluctantly, "but we did hear from some."

"Is Mrs. Fitzjohn?"

"No."

"Lord and Lady Carport?"

"No, isn't it a pity?"

"Mrs. Lalique?"

"As a matter of fact—no. You see, the Spring Show is on, and many of them, I'm afraid, are down in Dublin."

"Sir Thomas?"

"No."

Mrs. Protheroe began to look ill. "Countess de Roebuck?"

"No."

"Mr. and Mrs. Fauciter?"

"I don't know."

"Colonel Swift?"

"No."

The old lady gasped.

"My dear Mrs. Protheroe," said Louise, trying still to pass it off, "it was a very bad time and very short notice. Do have some tea."

Just at that moment Lady Agatha came up with the doctor's wife in tow. "Surely you know each other," she said, "Mrs. Whyte, Mrs. O'Neill—Mrs. O'Hara."

"Of course," said Louise and I.

"Mrs. Protheroe, Mrs. O'Hara."

"Miss Charlotte Protheroe's mother, I presume," said Mrs. O'Hara pleasantly, turning to her.

Mrs. Protheroe, ghost-like now, her eyes huge and burning, looked her up and down and ignored the proffered hand.

"Young woman, you presume too much!" she said, and stumbled from the room.

The silence was piercing. Mrs. O'Hara flushed; Lady Agatha, Louise and I all started talking at once, about the sandwiches, the flowers, the rain; Miss Protheroe twittered with nervousness; the Colonel announced that he must see to the fires, and Himself said loudly to no one in particular, "Tell me, what do you think of the foreign policy of Mexico?"

"Whew!" I said on our way home.

" 'Twas ever thus," he said. "The Ascendancy is not an aristocracy, you know.

> "I'm Burlington Bertie,
> I rise at ten-thirty.
> My people are well off, you know.
> I walk down the Strand
> With my hat in my hand.
> I'm Burlington Bertie from Bow.

> "Oh, it's Bert, Bert,
> I ain't got a shirt.
> When they ask me to dine I say 'No'.
> I just had a banana
> With Lady Diana.
> I'm Burlington Bertie from Bow."

CHAPTER 17

IT TAKES ALL KINDS

ONE DAY TOM MENTIONED that the hens weren't as fit as they might be.

"Goodness, what's wrong with them?"

Looking off into space, "Nothing, ma'am, to speak of, that is. They're excited, you might say."

"Excited?"

More scrutiny of space, even his voice became distant. "Yes. It's the banty, he'd need two bricks."

Giggles from Bridie in the corner.

I went to Himself, who smiled and duly translated, "The hens want a cock. The bantam is too small; he'd need two bricks to stand on."

"Oh."

"That's a common saying here, you know."

"Oh."

So we put the problem to Teresa O'Tuomey, who was a regular visitor and adviser by this time. "Whatever do you want with a nasty old rooster?" she asked in tones of great surprise.

"*We* don't know," I said. "Tom suggested one, he's in charge."

She blushed. "Very well, go ahead. I suppose he wants to rear chicks. Tell him to do as he pleases."

There was Teresa, looking wickedly sophisticated, blush-

ing over the thought of the cock, or Tom, or both. But I had
begun to realise that her appearance was deceptive—she was
not in the least worldly, almost completely unread and un-
informed. At I.C.A. meetings, where she stood out like a
fashion model in the midst of a girls' hockey team, she only
attended when Lady Crosby did, never said a word, and
hovered in the wake of Lady C. as if her presence were a
Royal Visit. Louise always dressed with the rightness that is
superior to fashion, but Lady C. was as dowdy as the rest of
us, likely as not wearing a fifteen-year-old suit and a raincoat
fastened by a belt of rope, while Teresa was a vivid page out
of the smart world. It seemed at first glance like mis-
casting.

But Teresa the *soignée* and svelte, the brisk and cryptic, was
in fact a simple type, a lamb in wolf's clothing. It turned out
that she was madly shocked by me and my breezy allusions
to such assorted topics as divorced friends, Michelangelo's
sculpture, New York restaurants, modern writers, progres-
sive education and ancient Irish myths. For just this reason,
though, I was a social advantage to her; and from time to
time she brought me to meet various friends in the county,
wives of 'big farmers', women whom in the ordinary course
I should never have met, because they were much too involved in household and farm chores to be free. But under
the influence of Teresa's descriptions—goodness knows how
purple—of 'the American', they were lured out of their
accustomed ways. This was how I met Mrs. Maher.

Teresa called for me early one afternoon—or evening in
Irish terminology (very confusing, and resulting more than
once in mixed-up appointments). The idea was not to stay
late, as Teresa had to bring me back to Barravore and then
go on down to Dublin. The Mahers lived in one of the old
big houses, middling big anyhow, which was set on a
glorious beech-lined avenue which had once been a coaching

road. It was named on the old maps Himself collected; in those days it would have been only three miles from us. Now, with a new trunk route and the old roads gone, Teresa had to drive twelve miles through the hinterland to get to it.

The house, of course, faced the avenue, but the avenue now came to an abrupt end; the approach today is from the rear: very ugly—uglier than need be. Outbuildings dangle from the original structure, go on and on with no apparent plan; and various cattle and pig sheds branch out from a yard deep in mud.

To please me, Teresa drove towards the front of the house, where the Georgian sense of proportion still imposed its authority. But the lawn is overgrown; rose bushes drag along the grass like barbed wire in bloom; the beautiful door with its fanlight is cracked and peeling, even the hand-wrought window guards have slipped awry.

"They never bother with the front," Teresa explained. "Some years ago the rains flooded the rooms on this side, and the people who were the owners at the time never repaired the damage, and neither have the Mahers. He bought it for the grazing, and she hopes he'll sell it and move nearer her family. It's a pity for the house, I suppose." I was only glad that Himself had not seen it, as he would undoubtedly have bought it and we would have been twelve miles further away from electricity and phone.

We tried to negotiate the back yard on foot, but the mud was highly organic, so Teresa drove nobly right up to the back door. (Nobly because she took great care of her car, putting her own raincoat on its bonnet every night to keep it warm and washing it every morning with a face cloth. Good luck to the face cloth after this.)

Mrs. Maher was waiting for us, a thin, fair woman in a new dress, her short hair parted at the side and held with a barrette like a schoolgirl's. "Come in, come in," she said warmly, "and welcome, Mrs. O'Neill! We have a trades-man in the house fixing the chimney. Need I say more? Mrs. O'Neill, how did you bear it with all those workmen at Barravore? We'll sit in the dining-room instead. Come this way. Forgive me for leading you through the kitchen, but the hall is unsafe since the flood there some years ago. Here we are now; did Teresa tell you I've been begging her to bring you? Sit down here by the fire, I'll put the kettle on and we'll have a cup of tea."

"Mark now," said Teresa, "she'll be all afternoon getting that kettle boiled."

From the glimpse we had had of the kitchen on our walk through, I was not surprised. The stove consisted of what must have been the first evolutionary step up from an open fire. The centre part was an open fire, but metal boxes on either side, rickety and fancily decorated with embossed work, apparently served as ovens and boiling surfaces, and a crane hung over the top. A cat was asleep on one of the boil-ing surfaces now, and the whole thing looked as though it were ready to fall apart. Mrs. Maher must have been richly endowed with forethought, alertness, know-how and luck to be able to cook and bake with that two hundred-year-old 'range' without going bats. The rest of her kitchen, scrubbed but murky, was the usual picture of depression. One dingy little window high up, flag floor, benches loaded with boots and brushes, coats hanging on wooden pegs, an old dresser with cracked and odd plates, a table and dusty stuffed easy chairs, and the gigantic fireplace.

"Never mind her, Mrs. O'Neill," called Mrs. Maher. "She's terribly greedy for her tea."

"If you lived in my digs, you would be too."

"You may get married, Teresa," Mrs. Maher said, rejoin-ing us. ('May' has the force of 'must' in our locality.)

"Oh?" I said with interest. "Is there news?"

"Heavens, no!" exclaimed Teresa. "Mrs. Maher is forever trying to make a match for me."

"Not forever. Just when I hear of a rich bachelor ripe for the picking. But Teresa is hopeless. I've never heard her speak a good word for a man—except for Lady Crosby's son-in-law."

"Yes," replied Teresa dreamily, "the Duke de Neville. Lavinia Crosby married him. Did you meet them?"

"No, they went abroad just before we came."

"They lived in Crosby Lodge until then. He's perfectly handsome. D'you know who looks very much like him? Your Tom."

"Tom Malone?"

"He's your steward, isn't he?" Mrs. Maher remarked. "He's famous already with all the young girls around here. A Valentino, isn't he?"

"Would you say Tom would be good class?" observed Teresa.

"I wouldn't know," I replied. "As a foreigner, you know, that sort of distinction escapes me."

"Mrs. McQuade I think it was, was telling Mrs. Griffin he was from the glen—a distant relative of your husband?"

"Could be."

"The O'Neill-Barnas, the whole family and all their connections, were at one time very rich," added Mrs. Maher, helpfully.

"Not any more, I'm afraid."

"Ah well," said Teresa with a heavy sigh, "it doesn't matter."

Rather a long silence ensued, but Mrs. Maher knew how to change the subject. "I well remember the excitement at Lavinia Crosby's wedding. We were all hanging on word of the latest news. You were there, weren't you, Teresa?"

"Not exactly. I helped Lady C. with the invitations and arrangements."

"They were married from Castlecrosby, you know," Mrs. Maher said, turning to me. "Such a to-do! Tell her about it, Teresa."

Teresa began somewhat absently, but then warmed up to her subject. "He had his friends from England and they were all staying in the next county at Lord Park's. Lavinia had her gown from Paris, all bits of tulle and lace, ravishing, with a long long train of rose point that Sister Ambrose whipped from the convent—Reverend Mother had practically promised it to someone in London for the Court. They were married in the chapel at Castlecrosby by the parish priest, assisted by Lavinia's cousin, a young Dominican I think he is, and four other priests connected with the family; and the chapel was simply thatched with flowers; and they had breakfast for over a hundred with champagne. Lady C. told me all about it; it was catered from Dublin. Poor Lavinia! I think all that would be too upsetting, don't you?"

"Dreadful," breathed Mrs. Maher.

"I don't think I'd mind too much," said I.

"Oh, it's all very well if one has money," said Teresa with a heavy sigh. "But Tom does look like the Duke. He's stationed in Germany now, and they have two children, and Lady C. says Lavinia loves it, their house has four servants and no draughts."

"Who wouldn't love it!"

"Surely you have that in America too?" said Mrs. Maher.

"Not servants. Very few people have full-time help these days. Too expensive and hard to get."

"Why, we're told that in America you can shovel the money in off the street."

I assumed this was intended as a joke and smiled accordingly.

"Never mind," said Mrs. Maher, "if you knew some of the eejits that have gone rom here to the States and returned with fortunes, you'd believe it too."

"Well, perhaps the odd person still strikes it lucky, but the days of easy money are over, I'm afraid. Income tax for one thing."

"Ah yes, that's right. You're very regimented now. The government tells you what you must do and must not do——"

"Oh no. You're thinking of England, aren't you?"

"No. America. I've read this often in the Irish newspapers. America gives its people freedom from want and freedom from fear, and in return the well-fed beast does everything the government says. Individual rights are no more; and over there conscience is a thing of the past, so that you have an ungodly system and the country destroyed with juvenile delinquents and Socialism."

"Good Lord, no! What nonsense. Who published this sort of thing?"

"Oh, you see it everywhere," said Teresa vaguely.

"A lot of lies!"

"Don't be offended," begged Mrs. Maher.

"I suppose everything's better in America than in Ireland," said Teresa sarcastically.

"Actually, I suppose people in every country are more or less the same and have more or less the same problems. We do have some delinquency and some regimentation, but really we have an overwhelming majority of happy, law-abiding citizens who stand on their own feet. I think there's no doubt that the mass of people in America are materially better off than the mass of Irish; and they are also much more independent, it seems to me, and therefore more courageous in holding firm for their rights against the government or any other encroaching power."

Silence.

"Americans speak more openly than we, anyhow," said Mrs. Maher.

"Well, any way you take it, that's significant, isn't it?"

"It *is* true," said Teresa, returning as ever to her muttons, "that Ireland is hundreds of years behind, don't you think? Take the men here, don't you agree that they are backward?"

"Do you think so?"

"I think they're hopeless. I've no use for them. Many a time people have made matches for me, but I simply have no interest."

"I suppose you're cold."

"Cold?" echoed Mrs. Maher, as though puzzled.

But Teresa went on. "Perhaps. Men just don't interest me at all. I have a little money of my own—what do I want with a husband? Look at my sisters—married, one has five children and the other eight, when the doctors said she should never have any at all, the creature! And what do my sisters get in return? Up to get breakfast, in the kitchen all day, or the farmyard, caring for cattle and pigs and children and farm workers. Their husbands have to be fed all day, and then they're off to the pub every night. They have plenty of this world's goods too, but do they buy their wives an electric pump, or a washing-machine, or do they ever bring them out? They do not. I'm much better off not married, thank you."

"You probably have never met the right man, that's all."

"Just because I have a little money, they think I'm a good catch. Haven't you heard them? 'So-and-so married five hundred pound.' You see them, sixty, seventy years old, horrid old men, 'big farmers'. Just because they've a few hundred acres of land, they think any woman would be lucky to have them!"

"And they would," put in Mrs. Maher.

"But there must be younger men around too?"

"I'd like a fine man," said Teresa wistfully.

"Just what is meant by 'fine'?" I asked.

"Big, you know," Mrs. Maher explained, "handsome. The Duke de Neville is a fine man."

"And Tom?"

"Tom's a fine man too," said Teresa, "but he's no class, I'm afraid."

"You mean he's a working man?"

"Yes. He simply couldn't be considered, you see."

"That's where you're making a mistake, Teresa," I said. "He may be a working man, but he comes of a highly respected family."

"Does he?" she said eagerly. "But then, it's the money too. If one of my sisters, for instance, married a labouring man, the family would feel disgraced. We wouldn't have a thing to do with her. Why, in no time at all, she'd be at the door with half a dozen children hanging to her skirt, each with his hand out for bread. My family are all farmers, you see. My sisters have all married very well."

"So you were saying."

"I mean, as marriage goes. Ah well, alanna, it's all the same in a hundred years." Relapse into gloom.

"You don't understand, Mrs. O'Neill," said Mrs. Maher, looking away from me and searching for words. "Courtship here in Ireland isn't like what it is in America, romance and all that. We're very practical and sensible. Most of the time I agree with Teresa. I don't know why we get married at all."

"Surely companionship, children——"

"Companionship. My husband and I are very happy, but could he and I ever talk as we are talking now? Never in a million years. He has his work and I have mine; but for

conversation, give me a woman any time. That's why I was
so eager to meet you, Mrs. O'Neill. Teresa told me of some
of the conversations she has had with you—only an American
could speak of things so frankly. And as for marrying for
children, I think of my four. They're all at school now, in
their teens. What are we going to do with them when they're
grown? One boy can have this place, but the others? It's
the export market for them, I'm afraid; what can Ireland
offer? We rear them, and then part with them, a painful joy
at best."

There was no answer to this. In fact, as our own family
increased and grew up, I could see that this might be a
problem for us too. Ireland, which I had once envisioned as
an undeveloped country and consequently a land of opportunity, as, say, Canada was fifty years ago, or the States were
a hundred years ago, now seemed not so much undeveloped
as stratified, rigid in its old ways, conservative past hope of
progress, a bottomless pit that swallowed and obliterated
enterprise. Young people had to emigrate to find employment; the possibility of creating it at home was very slight.
But while I was trying to formulate some sort of encouraging
reply, Mrs. Maher brushed the subject aside and came out
with what had evidently been her reason for wanting to talk
with me.

"I haven't had an intimate talk like this," she said, start-
ling me somewhat, "since I was in school. How I love it!
Tell me, Mrs. O'Neill, isn't it true, don't women everywhere
feel the same about marriage as we in Ireland do?"

"What do you mean?"

"Isn't it just a big bore? The marriage act, I mean. Not
painful, not horrid, but on the other hand, not pleasant at
all?"

"Good Lord!" I exclaimed, completely taken by surprise
and a little annoyed. Coming as I did from the liberal con-

versation of the U.S.A., was I going at this age and station to have to discuss sex? It seemed to me it was over and done with as a topic of vital interest. Surely all has been said on the subject that can be said—it's as pointless as to discuss should women vote?

"That is *too* banal and sophomoric——" I began. But Mrs. Maher was intent on expressing her thoughts, which were slow to form but evidently represented years of questioning. I felt that there was a dignity in her doubt, that her mind was hemmed in by repressive teaching and dreary circumstance; but she still, at least, wondered. I couldn't cut her off.

"A bore, a bore. Wouldn't you rather pretend to be asleep than to put up with it?" she continued. "How many times have I done just that!"

"That's just what my married sisters say," remarked Teresa. "They say it's a tedious cod."

"I admit," said Mrs. Maher, "that at moments when one was courting, there was a thrill. Perhaps just in a kiss, or a squeeze of the hands, but in marriage—nothing."

"Lavinia and the Duke kiss each other still," said Teresa thoughtfully. "The Tierney girl wouldn't clean for them, she was so disgusted at the goings-on. She said the cook never got the dishes washed, for watching the two of them sunning in the garden and calling each other darling!"

"How nice," I said.

"Nice!" snorted Teresa. "I suppose you'll think this is nice too. Mrs. Griffin told Mrs. McQuade and Mrs. Griffin had it from someone who saw them do it—Lavinia and the Duke went into the bathroom together!"

"No!" gasped Mrs. Maher.

"You mean, before they were married?" I asked innocently.

"What!" they shrieked. They were literally horrified.

Mrs. Maher recovered herself by going in to see about the tea, and Teresa rushed after her. Only when they finally had it made, and we had consumed it, along with delicious home-made bread and home-churned butter, and conversation had picked its way safely in the interval, only then did Mrs. Maher pluck up the courage to come back to her original point. In fact, it was a measure of its importance to her that she came back to it at all.

"But Mrs. O'Neill, don't you think that every woman feels the same? The marriage act isn't pleasant, is it, as one is led to believe, but rather something to be endured, to offer up?"

"Oh no, Mrs. Maher," I said firmly (thinking, 'This ends me but I can't let it go'). "That shouldn't be. You're sup-posed to enjoy it."

"Enjoy it!" she cried, hurt of course. "Enjoy it! If I enjoyed it, Mrs. O'Neill, I'd have to confess it!"

Teresa was in a mood while she drove me home, but my feeling was: 'She may be shocked but so am I.'

But when we got back to Barravore we found Himself and Tom—Tom all dressed up—waiting for our return. It seemed Tom had to get back to the glen that night and our car wouldn't start. Would Teresa give him a lift as far as Dublin?

"Why certainly," she said, "and would you like me to give the car a push?"

"It won't do any good," said Tom, "I've tried everything. If I was to go and kiss its exhaust pipe, the damn thing wouldn't start."

I thought Teresa would be offended at this egregious lack of class, never mind what else, but not at all. She giggled. "Come along," she said, "I'll get you to Dublin anyhow."

We waved them off and entered the house. Even from above stairs I could hear Bridie banging pots and pans in the kitchen, sure sign of trouble. As soon as I could I went down to investigate. "What happened, Bridie?"

"You was out this evenin' an' the Master was out, an' the kids were in the garden an' Tom was in the far field, an' the 'fridge man come, the feller that was here before. He asked fer all of ye an' I told him ye was out, an' what do ye think?"

"Tell me."

"He tried to attack me, or whativer ye call it."

"No!"

"Good job I could make mince o' him, if I wanted to."

"What did you do?"

"I trown him out in the yard an' locked the door."

"Poor Bridie! How perfectly horrible! How did it happen?"

"He come in to look at the 'fridge, he said, and thin he backed me up agin the wall an' put his hand on me."

"Disgusting!"

"And thin he says, 'Stand still, an' I won't tell anyone'!"

"The nerve of him! The horrid little man."

"And he half me size!"

Really, I thought, that takes the cake. "I won't tell anyone." A perfect précis of the national masculine attitude. "Never mind, Bridie, I'll tell the Master and he'll see to it that it doesn't happen again."

That night I had plenty of conversation for Himself, but he was much more exercised over my encounter with Mrs. Maher than with Bridie's Awful Experience.

"For God Almighty's sake, when will you learn sense? What possessed you to talk that way with her?"

"Now what have I done?"

"Why did you have to go and say you enjoyed it?"

"I was just trying to be honest—she was."

"Honest! A simpleton is honest. You'll have us run out of the country. She'll spread the news everywhere, she and

Teresa O'Tuomey. We'll be boycotted, that's what—grocers won't supply you with bread, butchers won't sell you meat, nobody will give us the time of day. My God, were you born yesterday? Do you want us read from the altars? I can just hear it: 'Strangers have come into our midst, with their pagan practices.' This is disastrous!"

After a while he calmed down and decided that if we weren't boycotted, it might be that the house would be full of women coming after him. This was obviously a comforting prospect. However, he gave me a lecture on the things that could be said and the things that couldn't. The gist of it was that there were ways of making your meaning clear without putting it in words.

Tom had his own way of dealing with situations, of that there was no doubt. Off he went to Dublin with Teresa, and as luck would have it, they decided to stop for tea on the way, at the only hotel, and who should also be having tea there but Lady Crosby? She waved. Teresa went over to her table and spoke a few words, rejoined Tom and explained to him the eminence of Lady C. The waitress brought their cups and served them, and Tom, who up to this point had seemed every inch a gentleman, now poured his tea into his saucer and drank from it holding it in his two hands and making loud snorting noises.

Teresa beseeched him to put it down, uselessly. She could see an incredulous glance from Lady C. as well as from everyone else in the room before politeness clamped blank disregard on all witnesses. Tom blandly ignored all that, chaffed the waitress, called her "Hey, sister", and "Hey, good-lookin' ", loudly ordered two stouts, offered to fight the proprietor when they weren't forthcoming, and in short completely humiliated Teresa. As soon as they were back in the car, Tom reverted to his quiet poker-faced self and they completed the trip in frigid silence.

Teresa told me all this in tears. She didn't know how to approach Lady C. again; she thought she had detected a snub from her; the whole foundation of her life was blighted. She wouldn't look at Tom, I never dared ask her about our hens again, and not long after she sought and got a transfer to another county. I'm sure she's still single. (After that Tom once, and once only, referred to Teresa to Himself. "I wouldn't," he said. "Not if her belly were on fire.")

"Anyhow," said Himself, resuming our discussion some time later, "never *say* what you really think or feel, not in this country. It's not only dangerous, it's unnecessary. Bide your time, and the opportunity will come to make your point. Take Bridie and the 'fridge man, for instance. That won't happen again."

"Did you threaten him in semaphore or something?"

"Don't be sarcastic. No. We simply let him know we knew about it."

"How?"

"The next time he called, Tom put two bricks in his van."

*

CHAPTER 18

HEDGIN' AND DITCHIN'

FROM HAVING BEEN the Great Unwatered, we became suppliers of water to the countryside. The local wells, supposedly maintained by the County Council, had been going dry regularly every summer and, come the second June, they gave out again right on time. Himself let it be known that anyone was welcome to come to our yard and get water from the tap there. He probably had had it installed with just such a thought in mind. Consequently, we became the village well.

All morning, farmers with tractors kept the tap busy, fastening a hose to it and filling tanks for their cattle. All afternoon women came on bicycles with pails to fill and carry home. At any hour children would arrive in pairs and take back buckets strung on a pole between them. After tea at night the young folk straggled in, painfully shy at first, but eventually to come into the kitchen and make a social occasion of it. Somewhere along the line, in the autumn, the County Council wells must have filled again, but no one bothered with them any more. We were it.

It was in this way that Bridie and Tom met all the young people for a mile around and got really acquainted. Himself and I were delighted to hear the laughter and squeals ascending from below stairs every night and felt it was the best kind of help insurance we could possibly have. Young

Mrs. Carthy was jealous of Bridie once—she thought her husband was taking too long when he came here. The others egged her on with such cracks as "There's no water like Bridie's water", but this was soon smoothed over, and the visits to our yard remained good fun for all.

Tom sat around with the others for a while, and then ordinarily went out, because he liked to ramble over the place on his bike, checking gates, lamping rabbits and watching fences for trespass before he went to bed. Often Himself and I joined the crowd in the kitchen for 'nineses', which were usually served at ten, and usually Jane was there too, and very occasionally Mrs. Cobley, as they apparently found night a good time for this errand. We grew used to unfamiliar figures making their way to and from the yard; and on the rare occasions when we walked out at night (as against driving in the car), we just tried to be inconspicuous and not spoil their fun.

That's how we got in on the beginning of this. Nineses were over, and we were reading by the fire in the sitting-room, when it suddenly struck me that rain was bound to come and I had better see if the laundry that should have been brought in during the afternoon was really off the line. Himself is always willing for a stroll, so he joined me. We went out of the front door and entered the yard from that direction, conscious of, but not paying much attention to, two figures who had emerged from the kitchen door and were heading for the barn wall, where the bikes were parked. Their path came very close to ours, but they did not seem to hear us, nor, since it was a pitch-black night, to see us.

"Nice night, Tom!" said a voice from one of them. It was Jane.

Silence.

Tom turned his bicycle down the barn lane towards the back gate.

"Lovely night, Tom!" said Jane again.

"Aye."

"What's it going to do tomorrow?"

"Rain."

Tom seemed unusually tongue-tied, and Jane, normally a brisk walker, was taking a very long time to get down the lane, even though Tom was carrying her pail. But there was nothing about their conversation to indicate anything private —in fact, there was nothing about the conversation to indicate anything, period—so we kept on our way without calling out. Tom opened and very carefully closed the gate, and then, to our amazement, hesitatingly said, "Any chance of comin' on the road with you, Jane?"

"Not tonight, Tom. I'm in a hurry."

"Well, what evening can I see you early till I get a good hold o' you?"

"What!"

"Till we get acquainted?"

"You see me here every night."

"Right. We'll leave early one night. I'll tip you off."

"You'll what?"

"Aye. You're not too well up yet, I see. Now if I'm readin' when you walk in, try and sit opposite me and be on the look out, and when I bat me eye over the paper, you say it's time to get the water, but if you happen to be in before me, I'll get to sit beside you and I'll give you a dig in the ribs when I'm ready to go. But let me get off first."

"My God," said Jane sarcastically, "I can hardly wait."

This did not deter Tom a bit, if he noticed it. He said casually, "It's a date then for this week. Good night now," and cycled on down the road. Jane stood staring after him, then picked up the pail and went off in the opposite direction, towards her cottage.

"Well, what do you make of that!" exclaimed Himself.

"Why, it's cuckoo. It won't do at all."

"That's what you think, lassie."

"Who would have suspected that they were interested in each other?"

"You'd never know. Tom is a deep one."

"But he has all those other girls on the string. Can't he leave Jane alone?"

"I'd say she didn't mind too much."

"Oh you *men*. You're all so conceited. She won't be bothered with him."

"Oho, just wait till he gives her that dig in the ribs."

"It just won't *do*."

"Don't assume that he has serious intentions. This is just a spot of courting."

"That's worse!"

"Not necessarily. But in any case, it looks as though we'll see how the cat jumps."

The next night, Himself made it a point to call into the kitchen and look over the crowd. No Jane. The next night it was Mrs. Cobley who came for the water. But the third night Jane arrived, much, much earlier than usual. I went down to greet her, and could tell at a glance that the lipstick was on with extra care, a touch of perfume had been applied, the scarf was a most becoming shade of blue, and that she was telling herself she had come quite regardless of whether Tom was there or not and was going to go home immediately.

While we were chatting, Tom materialised out of nowhere and sat down next to Jane at the extreme end of the bench, first arming himself with a newspaper and muttering, "Good night, all," before he ducked his head behind it and began to read. Himself observed out of the corner of *his* eye that the paper was three days old and that Tom was reading it upside down. We went back to the sitting-room and I began to sort out Tom's love-life in the light of this new development, and to wonder whether Jane would come and live with us (what a help she'd be) or whether Tom would move in with her and her mother.

But down in the kitchen things were not going according to plan. After a few minutes' talk with Bridie, it seems that Jane 'riz'. "I'll have to get the water now, and be off."

"It's early yet," said Bridie.

"Well," said Jane tartly, "Tom can cheer you up from now on."

At that Tom jumped up and made precipitately for the door. Bridie was baffled by all this leppin' about and asked, "Are ye goin', Tom?"

"Yes," he replied, "in me bed I ought to be. I've an early start in the mornin'." And he bolted out.

Bridie then walked to the yard with Jane and tried to make conversation while the pail was filling with water, but Jane was brusque and in a hurry. The truth was she was piqued by the turn of events and also wondering if Tom might be outside.

"Wasn't Tom in a terrible hurry tonight?" remarked Bridie.

"Was he?" said Jane, trying not to appear in too much of a rush. "I wouldn't know."

"Oh wouldn't you now!"

Jane stepped round her almost rudely. "Good night, Bridie."

"Safe home," said Bridie pointedly.

Jane told me the story herself. She arrived outside the first gate fairly heated. There was no bike, no Tom, and thinking now that he might be out on the road she hurried on with renewed hope, leaving the gate open. Then she decided this was ridiculous, she was getting altogether too excited, so she went back and closed the gate, and then found herself hurrying again out on to the high road. Not a sign, not a sound, not even a stir. She stood there for a few minutes and then scanned the road in both directions, bending forward with her hand shielding her eyes. Not a sign of him. Feeling like a pricked balloon she turned round in her own direction.

Voice from the hedge in a husky stage whisper: "What the hell delayed you?"

"Oh!"

Tom emerged from the hedge, dragging his bike after him. "Did you think I'd gone, me darlin'?"

Jane, totally rattled, snapped back, "I wasn't minding."

"Oh yes, but you were. Wasn't I watchin' your antics?"

"You're impossible!"

"Any chance of comin' up the road with you tonight, or are you still in a hurry?" This time he didn't wait for a reply, but took the pail and swung it over the handlebars of the bike. Then, with one hand pushing the bike and the other round Jane, he moved off. Jane had to do two steps and then three and back to two trying to fall in with his long strides.

"What ails you?" Tom asked her.

"Nothing," said she, trying not to shift her gait so obviously.

They had only gone a few yards when Tom abruptly stopped. "Whist! There's someone coming down the road."

This nettled Jane. Here *she* was, hopping about because it didn't occur to him to accommodate his pace to her, and here *he* was, being difficult because someone was coming. It was *her* right to be difficult, not his! "So what?" she said.

"So what, me London hawkie! Do you want the whole bloody countryside to know we were up the road together?"

"Go on back then. There's nothing stopping me from going on alone."

"No," said Tom, "me mind's made up, and I'm not goin'

I

to be done out of me bit of courtin'. Come on up with you on the bar, we'll beat them to it."

Before she could protest or agree, he lifted her on to the bar and pedalled away at a great rate. In a short time, he stopped suddenly, so that Jane almost went flying into the fields. He pulled her up quickly and jerked her to her feet. She was thoroughly shaken by now, and that 'London hawkie' bit rankled; what's more, they could still hear footsteps. She couldn't refrain from remarking bitterly, "Why didn't we just hop on a bus in the opposite direction?"

"Bus me foot! This is the spot. Come on, let's dive down there. Come on, hurry!"

"Spot? Dive? What, me?"

"No, the woman next to you, of course! Quick with you now."

She found herself doing a nose-dive into a gap in the hedge and then into the ditch on the other side, Tom landing along with her and the footsteps coming quite near now.

Tom whispered, "God between us and all harm, we only just made it. Don't laugh, you now. Make no sound."

After being shot off her perch, grabbed, jerked, hissed at and made to dive and crawl, and after hearing language no lady should tolerate, all within a couple of minutes, Jane didn't feel in much form for laughing *or* sound. The footsteps grew louder, very near now, but then they began to pass and presently faded on into the distance. This breathing spell gave Jane a chance to come to a little. "Drat it, my skirt's torn. Where's your bike, Tom?"

"Up on the road."

"Who owned those footsteps, do you know?"

Tom said between his teeth, "McQuade, the Blessed Man."

"Are you sure?"

"I'd know his miserable pigeon-toed footsteps anywhere."

"Would he recognise your bike? Any chances of his sneaking back?"

"If he as much as shows his dirty nose down here, be Christ I'll have his life!... How do you like this spot, Jane?"

"I've been in worse."

"I've had this spot located for a long time, and sez me to meself: 'With luck when I can get Jane cracking, this will be the place.'"

Jane couldn't help a snort of suppressed amusement and deflated vanity. He was so sure of himself! And yet she thought, 'He *has* got me cracking, all right,' She covered up by asking innocently, "Don't you like Kevin McQuade?"

"To hell with him. Isn't he in love with you?"

"What!" exclaimed Jane, to whom this was genuine news.

"What!" said Tom, imitating her. Then, changing his voice, "I suppose if I told you that I was in love with you, that I was mad about you, you'd hardly believe it?"

"No."

"And it wouldn't be true, either."

"Oh my God," cried Jane. "These Irish!"

Later on, however, she had occasion to ask him, "Who taught you to kiss?"

"No one taught me. I've kissed dozens and dozens of girls in my time."

"Yeah."

"Honest now, I haven't had a hold in four years. The last bitch let me down and I promised meself I'd never look at another woman, never mind kissin' one, and now you come on the scene. . . ."

Jane was touchy. "I was pushed on this scene."

Tom answered in a low throaty voice, "I'd love to be courtin' you in earnest. I wonder now how we'd measure up?"

Jane felt anxious about the measuring. "Come on, Tom," she said briskly, "let's go. The danger has passed."

Tom refused to stir. "Don't be coddin' yerself now. Come on, sit down, it's early in the night yet . . ."

Much, much later, trying to get her breath, Jane asked, "Who *did* teach you to kiss, Tom?"

"I told you, no one taught me, but I've watched them at it on the pictures."

"You keep away from the pictures."

Tom looked into her eyes and said, "Jane, that kiss wasn't pictures, that was real."

But it seems the pail of water was stuck in the hedge (spilled, of course) and Tom's bike with his special lamp was visible to anyone inquisitive enough to poke around a bit, and Blessed McQuade *had* been following them. Jane carefully mended the snag in her skirt, but the next evening Bridie greeted her with a grin and said, "I hear you been doin' some hedgin' and ditchin'," and the fellows held a long indirect conversation about London and the great good times there, and was Tom ever thinkin' o' goin' in ower that. Tom never batted an eye, but went along with the talk and then departed. He left Jane severely alone for weeks, and busied himself with poaching at night or other exclusively male occupations, like doing the round of the pubs.

Jane made me her confidante, and together we went over the ground, puzzling it out, and came up with the reluctant conclusion that in Ireland half, nay, three-quarters of the game lies in 'keeping it dark'. We pulled Himself in to get a masculine reaction.

"You wouldn't think," mused Jane, "that when two people are interested in each other, really interested, that a man would care if other people knew about it. Not a *man*."

"Everyone is so afraid of being made a fool of. It's pride."

"But to run away like that, from a creature like McQuade!"

"But you see," Himself pointed out gently, "McQuade did talk."

"Well, what if he did? Isn't Tom man enough to stand up for his own feelings?"

"That would be rushing him. My dear girl, you have to be very careful about rushing a man. Once McQuade spread the news, for you two to go on 'walking out' together would mean you were as good as engaged. If no one knew about it, why then you could keep on all you liked. But the whole thing depends on its being a secret."

"I'm not cut out for that sort of thing."

"Oh, it's not so bad," said Himself with a reminiscent smile, like Casanova reading Kinsey.

"Humpf!" said I. "I don't see how couples ever *do* get together. To have to meet outdoors all the time, and in secret, and the parents never knowing about it till they're ready to be married, practically. Still, there must be a special, clandestine thrill that the rest of us miss."

"Rather!" grinned Jane and Himself simultaneously.

"Oh, you both make me sick!"

"No, really," said Jane eagerly, "it's much more exciting than a date for a dance or a play, don't you know? The moon and the stars, the fragrance of the flowers *and* the uncertainty——"

"Look, who's giving advice to who?"

"No one can give Jane advice," summed up Himself. "She'll just have to sweat it out. He'll wait till all the talk dies down and then try and see her again."

"Well, he can jolly well jump, if that's what he thinks! I'm not one to blow hot and cold. It's too upsetting—knocks me right off my stride. If things are off, let them stay off. Just wait till he comes around again, I'll send him packing!"

All of which we'd heard before, of course.

*

CHAPTER 19

DUBLIN

THE DAY IN DUBLIN started with the unaccustomed discipline of dressing up the first thing in the morning: nylons, instead of the lovely warm woollen socks and the lovely warm slacks on top of them, high heels, dress, make-up. Thus bedizened, I had to run the gauntlet of breakfast conversation, "Oh, Mummy, you're wearing your good clothes!" and the baby's "Mummy going to 'chool?" (that being her idea of the pinnacle of social occasions). Next the ordinary furore of getting satchels, coats, sweaters, pencils and children into the car, complicated by the jumping dogs and now by my own fuss-fuss—books to go back to the library, parcel for the dry-cleaner, box of shoes for the shoe repairer, marketing list, shopping bag, cheque-book, money. The relatively calm drive, first to drop off the children, and then the early, empty roads down to Dublin, sixty miles of driving in freedom and quiet, with the sense of owning the road and the earth and one's destiny.

New car sales are mounting every day in Ireland; and even the poorest country people seem to have old jalopies—even, for example, the widow who lived in the cottage down the road. She received milk from Louise, children's clothes from me, and steady assistance from the Vincent De Paul; and incidentally, she looked more or less like the remains of a sailor's Saturday night. Even *she* and her current boy friend owned an ancient automobile. "Why," said Tom when I expressed surprise, "everyone drives a car now. These days it's only a decent way of walking."

But very few of these people ventured onto the main roads. The frugal farmers, on the one hand, expected their cars to last at least fifteen years and used them only when absolutely necessary, while the widow-down-the-road type of owner, on the other, dispensed with such formalities as licence and tax and never dared drive where a guard might be observing. Neither group took a car to Dublin. Quite apart from everything else, to them it was an unthinkable distance away. Sixty miles! A day and a night's journey! Himself's gay charges around the country were regarded as mad, though, if one needed a lift, convenient.

Anyone in Ireland can have a licence by paying for it. This done, you just get behind the wheel and eat up the road, only the very cautious taking a trial run around a field first. It thus follows that roadmanship is not what it might be. "On the continent they drive to the right," commented Himself; "in England they drive to the left; so Irish drivers, wishing to please, stay in the middle." They seem to feel more in command of the situation when they are plunk centre, and of course they are, because no one can pass them —and passing, or any other method of escaping, as you can see, is not only desirable but healthy. However, driving tests are nearing. At least there was considerable protest recently when it was discovered that a man who had been given a licence was an old-age pensioner who was also blind.

But the main roads had little traffic, except occasional lorries very near Dublin; and for one used to the nightmare highways around New York, to the four-hour friendships struck while waiting bumper-to-bumper, three lanes deep, in New Jersey thoroughfares to the almost fatal exhaust fumes as one inched and stopped in the Holland tunnel, this ex-

perience was intoxicating. Unleashed, free, solitary, I in-
haled, I worked out my daily shopping route, I communed
with my soul, I brooded on decisions, but chiefly I felt like a
prisoner let loose, like the inventor of motor-cars, like a poet,
a bird, a spirit, a monarch. It is much better to attack a
day's business in this frame of mind, than as one of a long,
frustrated, over-heated line of traffic, battered and beaten
before arriving.

Dublin is a red-brick city on a plain. Its industries are
banished to the fringes, and it still gives an eighteenth-
century impression—rows of houses, domes and church
spires. It is divided in two by the river Liffey, immortalised
by Gandon's architecture, by Joyce, by Gogarty's swans and
Guinness' barges; but it is stitched by frequent bridges and
by streams of green double-decker buses, thousands of cars
and millions of bicycles.

The main streets are thick with traffic, but a striking thing
is the quiet, for neither the vehicles nor the crowds of pedes-
trians give forth a tenth of the noise an American would
expect. Streets are narrow but the cars are small; a Ford
V-8 here is considered a giant among cars and a luxurious
one at that. Jimmy's awed comment on a funeral, for instance, was: "A V-8 pulled the coffin away!"

Because of the river, I suppose, which when these things
started perhaps was a real barrier, there are two main shopping centres, one on either side, Grafton Street, and O'Con-
nell-and-Henry Street; and my problem was always to
organise my time so as to cover one side completely before
beginning the other.

Grafton Street and the streets around it are more elegant,
both from the point of view of clothes and food. If my time
in Dublin hadn't usually been so limited, I should have loved
just hours of window shopping. As it was, the fact that Irish
sizes do not fit me saved me from many an impulsive buy. I

admire tweeds, in bolt, in suit, in coat, in dress. Anything handwoven, in fact, charms me with its texture and colour, and every year, more and more, Dublin styles grow better and better. It's all very tempting.

The food shops, too, improve with time. When I first came, there were three, to us, indispensable items which could not be got—maple syrup, soy-bean sauce, and unsweetened cooking chocolate. Now there is only one, the chocolate; and maybe if I look tomorrow I'll find that. (You can't imagine till you do without it how many recipes call for it.) When I first came and asked for garlic, the saleswomen thought I had rheumatism and sympathised for five minutes. Now, they think nothing of a request for it. Ditto whole wheat bread. At first they hadn't heard of it, just of 'wheaten meal'; now there are several shops which stock it. Ditto compressed yeast. At first you had to buy baker's yeast and use it immediately. Black-strap molasses—at first they had only 'treacle'. Celery salt, poppy-seed (in desperation I asked the chemist for that, and she thought I was trafficking in opium), monosodium glutamate, cake mixes, pudding mixes, gruyère cheese—really, when I think back on the will-o'-the-wisp errands that had me darting around Dublin!

In America I never appreciated how exotic our menu is, nor, on coming here, did I grasp the fact that dishes which charmed in the States because they were not only delicious but inexpensive (pizza, chili, chow mein, spaghetti) cost more than steak in Ireland. It was very simple to revert to sirloin, I found.

Another thing that was disconcerting was the fact that prices varied so, from day to day and week to week. Just when I thought I'd discovered a good buy it would turn out that next week lobsters imported from Maxim's would have been cheaper. However, thanks to Dublin and the freezer, we ate a fairly balanced and varied diet, more typical of the

r*

city than of the countryside, for though the rural housewife, God knows, has her problems, meal-planning is not one of them. Corned meat, sausages, potatoes, and sometimes cabbage, is her gamut.

Many grocery prices defied comparison with home, because they varied with the seasons. Eggs, for instance, were two shillings a dozen in May and eight shillings a dozen in December. Tomatoes were two shillings a pound for the Dutch ones, early in the summer, and five shillings later on, when the Government-protected Irish crop came in. Tiny bananas were anything from threepence to sixpence each; oranges were sometimes cheaper, but usually sixpence each. I once paid one and twopence each for apples, but that was in a fancy shop.

Shopping in Dublin involved parking, and parking can be a real problem. We solved it on the Grafton Street side by joining the Automobile Club, which provides parking facilities. On the Henry Street side we had to depend on luck and the Irish Guards who are, without doubt, the nicest men on the face of the earth. Tall, handsome, wearing white gloves as immaculate as butlers', they are also slow to wrath, quick to understand, and they *never* give you a ticket! If you park for hours over time in a place where you oughtn't, at the worst there's a polite little sticker on the car window asking you please not to do it again. If they rebuke you in person, they're really interested in your explanation. Their attitude is a combination of us-working-girls-together, with a touch of paternalism. Very sympathetic.

One more note on marketing in Dublin—it seems to occur on Thursday. Thursday is the traditional day for ladies from the provinces to come in and do their more exacting 'messages'. Trains run excursions then, and the streets are jammed with housewives. I sometimes went on other days, just as a gesture of independence; but Thursday really was best, because of fish. Monday Himself always went; Wednesday was half-day, Friday would have left the house without fish to eat; so that left Tuesday and Thursday, and by going on Thursday I could get fresh fish in great variety, and thus take care of Friday. I suppose that's why all the other women went then too.

Shopping days zipped along in a great rush, their further limit being the necessity to call for the children at school on the way home. But there was another Dublin too—the social one. This was the Dublin of restaurants and theatres, films and parties. A magic city for us, entered after the preamble of the drive in. For a country of only three million people, Dublin is an extraordinary capital even in its most workaday aspect. It is like a top-heavy head, holding one-fifth of the population, almost all of the business, a huge amount of industry, the arts, the chief universities; and, with few exceptions, all the intellectual life, as well as the Government and the national library, museum, gallery, and so on, which would be expected of any capital. The hotels are famous; there is a literary aura about many of the restaurants; and the pubs of course are historic.

There are four theatre groups constantly in action, plus other sporadic offerings—opera, ballet, concerts, musical comedies, Spring Show, Horse Show. The drama is almost always excellent—the Irish talent for acting being unsurpassed, I think. The diversity of plays is all one could ask, ranging from the Abbey Theatre's speciality of drama laid in rural Ireland, to the very sophisticated, international 'advanced' productions of one of the other groups, which is best described by mentioning that this theatre and the Abbey were referred to as Sodom and Begorra. Dublin has beautiful cinemas too; the people are cinema-mad, and orderly and cheerful queues for the shows are lined up for hours ahead. Most of the cinemas have restaurants and thus serve a double function—you go for a meal or a show—which is one reason why restaurants in Dublin are not very much in evidence. The other reason is that most of them are concealed in hotels.

Conversation is the city's lifeblood. Pubs which installed TV 'on appro' returned them because their customers liked to talk while they drank. Himself used to hear marvellous bits—a chap talking about a duplicating machine supplied by a Dublin firm to the Vatican: "They bought it for the artificial dissemination of the Papal Bull"; or the fellow with a good few scoops in him holding forth on "the jiys and delights of married life": " 'Hey, Joe, is that you?' she called out. 'Jasus,' I said, 'it better be!' "

Dialogue springs up all day too, in the many cafés where Dubliners like to go for elevenses in the morning and fourses in the afternoon, and for lunch. I listened to intriguing conversations as I sat silent, practically invisible, sipping my own coffee.

Two pretty girls nibbling at iced *petits fours* (which the Irish adore).

"So-and-so is engaged."

"Oh, I didn't even know she was pregnant!"

"She isn't."

"Hmm! I always knew she was a snob."

Similar scene in another café, similar girls.

"The new boss is grand, isn't he?"

"Yes."

"And he dresses so well."

"And so quickly."

But the best talk of all was among the men, or at mixed parties. Usually Himself was clapped on the shoulder and hailed as an old acquaintance by this one and that who would explain to me, "We were in jail together at Kilmainham," or, "I was in prison with him at Mountjoy—Newbridge—the Curragh—Arbour Hill——" as the case might be. Having been in jail for the Cause is a social distinction in present-day Ireland, and politicians brag about it and make political hay of it. Himself despises this and other name-dropping on the same principle which made him refuse a government pension. "Why batten off patriotism? Why take pay for acting of your own free will?" But, as far as I know, he is unique. His back-slapping buddies were usually well 'in', prosperous, active in Government and business both, and pensioned besides.

For a proper discussion, Himself preferred freer agents. I remember a bar lounge one evening when one of the company was an ex-Kilmainham southern businessman and the rest were from the North. They included an Oxford-accented Englishman and an evangelical Presbyterian; and the subject of Partition was as inevitable as the whiskey. Himself started it. "Don't you feel a little nervous down here?" he asked, grinning.

The Englishman laughed. "We're not so timid as all that. Business is business, no matter about borders."

"I agree with you. That's why we deplore it."

"I deplore it too," said the Presbyterian. "I'd like to see all Ireland united."

"Under the Crown, I suppose?"

"The Crown? Think again, mon, I'm a Nationalist!"

It turned out that the evangelical Presbyterian was a rabid patriot and spent two hours a day learning Gaelic from Linguaphone records. The Englishman, very upstage, was a Roman Catholic, and strongly pro-Partition and the return to the English of all Ireland, if possible. The businessman, who was making a good thing out of a string of shops in Cork, said "Partition? Jasus, I wish the Border was just north of Mallow!"

To me, it seemed everyone was saying the wrong lines.

Clearly this wasn't the simple religious issue it was made out to be.

"It's regrettable," said the English Roman Catholic to the Ulstermen, "that your compatriots in the North would like to see you all united under the Pope."

"Leave the Pope out of it," exclaimed the Presbyterian. "North and South, we want to be one, that's what!"

"The National cause," said the businessman piously, "has always championed Catholic rights. Think of all our Catholic martyrs for Ireland."

"E-a-u-x!" cried Himself. "Think of all our Protestant leaders! Humanitarian, liberal, democratic."

"Surely the thing is economic," put in the Englishman. "Belfast's connection with England is too valuable to break."

"Belfast shared in the English industrial revolution," said Himself, "the only Irish town that did. Industries elsewhere were forced out of business. The only reason Belfast was spared was because its one industry, linen, did not conflict with any English interest."

"You Irish always rake up the past, don't you?"

"He's entitled to!" spluttered one of the party who had previously been silent. "I'm a member of the Orange Lodge, but I'm an Irishmon, and I'll say this—England never did onything for Ulster but what she hod to!"

"Hear, hear."

"I'm no Nationalist, like yon wee lad," he continued with a great roll of r' 's. "I r-r-regard the r-r-rise of Cotholic political power as a threat to the r-r-rest of us!"

"Isn't that the trouble?" asked Himself. "Those who are disinterested, sincere fellow-countrymen, who happen to be Roman Catholic, are deprived of your support. As recently as the Trouble, and that's only yesterday, weren't we Protestants and Catholics together?"

"Deprived of our support? Hoven't we our honds full with

the growing Cotholic population in the North, and so mony of us Protestants emigrating? And you want us to join this priest-r-r-ridden state of yours?"

"If only we had you, it wouldn't be priest-ridden. Protestant representation in the Government would prevent clerical domination."

"You must admit," said the Englishman, "that the South would have everything to gain and the North would have everything to lose."

"Everything to gain! God between us and harm!" said the businessman. "If the Border were to end, my shops wouldn't make a third of the profit they do now."

"Shoneenism!" hissed the Presbyterian reproachfully.

"Instead of being part of a British r-r-religious majority," objected the Orangeman, "we'd be an Irish r-r-religious minority."

"But," Himself pointed out, "you'd join your co-religionists in the South and give them a voice. As it is, Trinity College is our one bulwark against the power ambitions of the Catholic hierarchy. We need you."

"Begob, mon," said the Orangeman, "if ever a mon could make me see things another way, it would be you!"

"Let's drink on thot," said the Presbyterian.

"I can't get over all this," I said wonderingly. "Partition is supposed to be a great big fight—you're all supposed to be at dagger's points!"

"Ah, you've been reading the newspapers!" accused the businessman.

"You don't want to do thot," cried the Orangeman, "they're the greatest cod since Moses struck the r-r-rock! We're all Irishmen."

"We are," said Himself, "for what it's worth. Sure, if things go on as they're going, we'll probably be hoisting the next one together in Canada."

The barman moved with the bar rag along the counter. It was nearly closing hour. "Come on, now, lads," he said reproachfully, "less talk and more drinkin'."

We often dropped in on Enid and various other friends, and sometimes stayed on for dinners and receptions. One in particular was a big affair. It was like entering the Isles of the Blessed to step once more into central heating and the open arrangement of rooms. "Close the door!" was our theme-song at Barravore, but here room led out from vast room. Ash-blonde parquet was covered with thick carpets, mirrored walls reflected the glorious curves and prisms of Waterford chandeliers, looking like huge flowers crystallised with dew. Period furniture, inlaid. Butlers and footmen with trays of drinks edged their way through crowds engrossed in conversation.

This reception was for an international convention of astronomers who were meeting in Dublin. Hundreds of people were present, yet I knew with sure anticipation that whomever one talked with, on whatever subject, the going would be good. Dubliners are entertainingly articulate on almost any (Irish) topic, and it was at big, rather anonymous gatherings like this that rural dead-ends such as the censorship of books, the archæological finds at Lough Gara, or the Archbishop's latest taboo of a football game were likely to come up. Dubliners *cared*.

I talked with a sardonic writer whose books had been banned, with some gorgeously clever young people associated with Radio Eireann (a nest of genius, in my opinion), with various astronomers whom I had thought were at least Iron Curtain, because they wore beards, but who turned out to be bright young professors from Columbus, Ohio. But Himself searched out and found the Soviet astronomer, the real thing.

"And what do you think of our Irish stars?" asked Himself. "Not red enough."

See what Dublin does to you, I thought. Then someone presented me to a lady from Nebraska with an Irish name; she had come to live in Ireland for a while and had taken a flat in Merrion Square. She had a kind face and shining eyes. She had only arrived a week before, and her first words to me were, "I do think that Ireland is wonderful, and I do believe very strongly that the young people shouldn't leave the land, don't you?"

Suddenly feeling queer I smiled wanly and moved off. See what Ireland does to *you*, I thought.

On the way home that night the black highway seemed rather suddenly to leave the magic city behind, as though the lights and laughter had sunk once more beneath the sea. What struck me was the contrast—this flowering city and that barren countryside. Dublin, combining civilised leisure and wells of wit, filled with charm and brilliance, seemed to exist for the benefit of those living sixty miles away, to come in when they wished, to sip and then retire. We were having our cake and eating it too, I decided, existing in the slack backwaters of Barravore, comfortable, lazy, prodigal of idle projects and uncritical consumption of reading matter; and then presto, when we wished, life on the *qui vive*, smartened up, sharpened up, engirdled, high-heeled, ready for the centre of things, for stimulus and elegance, ideas and people.

I thought of Barravore now without distress. The implications of living in the country flashed through my mind. I thought of diverse matters such as, for one thing, the slant on life it gave the children. To them, animals never died of sickness or old age—they were felled and eaten. The baby carried her doll around by the head, the head came off, she wailed, "Tom killed mine dolly!" And Dorothy saw a bone on the ground and asked with interest who had been killed.

I thought of how Brady the publican's wife had opened a shop, and the inferences from that—that he was a bad provider or had made a pass at a girl at a town dance—for a wife's self-assertion in opening a shop was the Irish equivalent of divorce. I thought sleepily of the McQuades, all Pioneers, who schemed and fought to get a contract to grow malting barley. Of the MacAndrews' new bull, whose presence in a field had cut off one of our nicest walks. Of the Irish so-called summer—if one hour of lukewarm sunshine appeared, everyone immediately put on straw hats, as though they had been sitting by the window, coiled and waiting, all year. Of Enid saying thoughtfully, "The trouble is, one no longer has to go to America in order to dislike it." Of the priests, who had eased up on the States, and were now taking over emigration to England. Of the neglected garden, and my devout hope that what once had been spinach would, with luck, one day be spinach again. Of how fortunate we were to have servants, however amateur, and time, however wasted. Of the hidden Ireland, slipping past us in the darkness field by field, and ours to explore. Of Dublin . . . and by this time I myself was dreaming. The most superlative, the most passionate of words failed, and Dublin seemed a dream world, only an hour's drive away.

CHAPTER 20

HIMSELF AND THE TINKERS

DESPITE HIMSELF'S ARDENT LOVE OF SPEED, he is a great one for giving lifts; in fact, the road from Barravore to Dublin was lined with his regulars, ranging from the ultra-respectable McQuade girl who worked in Dublin, to the widow down the road who was having a series of children long after the gallant departed, and was always needing rides to the hospital. Locally, it was different. When he drove to town, women and children screamed and hid. "Sure the wind would lift your skirts over your head," one of them commented to me.

In four years he went through eight cars, having assorted adventures such as floating down the Boyne in one, overturning in a drain with another (he got out by kicking in the back window), and rolling down a mountain in a third. When they hauled him out of this one he was observed to be laughing.

"God help us, are ye hurt, Mr. Neills?"

"No, I'm just thinking of what the insurance company will say."

Enid's customary toast to him became, "Well, here's one for the road, Billy—and one for the ditch."

When the rest of us were in the car, we, of course, cramped his style, as there wouldn't have been room besides us for an infant pigmy. But often when I alone was with him we'd be

269

whizzing along, and I'd be startled out of my usual prayerful attitude to find us slowing down to take on a series of passengers—gay young things, decrepit old things, Australian hitch-hikers, salesmen, soldiers and, very particularly, guards; for as Himself would inform me later, "You never know when you might need one."

Once he stopped for a guard who turned out to be drunk and refused to reveal his destination. "Mind your own business," he commanded, and sang glorious bits of opera, with gestures. We drove along and Himself asked again, "Where do you want to go?"

"Mind your own business—proceed."

More arias. After miles and miles, Himself slowed down in front of a guard barracks. "Do you want to get off here?" he asked.

"Mother of God! Don't drop me there!" he begged, suddenly sobered, and divulged his home address some distance farther on.

The one requirement Himself made of his clientèle was that they be sociable. Once we picked up a taciturn man and, after twenty miles or so, Himself stopped the car and opened the door. "Get out," he said to the puzzled passenger, "there's never a word from you."

Children, on the other hand, were forbidden to speak. "Keep quiet, Bridget! Can't you see I'm driving through traffic!" "Sally!" "Dorothy, if there's one more squeal out of you I'll dance on your carcass." "Jimmy, how dare you distract me, and I concentrating on the road?" They early learned to follow me in silence if not in supplication.

Whenever we waved him off in the morning, I used to wonder if we'd really and truly ever see him again. He suffered a black-out while driving once. The summer sun, particularly when intensified by car windows, sometimes made him ill. He would come home and stagger up to bed, full of alarming symptoms but absolutely forbidding me to call the doctor. His technique was to lie in his room, groaning. Everyone had to tiptoe; all children had to be gagged. "Ah, you won't have me long," he would mutter, clutching his stomach or his head or his chest or whatever was ailing. "What have I done to God to deserve this?"

Then, when he felt we were sufficiently intimidated, he would rise slowly, nobly, lower himself down the stairs with the help of a cane, and then pound on the floor and loudly demand tea.

But so far as children are concerned, Himself was as nervous as an old maid. "She's punctured her ear, get the doctor." (Doctor reports ear is perfect.) "She has a red spot on her neck, get the doctor." "This child has a temperature, see after it." Dr. Carmody and myself consequently became great buddies, and had long chats in the sitting-room while the child in question romped about, healthy as a fish. In the course of these discussions, the usual wide variety of topic was touched on—Ireland, the American view of Ireland, the Irish view of the American view of Ireland, the American view of the Irish view of the American view of Ireland, and so on, new changes being rung as time stumbled on.

For instance, the familiar, "Tell me, Mrs. O'Neill, what do Americans think of the Irish? No, I'll tell you—they think we're all running around with bare feet and shawls."

"Oh no."

"Did you see that article in *Life* on 'The Vanishing Irish'?"

"Yes. Did you?"

"Bother the article, I didn't read it, I just read about it in the papers here. Did you see the photographs that went with it?"

"Why yes."

"Did you know that they took a girl who was a model and specially posed her in a shawl, for American consumption?

The whole story about it was in the *Press*. It's scandalous. Are they trying to insult us? And did you see *The Quiet Man*?"

"Yes, wasn't it charming?"

"Charming! Certainly not. And what did Maureen O'Hara wear? A shawl. You'd never see a respectable farmer's daughter dressed like that."

Dr. Carmody also came to us to give booster shots for this and that, which having been started in America had to be kept up; and vaccinations which some one of us was always needing to keep a passport current. Hardly would he finish when it would be time to start the round again. I noticed that vaccinations in Ireland are done with four scratches instead of one. Poor Dorothy, who got her first one here, has her whole leg practically given over to it. (When Sally's turn came I was firm, and he did it American style.) Another thing I noticed was that temperatures are taken under the arm. I commented on this to Himself.

"Well, where did you expect them to be taken?"

"Mouth or rectum, of course."

"Rectum, ye gods! Can you imagine Dr. Carmody going up to an old Irish farmer and trying to take his temperature there? I'd have you know that the rectum's a very private place in Ireland."

Actually, I sometimes got the impression that no one in Ireland called the doctor but us. The poor went to the dispensary, and, when they were dying, to the Country Home. The farmers had little use for doctors' prescriptions, though they dosed themselves with all sorts of home-made brews, patent medicines, and mixtures from the wise woman or the quack (a term without disrespect, used of the many unlicensed practitioners). Tom, who was fairly typical, had heroic health, but occasionally he looked haggard. Once this occurred after a period in which we had experimented with rabbit cooking. I had been charmed to find such an economic meat so abundantly to hand; and we had had southern fried rabbit, rabbit salad, rabbit soup, curried rabbit, rabbit in béchamel—fascinating.

"What's wrong with you, Tom? Would you like us to call the doctor?"

"It isn't a doctor I need, it's a ferret."

But he would carefully unwrap a bottle of vile-tasting pills that he had bought at a carnival from a character called 'The Black Master', and the next day claim that they had cured him.

The Whytes were rather anti-M.D. too. Louise, who seemed to have spent most of her life at the mercy of the Harley Street type, felt that many of them were only after money. Devotion to one's obstetrician and pediatrician was, according to her, not a British phenomenon, and she thought I was rather rash to hand on to Dr. Carmody the boundless faith that the doctors at home had inspired. She and the Colonel, led on by their interest in organic gardening, wouldn't touch white sugar, white bread or pasteurised milk; they used brown, brown and raw respectively. In fact, they subsisted on a variety of organic produce designed to prevent sickness, aided and abetted by garlic powder, blackstrap molasses, wheat-germ, barley coffee, dandelion tea and a blend of herbs, a dose of each of these being taken daily. This was to supply trace-elements and make up for mineral deficiencies, as they carefully explained to us. Most people's diets were lacking in those.

"Now that you put it so cleverly," said Himself, "I grasp it all. There's one mineral I've never had enough of."

"What's that?"

"Gold."

"Aren't you horrid," said Louise. "Don't laugh, we really do think it helps."

But somehow she was sick rather a lot. The Colonel's troubles ran more to sessions with osteopaths and chiropractors, and to consultations with a Dublin healer who turned dials on a little black box and diagnosed from the distance. Naughty Peter Griffin listened in on a phone conversation between them and reported it to all.

" 'Good morning,' says the Colonel. 'How am I today?'

" 'Oh, you're fine, Colonel Whyte.'

" 'Thank you, that's very nice indeed.' "

But the Whytes weren't completely satisfied with their efforts on the score of health until they met a Mr. Grimm, who was a water-diviner, a layer-on of hands and a finder of lost objects. He introduced them, and they to us, to pendulum-swinging as a sort of universal panacea. The Whytes tested their food for it—if it swung, the article was good; if it didn't, don't touch! But both Himself and I turned out to be mad geniuses at pendulum-swinging; for us, the darn things whirled all the time, over anything—white bread, white sugar, whole-wheat bread, brown sugar, herbs, whiskey, chicken feed, arsenic. So embarrassing. Himself even began to enjoy a modest reputation as a water-diviner. And one day the tinkers, who are supposed to be fortune-tellers and workers of magic themselves, appealed to him to locate a missing pony.

"Well, now we've seen everything," I said.

Meanwhile the Whytes were suffering from roving animals too. Croesus disappeared twice, and each time, sifting a welter of clues raised by 'dead spits', Mr. Grimm was able to tell them in which direction to look. Then a cow vanished and, for a somewhat larger fee, Mr. Grimm swung his pendulum over the map and located the cow on such-and-such a road. Sure enough, when the Whytes drove there, they found her being led towards them by a small boy. They brought her home, but a few nights later she broke out again, and this time it took several quite expensive visits to Mr. Grimm before she was found. Louise was really upset, and Kinch bewildered by all the goings-on.

"God knows, Mr. Neills," he complained, with a somewhat confused effect, "she has a Christian made o' that cow, takin' her out fer walks and me tryin' to put a bit o' mate on her! Haven't I kept her a year after she should have went? Well fer her if she niver come back!"

When news of Himself's prowess reached them, Louise also asked *him* what they should do pendulum-wise to secure the cow.

"Just one thing," he said. "Lock the blasted gate."

They had no more trouble.

But we began to suffer from the opposite problem—stray animals came to us, the horses and donkeys which the cottagers used for carrying turf on the bog. At the end of August, we noticed that they were turned out into the road, to graze 'the long acre' at no cost to their owners. "Aye," said Himself, "the turf harvest is over, so bedamned to the poor creatures now."

"Bedamned to me too," said Tom. "There'll be gaps made in all the fences and horses in me corn."

This was only too true. Tom spent his days mending holes in hedges and barbed wire and his nights chasing horses and asses out of the fields. All the farmers around us were similarly occupied, but no owner to any of these animals could ever be found. If a horse or donkey could be identified, the man who had been seen working him merely said, "It's just a mane shtraggly beast, I found him shtrayin' on the bog." So the horses and donkeys fed at everyone else's expense, and a land-owner foolish enough to talk to the guards about trespass or make any outward complaint just provided the neighbours with an extra good laugh.

Blessed McQuade turned up in our yard one afternoon, when Himself and Tom were making a bench, filling in another wet day. It was harvest time and raining unmercifully. They were getting nervous about the oats.

"Ah, the blessed work," said Blessed, "the carpenter's work!"

Tom sawed away in silence. Himself lit a cigarette.

"The sanctified work! Glory be to God, when Our Lord was amongst us, He was a carpenter!"

"So was the so-and-so who made the cross," retorted Himself.

The Blessed Man swallowed hard but made another beginning. "Do you think it will hold?" gazing at the sky which was momentarily inactive.

"It will rain," answered Himself, not bothering to look up.

"It's America sendin' off them atom bombs. But maybe it's the Panama Canal," he amended hastily. "They say in the old days there was always good harvests, until America built the Panama Canal, and deflicted the weather."

"Jasus!" said Himself.

"Ah, rain falls like a benediction on the parched land. Where would we be without God's rain?"

Blood-curdling squeak of the saw from Tom, and then he walked away in disgust.

"What's on your mind?" asked Himself.

Blessed seemed relieved that Tom was out of hearing. "Ah, Mr. Neills, each night at the Rosary we say special prayers for the salvation of your soul. We never forget you."

"Now I think there's something else on your mind besides my soul's salvation, so out with it."

"You're a very direct man, sir. You're so kind to Eileen, bringing her to Dublin every Monday, God bless you. You're always in our prayers."

"Well?"

"We have only a small place, but I suppose it's the will of God that we must struggle. With the help of God we'll make out."

"Well?"

"Well, as a matter of fact, 'twas only at dinner the aunt was saying maybe you would let us graze our donkeys on that spare field of yours? God loves the poor, but we're always short of grass. They won't be any trouble."

"Is that all? Of course," said Himself, always willing to oblige. "Bring them around tonight if you like."

Tom was leppin' when he heard the news. "That miserable craw-thumper! Him with his inside line to heaven! He'd come for the grass all right, but he wouldn't come to give a hand to save the hay. He thinks he has a soft head in you, and begob, he's right!"

"Keep your shirt on, Tom."

"I'd like to set me hands on him an' the rest o' his mis-faytured family! They're so mean they'd get up an' blow out the candles at their own wake."

"Look at the fun we have with him."

"He's no fun fer me."

The McQuade donkeys were bad enough, but Tom was in a worse torment when two horses suddenly appeared and joined them. He couldn't chase the horses and leave the donkeys, the dogs were equally baffled, and Tom was sore.

"The Blessed Man does be cute enough," he complained. "When he sees how it is, wouldn't he take them donkeys and leave me a night's sleep?"

"Ah," said Himself, "it's not Blessed's fault. You know, Tom, he's shy."

"Shy but willin'," muttered Tom, "like a cat in a dairy."

"Surely the owner of such a fine pair of horses will come to claim them."

"Sure as a house on fire."

Himself inquired all around about the horses, but no one had a clue. Not even Blessed McQuade, whom the mare nudged with an air of old acquaintance.

"You seem to know those horses well," observed Himself, off-hand.

"Oh no, sir," said Blessed hastily in his high voice. "It's just that they always do be strayin' on the bog."

"That's a handsome cob. I wonder that he's allowed to stray."

"That's mother and son. They're both wonderful jumpers. That is," he cleared his throat, "I—er—seen them on the bog."

"I'd like to buy that cob, if you can find out who owns him."

"Sure now, I'll try, sir," said Blessed quickly, "—with the help of God. It might be Flannery's now. I'll go and ask them this minyute," he added helpfully. "God bless!" And off he went, apparently very glad to get away.

But no owner could ever be located.

The weeks flew by. The children went to school. The I.C.A. started a new season. And the horses and donkeys grew fat and sleek. Tom's gloom could be felt for miles around. He not only had to mend outside fences but inside ones too, and in spite of all his work the horses trampled a field of wheat just before the harvest. He began to look peaked.

"What's wrong with you?" asked Himself.

"It's them damn horses and asses. I'm bet for lack of sleep."

"Wouldn't you take a nap during the day?"

"I couldn't sleep in the daytime."

"Even if you put a heavy shade on the window?"

"Not if I was to put my head in a sack. It's them horses

278

has me run off me feet, tryin' to keep them out of the fields at night. I haven't had an evenin' to meself for weeks."

Bridie giggled.

"Oho," said Himself, "so that's the way it is. And her golden hair was hanging down her back."

Tom laughed too.

"Well, well," said Himself, "enough is enough. We'll have to take steps. I don't mind about you, but if there are other people involved——" and innocently he sang:

> "He bought me a petticoat bordered in blue;
> Before we got home, he tore it in two.
> Still I love him, I'll forgive him,
> I'll go with him wherever he goes."

One evening, driving back from Dublin, he came on a family of tinkers travelling on the Barravore road. The usual dingy pink curtains flew in the breeze over the wagon's half-door; but there were none of the usual calico ponies and donkeys following along; and most unusual, there was not even a horse between the shafts of the wagon itself. Instead, it was being pulled by two men, red-haired of course. Himself stopped the car abreast of them. The men halted and mopped their brows. "That's not work for you," said Himself. "What happened to your animal?"

"We were snaggin' beet, sir, over in Cavan, and our horse was hit and killed by a lorry."

"And you have pulled that caravan all this way?"

"Yes, sir."

"Would not the Brians or the Doyles give you an animal—they should be on the road, surely?"

"We'd have no trouble gettin' a beast, sir, but we're late on the road ourselves. The others are already gone on."

Himself knew that they were headed for the place of

assembly for the winter convention, outside Cashel, in Tipperary.

"You'll never be in time travelling as you are. How long does it take you?"

"We're five days on the road already, sir."

"Come on," said Himself, "sit into the car and I'll give you a horse."

The men stood stock still, staring at him, suspicious stares, from under lowered brows. "Are ye coddin'——?" began one of them angrily. With that, the greying, tousled red head of a woman appeared over the half-door. She said quietly, "That's Mr. Neills. Do anything he tells ye. You, Tim, sit into the car with the man. He's a good friend and won't let you get into trouble. Go in, now, and don't delay him." To Himself she said, "God bless you, sir; the old blood is still strong. But 'tis seldom found today and, sure, the lads are dead from pullin' the wagon. The Brians were askin' for you, and the Sheridans. They couldn't stick the houses— they're on the road again. God bless you, sir."

Tim obediently sat into the car, and Himself drove the journey to the house. If anyone identified his passenger by the shock of red hair, it was put down to Himself's well-known eccentricity and no more thought about it. Dusk was creeping in, a cold miserable drizzle of rain was falling, and on the lawn field the horses and donkeys were busily grazing.

Tim looked them over and remarked, "They're lovely animals, sir."

"They are indeed."

"Which one should I take, sir?"

"Take your pick. As a matter of fact, take them both."

Tim whistled softly. Then, light dawning, "Are they yours, sir?"

"I'm surprised at you," said Himself indignantly, "asking

me such a question! Did I ask you if you owned the caravan?"

"Well, beggin' your pardon, sir, you know—it's the guards."

"What about them?"

"They might be stoppin' us and askin' awkward questions."

"Don't worry. Answer their questions and tell them the truth. I'll stand behind you if anything arises."

"All right then, sir. Will it be all right if I wait till dark? I'll have to get a few ropes and Jack to help me."

"Fine. Come any time you wish."

Sitting at our fireside that night, the children regaled Himself with the day's news. "We learned all about how Newton discovered gravity."

"You have that wrong. You mean, you learned how gravity discovered Newton."

"Was that it, Daddy?"

"Yes, Newton was sitting under a tree——"

"That's right!"

"And an apple hit him and he said, 'My God, gravity!'"

That delighted them. "An apple hit him!" they chortled.

"Mine apple!" put in Sally, just to be on the safe side if apples were going round.

"Ho ho! And he said, 'My God, gravity!'"

"Shhhh!" hissed Himself. I *thought* I heard, through the quietly drizzling countryside, the sound of hooves unhurriedly retreating down our avenue. "What is it?" I asked.

"Rain," said Himself, smiling in a pleased way.

For days afterward the McQuades seemed to be in an aimless bustle. Mr. McQuade, Blessed, even Nora, were on our land more than they were on their own, cycling down the bohereen leading to the bog, peering over fences into fields, but going away without conversation if one of us drew near. Other locals, too, were in on something which they suspended in our presence. We caught phrases like "They're not down there", "Did anyone seen thim since?" "God blast thim any-way!"

Finally Blessed came to remove his donkeys. "I don't see the horses around any more," he said with elaborate casualness.

"Now that you remark it," replied Himself, "they do seem to have gone."

"God save us, they niver went like that before, sir."

"Perhaps the owners came for them. Yet that could hardly be, since no one for miles around did own them."

"True for you, but all the same you'd miss them around."

One afternoon the Sergeant of the local guards stopped us in the car. "Any trouble with straying horses, sir?"

"Sergeant, a horse is so rare these days that I'd hardly know what it was unless it kicked me."

" 'Twasn't always like that," remarked the guard con-versationally. "I suppose you have no bother with tinkers either? You know, when the Singletons owned Barravore they used to be tormented with them—they camped at the front gate, and when one caravan moved on, another would take its place."

"Sure," said Himself, "I wouldn't even notice. They can camp on the front lawn for all I care."

"Ah, from the look of things they'll never trouble you. Well, good day, sir, good day, ma'am, and good luck."

"How nice," I exclaimed. "Isn't it nice of the police here just to check on one's comfort, so to speak. Gosh, they don't do that at home!"

But he was smilingly humming 'The Little Red Fox'.

A few months passed, and it was fair day, good prices for cattle and horses. Hustle and bustle infected everyone, and all kinds of merchandise changed hands for cash, sales being consummated in the pubs where the pain of parting with money could be dulled. To be drunk at 11 a.m. didn't mean that the man of the house was a no-good tramp, but simply that he had done business. Blessed McQuade hit the road for town early, dressed in his best black clothes. Old Mrs. Carthy rode in, starting at dawn, with a cart full of trussed hens to sell. MacAndrew drove his bullocks in for the umpteenth time—perhaps he'd get his price today. Peggy and Nellie passed on their cycles; Mike Kinch turned up to buy pigs for the Colonel (the Colonel's latest idea). The road was full of man and beast headed for town.

Towards noon Himself decided that we should go in to see the fun. The fair green was crowded; it was perilous to walk. Bullocks were jammed and milling; pigs were squealing in high-penned carts; sheep were standing in rosette formation with their heads tied together; horses were being trotted about. The animals often changed hands several times, so relatively few had been led away; yet in another hour or two the fair would be over. In the confusion Himself noticed a conspicuously good-looking mare and colt, groomed and shining like mahogany, and Tim the tinker parading them up and down. Among the cluster of would-be purchasers was our neighbour Blessed McQuade.

"A bargain, a bargain," called Tim. "Fifty pounds apiece —mother and son—it's a shame to part them. I'll let the two go together at seventy-five." He pulled on their halters and had them step along briskly.

Himself gave a start of recognition, despite the trimmed, polished hooves and burnished coats. Tim as he trotted by caught his eye and without breaking step gave him a knowing, slow wink.

The Blessed Man stepped forward, face flushed and anxious. "Forty pounds for the two."

Tim stood dramatically still. "It's only the kindness of my heart would let them go at seventy-five. Have you no feeling, man?"

K

"Forty-five."

Tim looked as though he would weep. "I reared that mother from a foal. She's me only friend. It's only the hard times at all is making me sell. Seventy-five."

"Fifty," said Blessed, "and God help me!"

The tinker gazed at him in sorrow. "Ye're not in earnest? Fifty is the least I'd take for any one of them."

"Fifty," repeated Blessed. The mare nudged him and he stroked her neck.

"Look, man, she has a feelin' for you! Sure you wouldn't part the two."

"Fifty," said Blessed, but his voice quavered a bit.

Tim suddenly whipped around and faced Himself. "I appeal to you, sir, a dark stranger, who never saw me before, be the Holy Mother and all the saints—am I not robbin' meself to sell the pair at seventy? That lovely mare that I reared from a foal, an' her bedded beside me on the roads of Ireland through the long cold winters!"

"F-f-fifty-five," said Blessed desperately.

"Not another word," said Tim. "We'll lave it to the gentleman."

"What's between ye?" asked Himself.

"No, no," said Tim, "I'll not split the differ. Seventy pounds, and me a traitor fer sellin' me own flesh an' blood."

"You'll leave it me," said Himself, "and give a good handsel?"

"Yes indeed, sir."

"And you, Blessed?"

(Shrilly.) "Whatever you say, sir."

"Seventy it is then, but ten pounds handsel to the Blessed Man."

Blessed made the sign of the cross and carefully counted out seventy pounds. After much spitting on hands and on the luck penny, the deal was closed.

Himself had a lot of humming to do that night.

> "As I was going to the Fair of Athy
> I saw an old petticoat hanging to dry.
> I took off me trousers and hung them close by
> Just to keep that old petticoat war-rum."

He was delighted with himself.

"Well, I suppose Blessed only got what was coming to him," I admitted.

"Lassie, don't be casting gloom on the occasion. He's a fortunate man. He got a bargain. In fact, all the neighbours are this minute down at Brady's pub toasting his luck at getting his own horses back, and regretting that the animals *they* bought are strange to the bog and will have to be trained to the work.

"And that'll be a lesson to them all," he added nonchalantly.

*

CHAPTER 21

THE I.R.A. ARSENAL

YOU DON'T HAVE TO BE A CITIZEN in order to vote in Ireland. Residence is enough, as we found when I received notice to cast my ballot. The Whytes, loyal subjects of Her Majesty, did, and so did the Danes, the local Czech, the local Pole and the local Dutchman; but, of course, I didn't. It was flattering to be invited, but from an American viewpoint they seemed here to be rather free with the franchise. We took a great interest, though, in the election; the Colonel had put Mike Kinch up again for County Councillor, and Tom offered his services—and our car—to one of the political parties to drive voters to the polls.

When the day came, Tom departed in the morning with the car enswathed in Irish flags and proceeded to ferry older ladies to the schoolhouse. Another fellow, he said, had them rounded up and he, Tom, cut them out three at a time. "I had the sport o' the world," he reported that night. "I'd look about me and say, 'Well, ye're all mothers. Tell me, does any of ye have a daughter?' We had great gas." He also mentioned Kinch to each lot.

Meanwhile the Colonel joined us and we watched a big crowd queue up outside the school. Even Old Joe appeared in the line; he was jauntily wearing a bandanna under his hat again, and he had in his lapel a badge which was a symbol of one of the parties. The guard noticed it and shook his head.

"Divil on ye!" cried the old man. "I wasn't afraid to wear it in 1916 and I'm not afraid to wear it today!"

"Come along now," said the guard peaceably, "ye're not supposed to wear anything belonging to a party when ye go to vote. Take it off."

Old Joe almost wept as he carefully unpinned it and put it in his pocket. "They couldn't make me take it off in '16, and ye upstarts make me take it off now. I was out then, and where was you? Niver mind," he cried, thumping his chest, "the badge may be off, but the heart's there still, and the heart is still true!"

Cheers from the crowd, interrupted when the sergeant came to arrest one of their number who was about to vote for the third time.

"Hell melt him!" lamented the Colonel. "He promised me he'd vote for Michael!"

But the next day, to his joy, word came that Kinch had been elected. The Colonel started immediately on plans for a town sewerage-cum-methane-gas scheme—which Kinch never discouraged but somehow managed never to forward. Politics must indeed be the whetstone of the Irish personality, for Kinch turned out to be a superb politician. He did not change, exactly, rather he matured. No longer did he evade responsibility; on the contrary, the weight of the county, of the nation, of the world, was on his shoulders. He was sagacious in office, and very, very dignified, but his sympathies were always those of a labouring man.

His first act was to make a speech of thanks to his constituents in the town square. Beaming with success, the Colonel drove him there, and Mike spoke from the bonnet of the Colonel's car. First he pledged "M-m-more and b-b-better unemployment", and then, encouraged by thunderous applause, he went on, waving his arms wildly and promising the whole country to the working class. "Ye see thim fields—

they're yours, that's what they are! Ye see thim cattle, they're yours, that's what they are! Ye see thim roads, that river, thim houses, thim tractors——"

"Oh I say, Michael," interrupted the Colonel nervously, "when you come to the car, that's mine!"

But Kinch revealed an independence of mind, an ingenious common sense which recalled the time when the cows did the ploughing. Tremendous local renown accrued to him when the town was trying to get housing grants to start a badly needed new development. It turned out that no grant could be made till the houses were completed, and for the purpose of the act completion was defined as "when the chimneys are finished and functioning". The town had no funds to build without the grant. What to do? "Be Jasus," said Mike, all stirred up, winking and jerking his head conspiratorially, "we'll put up thim f-f-finished f-f-functioning chimneys f-f-first, that's what!" It worked, and the new terrace was gratefully named Kinch Drive.

The Colonel of course took a proprietary view of all Mike's activities; wheels within wheels, Richelieu had nothing on him. Both of them came to Himself for advice, and so to a certain extent he too was drawn into current events, which, as an unreconstructed revolutionary, he had always avoided. Thus it was we supported Kinch with our presence when the meeting for An Tostal was called.

An Tostal was thought up a few years back by some tourist-minded genius in Dublin. I won't attempt to go into the Gaelic etymology of 'tostal'—debates on it raged long and hard in the papers for months—but the general idea was a home-coming period of several weeks. During this, Irish 'exiles' (an exile being someone who wouldn't come back to Ireland, not if you paid him) and even non-Irish travellers would be especially urged to visit the country. Large sums were spent on publicity and 'attractions'. Oddly, An Tostal was always set in the spring, which certainly limited the number of American tourists to less than the tens of thousands hoped for, but defeat was never admitted in Dublin. There it was announced each year, on the one hand, that it was a great triumph; on the other, that the provincial towns had not co-operated and so it was all their fault that An Tostal was a flop.

The country attitude was that the money allotted to each town was so paltry as to be an insult, while no amount was too much or no idea too ridiculous for Dublin. Perpetual Tostal bowl-of-light on O'Connell's Bridge! (A student threw it into the Liffey, and so great was the feeling, tourist authorities pro and everyone else con, that he was almost beheaded.) Expensive Tostal badges for foreigners arriving in Ireland! Glossy programmes for them, listing mythical Tostal events! Expense-account junketings for members of the three tourist boards! Only in Cork, a city blessed with imagination and community spirit, was the Tostal a success. The disgusted provinces, compelled to make some showing, strung ancient bunting across the main streets or stuck tired geraniums into window-boxes here and there.

So when word came from Dublin once more that the town must think up a project for tourists, it was received with something less than apathy, until word also came that An Tostal was this time providing a substantial sum. Immediately everything was changed. The committee was appointed, axes started grinding. All agreed that the money should be spent to the best possible local advantage, but what this was kept the countryside arguing for weeks. Finally the meeting was called.

This was in the spring when there is always confusion about Old and New time. The farmers keep to the old, but the town goes on to daylight-saving, and Mass and school hours switch over from the hour to the half-hour in the hope

of catching everyone. The Tostal gathering too was to start
at 'half-eight'. With some knowledge by now of Irish meetings, we groaned that this would be a very late night indeed.

"Sure, sir," Kinch remarked reasonably, "they can't be
more nor an hour adrift in ayther direction." But it was
along about ten before it started.

The town hall was jammed, everyone was there. The stal-
warts of the I.C.A. from Miss Protheroe to Mrs. Dooley, the
National Farmers, the Young Farmers (average age, fifty),
Muintir na Tire (more farmers), the Co-operative Dairy, the
Beet Growers' Association, the Wheat Growers' Association,
the Barley Growers' Association, the S.P.C.A., the town
Social Club, Sinn Fein, the Pipe Band, the Christian
Brothers, the Bridge Club, the Historical Association, Fianna
Fail, the Catholic Young Men, the Children of Mary, the
Girls' Friendly Society, Fine Gael, the Transport Workers'
Union, the Gaelic League, St. Conleth's School, St.
Michael's School, the County Council, the Town Council,
the Dominicans, St. John's Ambulance Brigade, the Antiquarian Society, the Labour Party, the Men of the Trees,
the Parish Priest, Clan na Poblacha, the Presbyterian
Minister, the G.A.A., the C. of I. Canon, the Football
Association, the Guards, the County Hunt, the Red Cross,
the four bank-managers, the twenty-three publicans and a
procession of Holy Children. Among the crowd, amazing to
relate, was even Brigadier Freyke, pulling on his moustache
and looking rather baffled, it must be admitted; but the very
fact of his being there was proof of the magnitude of the
occasion. Money to be had, free, gratis and for nothing!

As soon as the Chairman rapped for order, one of the town
shopkeepers popped up and read a long speech recommend-
ing that hundreds of pounds be spent on lights and decorations for the main street and improvement of shop windows.
A storm of boos and cat-calls ended that. "Do it yerselves!"

"Sure, isn't an inch o' counter worth an acre o' land?" "If ye're so hard up, go to the workhouse!" The Technical schoolmaster suggested a bus to bring country students to school. The Transport Workers wanted fewer buses and more wages. Mrs. Dooley demanded "a thousand pound fer the Countrywomen's Hall". Loud cheers and cries of "Good woman!" The Young Farmers said they needed a hall too. Boos. The Dominicans wanted a statue of St. Dominic in front of the Priory. Father Kelly said the nuns would like to build a shrine along the river bank. Mr. Comerford, who owned the biggest pub and a motor-boat, seconded this with great sanctimoniousness, adding that at the same time the river could be dredged. The Colonel wanted the sewage plant. Muintir wanted a theatre. The Pipe Band wanted kilts.

The Gaelic League wanted a festival in Gaelic, repeating with fervour the famous words that Ireland must not be free only, but Gaelic as well. "Jasus!" said the man next to us. "lave it to thim Gaelahoolies to think o' somethin' quare. Can ye see us leppin' about in a fistival? But sure, whin they could make 'Baille Athe Cliath' outa 'Dublin', nothin' could surprise me!" Still, there was voluminous applause.

The Hunt wanted a horse show. More applause. The Labour Party wanted a paid holiday for all workers. The Guards said that, in that case, they'd need a new jail. The County Council wanted a new road. In other words, everyone had his own special list for Santa Claus.

The Chairman, a patient and long accustomed man, reminded the meeting of its purpose. "We have this sum to spend, we may" [meaning *must*] "spend it, but none of you has put forward a suitable proposition. We want something which will improve the town permanently, not just for summer visitors" —[cheers]— "something which will enhance it for all, not for one class only. Something decorative, yes, but also useful. Something needed. Something we can be proud of."

Babel as everyone tried to convince his neighbour that *his* idea, and his alone, was just that.

"Any new proposals?" asked the Chairman.

There were several. Landscaping the town square. Mild approval. Turning the ruined castle on the Dublin road into a museum. "Hear, hear!" from the Historical Association and the Antiquarian Society, indifference elsewhere. A new fair ground. Loud cheers from the various agricultural organisations and hisses from the shopkeepers. Then the chief town councillor, in a sensible if somewhat embarrassed voice, said that for many years it had been recognised that as soon as the money came to hand six urinals should be built. There were no—er—amenities of this sort at all, he pointed out. Whilst some people might feel that such things were an unnecessary bother, foreigners were known to think otherwise. Surely, what could be more fitting than to use the tourist funds for this?

Buzz, as everyone mirthfully discussed it.

Kinch, up on the dais in his Sunday suit, had been sitting in appropriate silence, but now he jerked his head and scratched the receding hairline. "What's a urinal?" he asked in a loud voice, poking the man next to him. Everyone stopped talking.

Sotto voce, the explanation was given.

"Thim things?" Kinch exclaimed in the dead hush in tones of great surprise. "Thim things? Sure, that's only a quick job." Then, excitedly, as the inspiration hit him, "This t-t-town don't need any s-s-six urinals! What this t-t-town needs is one g-g-good arsenal!"

Wild acclamation and cheers! We all voted for it.

We were still laughing when later in the week the county

paper came out. Headlines screamed across the front page:

SUSPECTED I.R.A. ACTIVITY
BRIGADIER FREYKE REPORTS OPEN PRO-
POSAL TO BUILD ARSENAL

Brigadier-General Freyke, former Resident Magistrate, said he felt it his duty to report to the Tostal authorities an attempt by a subversive group to divert Tostal funds to an arms dump. "There's more to this than meets the eye," he said. An Tostal will investigate.

And to this day, when Himself drives visitors about to see points of interest, he always stops in town to show them what he calls 'the I.R.A. Arsenal'. "There it is," he says, "a graceful, decorative, useful little building, for all classes, permanent, the town's pride, and not free only, but Gaelic as well, with 'Mna' on one side and 'Fir' on the other."

CHAPTER 22

*

POSTSCRIPT

THE OTHER EVENING, at tea-time, Himself and I sat at the small table in the sitting-room. Bright daylight outside, bright but sloping, for the evenings are long now with summer and New time. Birds sang in the hedges, and swallows flew high in and out of the barn. A tractor chugged along the road. The children were playing in the garden, looking for the earliest strawberries, and Himself was humming:

"The Garden of Eden is vanished, they say,
    But I know the lie of it still."

"Umm," I said, startled to realise how contented, bovine, moss-grown we were. "Do you know we've been here for five years?"

"Notatall."

"Five years."

"That's only yesterday."

"Do you know what we've become?"

He didn't answer.

I poured his tea and mine and mused a bit, and between the pouring and the drinking the years slipped by.

Barravore as we first saw it, overgrown and obscured, and Barravore now, trim and clean-lined, with roses nodding against the windows and orderly fields stretching away beneath young trees. The children, growing into persons, these days chanting multiplication tables no American child has to cope with: "Five one's five, five two's ten, five three's fifteen one and three, five four's twenty one and eight, five five's twenty-five two and one——" The puppy biting Sally and Sally biting the puppy. Deaths, emigrations, births mentionable and unmentionable. Tom's and Jane's romance ("So sordid," reported Jane. "He calls on Mother now and all they talk about is money." "My God!" admitted Himself. "If he's doing *that*, it's serious!") The Colonel after a holiday in Italy: "I say, O'Neill—hello, Tadpole—I say, is there a volcano in Ireland? Lava makes wonderful compost." The waving of handkerchiefs and the cloud of dust as Mrs. Dooley and the I.C.A. set off on their latest bus excursion to the sea. Louise turning her head and smiling. The castle on the Dublin road with the sky showing through its tower. Old Joe, a flower behind his ear, strolling along on a spring day. Tinkers' caravans, camped at Miss Protheroe's front entrance, and their toothy grins as her car sailed out of the gate with alarming aim. Enid. Bridie dreaming over the dishes. Father Kelly on his way to a hurling match, "Are ye goin' to the game, Father?" "I'm going to pick up the pieces." The river winding past the convent garden. Driscoll the grocer growing indignant over American oranges—"Sure, they have to put colour on them to sell them in Ireland!" The rock in the glen and the sound of waterfalls. A hush in the laughter round the tap at Barravore as Peter Griffin tells the day's news: "Young Carthy's in hospital. He borried MacAndrew's ladder to do a bit o' paintin', an' he fell an' knocked down a picture o' the Pope an' broke his leg as well!" And Blessed's shrill voice asking, "What other luck could he have, usin' a Protestant ladder?" Kinch and the County Council. The road to Dublin, widened and straightened. Yellow irises at the edge of the canal, and three wild geese taking flight.